WORKERS IN INDUSTRIAL AMERICA

WORKERS IN INDUSTRIAL AMERICA

Essays on the Twentieth Century Struggle

SECOND EDITION

David Brody

New York   Oxford
OXFORD UNIVERSITY PRESS
1993

Oxford University Press

Oxford New York Toronto
Delhi Bombay Calcutta Madras Karachi
Kuala Lumpur Singapore Hong Kong Tokyo
Nairobi Dar es Salaam Cape Town
Melbourne Auckland Madrid

and associated companies in
Berlin Ibadan

Published by Oxford University Press, Inc.,
200 Madison Avenue, New York, New York 10016

Oxford is a registered trademark of Oxford University Press

Library of Congress Cataloging-in-Publication Data
Brody, David, 1930–
Workers in industrial America : essays on the twentieth century
struggle / David Brody. — 2nd ed.
p. cm. Includes bibliographical references.
ISBN 0-19-504503-3 (alk. paper).
ISBN 0-19-504504-1 (pbk. : alk. paper)
1. Trade-unions—United States—History—20th century.
2. Working class—United States—History—20th century. I. Title.
HD6508.B8113   1993
331.88'0973'0904—dc20   92-366

9 8 7 6 5 4 3 2 1

Printed in the United States of America
on acid-free paper

FOR OSCAR HANDLIN

Preface

This second edition contains intact chapters 1, 2, 3, 5, and 6 of the first edition. In Chapter 4, the historiographical pieces that have become dated are replaced by a more recent essay surveying the historical study of the CIO from its founding to its fiftieth anniversary in 1985. And a final essay has been added that tries to place in historical and comparative perspective the declining fortunes of the labor movement since the appearance of the first edition in 1980. For reprint permissions I would like to thank the Ohio State University Press, the Johns Hopkins University Press, and the editors of *Dissent*.

Davis, Calif.   D. B.
April 1992

Preface to the First Edition

The study of the American worker has undergone a renascence in recent years. Rich veins of information have been uncovered. New themes have emerged. Debate has grown lively and provocative. At such a happy time, the practicing historian finds his attention strongly engaged, apart from the demands of his research, by new trains of thought, sometimes provoked by the implications of his own work, more often by the work of others, occasionally by an inkling about a problem as yet unexplored. It often takes external prompting—an invitation to give a talk, or to contribute an essay, or to write a review—to get him to elaborate the idea and commit the results to paper. If he is lucky, the sum of that episodic writing finds a coherence of its own and perhaps warrants presentation in book form.

This is such a book. It represents fifteen years and more of thinking and writing about the history of American labor in the twentieth century. The earliest essays, "The Emergence of Mass-Production Unionism" (1964) and "The Rise and Decline of Welfare Capitalism" (1968), served as explorations for a longer-term project. "The American Worker in the Progressive Era," somewhat more narrative in approach than the other essays, was originally commissioned by the U.S. Department of Labor for its bicentennial history *The American Worker* (1977) and then, for reasons best known to the department, not used in that volume. The group of briefer pieces on the 1930s, written over the past decade, speak for themselves; they are offered here as a kind of personal intellectual history in a particularly rich period in New Deal labor historiography. The final essays, jointly titled "The Uses of Power," were written specifically for this volume and, of all the essays, were least prompted by any initial enthusiasm on my part. I started them at the urging of my editor Nancy Lane, who rightly argued that the book—and the field—needed to pay more heed to events since World War II. The resulting essays, especially the one subtitled "Industrial Background," should be read as first ventures into ground largely unexplored, by historians at any rate, and, as I see now, richly warranting their attention.

The unifying elements that emerge from this irregular history of composition have taken me somewhat by surprise. Excepting the short pieces in the historiographical section, the essays seem to have found a common level of historical discourse, both on the degree of detail and the pitch of the argument, somewhere midway between the journal article and the general synthesis. They reflect also a consistency of perspective toward the nature of American labor institutions and, more unexpectedly, regarding the central themes of the labor history of the twentieth century. From first to last, I have found myself occupied with the issue of power, with the efforts of laboring people to assert some control over their working lives, and of the equal determination of American business to conserve the prerogatives of management. If there has been any exceptionalist feature to the modern history of the worker in this country, it has been in the fury and persistence of this struggle. There is, finally, a consistency of intellectual purpose of which I have always been conscious. The starting point of every essay was a problem that I was trying to work out. The reader will thus find in these essays, not a full account of the subject, but an ongoing confrontation with certain of the central questions—substantive and historiographical—of American labor history in the twentieth century. The best I can hope for is that the reader will come away with a fuller understanding of the kinds of concerns that have so enlivened the study of the American worker in recent years.

A book such as this leaves behind it a trail of debts. As co-editors of the series in which those essays first appeared, John Braeman and Robert Bremner read critically "The Emergence of Mass-Production Unionism" and "The Rise and Decline of Welfare Capitalism." Richard B. Morris performed the same chore on "The American Worker in the Progressive Era." I am particularly grateful to him and to David Montgomery for urging me not to put that essay aside. It was my special good fortune to have been a visitor at the Institute of Industrial Relations at Berkeley while I was writing the companion essays, "The Uses of Power." Not only was my work speeded by its helpful staff and good library, but I benefited from associates who knew a great deal more than I about the recent history of American industrial relations. I am especially in the debt of George Strauss, a pioneer in that field, both for much advice and for a most careful reading of the essays. David Lewin and Sandy Jacoby also made suggestions that led to a substantial recasting of an earlier draft. During the summers of 1977 and 1978, I directed seminars for labor leaders under the Seminars for the Professions program of the National Endowment for the Humanities. It was, in truth, an educational experience in which the teacher was the net beneficiary. Much that was hotly debated in those sessions on the Davis campus has found its way into my treatment of recent American labor history. Those final essays were written while I was on a fellowship from the National Endowment for the Humanities. Over the years I have also been the beneficiary of the generosity of the University of California at Davis both for sabbatical time and research support.

D. B.

Contents

WORKERS IN INDUSTRIAL AMERICA

1

The American Worker
in the Progressive Age:
A Comprehensive Analysis

A door closed behind the American worker at the turn of the century. An earlier world of labor, weakening for many years under the impact of America's industrial revolution, had slipped irrevocably into the past, and after 1900 the wage earner stood wholly within the modern industrial order. Only now could he fully take in his fate—what it meant to work in a large-scale, mechanized, rationally managed, corporate system of production. And only now, when it was essentially fixed, had the time arrived for coming to terms with the industrial system.

The world of work

Late in his life, the CIO official John Brophy (1883–1963) thought back on his early days as a coal miner in western Pennsylvania. As he learned the trade by the side of his father, the boy became aware that the old man was "a good workman; that he had pride in his calling."

> It was a great satisfaction to me that my father was a skilled, clean workman with everything kept in shape. The skill with which you undercut the vein, the judgment in drilling the coal after it had been undercut and placing the exact amount of explosive so that it would do an effective job of breaking the coal from the solid . . . indicated the quality of his work.

All this the pick miner did with a minimum of supervision. He was a tonnage worker and clearly distinguished from the company men who transported the coal away from the headway, maintained the haulage ways, and did the surface work. The miner provided his own tools, knocked off early when he chose, worked at his own pace, and exercised his own judgment in his "room" at the coal face. "That was one of the great satisfactions that a miner had—that he was his own boss within his workplace." And he took pride in the craft. The miner "is inclined to lose face with his fellow workmen if he misses his turn [in the flow of coal cars] because of poor workmanship."

The shared dangers, the craft identity, the rhythm of mine operations promoted an abiding solidarity that was deeply rooted in an identification with the past. "The miner in my day," said Brophy, "was aware that all knowledge didn't start with his generation," that miners before him had lived and worked and struggled as he did, and "had passed this knowledge on to their children, and their children had passed it on." John Brophy himself sprang from at least four generations of English miners on one side of his family. The inheritance gave him "a sense of pride; very much so."[1]

Brophy's pride did not, however, pass on intact to the next generation. Undercutting machines, first introduced in the 1880s, deprived the miner of the most demanding part of his pick work. "Anyone with a weak head and a strong back can load machine coal," grumbled one Kentucky miner. "But a man has to think and study every day like you was studying a book if he is going to get the best of the coal when he uses only a pick." By 1913 half the nation's soft coal came from mines using undercutting machines. Coal loading yielded more slowly to mechanization. At the end of the 1920s, machines were loading 13 per cent of the soft coal output. Where this occurred, the miner became a machine tender or conveyor loader. Specialized crews took over the miner's other tasks at the coal face—the timbering, the track laying, sometimes even the drilling and shot firing. The subdivided work was brought under close supervision. Once loading became mechanized, the miner lost control over the pace of his work. The deadly speed-up began. The climax of this relentless drive for efficiency was to eliminate the underground work by stripping off the overburden and digging out the coal seams with power shovels. Only just beginning during the 1920s, strip mining, together with fully mechanized underground mining, clearly represented the industry's future.

The pick miner produced 2½ tons a day. The upward curve of labor productivity from that standard measured the operator's achievement: in mechanized undercutting operations, 4.76 tons per man in 1930; in fully mechanized mines, 7.12 tons; in open-pit mines, 16.2 tons. But the price was the inexorable destruction of the prideful occupation that John Brophy had known in his boyhood, and the transformation of the mine, as one miner put it, into "nothing but a goddam factory."[2]

The counterpart of Brophy's miner—the autonomous craftsman who worked at his own pace in his own way—had flourished in many branches of nineteenth-century industry. The technological advances only now affecting the pick miner had long since been undermining other craft workers, and continued doing so in ever more complex ways after 1900. The material-processing fields, such as iron and steel, paper, glass, cement, and chemicals, became increasingly continuous and automatic. In glass manufacture, virtually the entire transformation took place after 1900, when glass-blowing machines first broke the hold of the craft workers. For the others, progress principally meant fuller application and perfection of machines and processes invented earlier. Advances in fabricating industries came on two main fronts: first, making the power-driven machine tools faster, more precise, automatic, and multistage; and, second, introducing better layout, handling, and task subdivision to the assembly work. When Henry Ford applied the moving belt to these fabricating techniques in 1913, industrial efficiency leaped a barrier. The time required to assemble the Model-T fell to under two hours. Primarily as a consequence of Ford's achievement, output per man/hour multiplied an incredible four times for the automobile industry during the decade 1909–19.[3]

The impact on skill levels was by no means simple or one way. In the handling of materials, machines eliminated gangs of day laborers and replaced them with semiskilled operators of fork-lifts, skip hoists, and overhead conveyors. While iron puddlers, steel rollers, and glass blowers were thrust into the semiskilled ranks of machine tenders, the machines themselves demanded skilled installers and repairers. New products sometimes generated a fresh demand for craft skills. Auto manufacturing was a haven for the all-round mechanic before it became the model mass-production industry. And then the craft mechanic became the tool-and-die man who set the jigs and prepared the assembly lines. The census reveals the upward leveling effect of mechanization: from 1910 to 1930, the percentage of unskilled workers in the industrial labor force fell from 36 to 30.5, the semiskilled rose from 36 to 39, the skilled from 28 to 30.5. Even so, except for the maintenance workers, mechanization consistently undercut the worker's full relationship to the productive process.

The factory worker became the servant of the machine that performed the actual work or, if he did the endlessly repetitive jobs on the assembly line, he became himself a part of the machine. An observer watched the deadening task of one female worker: "One single precise motion each second, 3600 in one hour, and all exactly the same. The hands were swift, precise, intelligent. The face was stolid, vague, and vacant." The manager considered her "one of the best workers we have. . . . She is a sure machine." A shirt worker in 1903 described the "1000 souls hurrying from morning until night, working from seven until six, with as little personality as we could, with the effort to produce, through an action purely mechanical, results as nearly as possible identical to one another, and all to the machine itself." For the factory worker, there was "nothing tangible at the end of the day's work to which he can point with pride and say, 'I did that—it is the result of my own skill and my own effort.' "

Nor did he any longer exert much control over his job. In the American steel mill, an English steelmaster noted, the workmen "do not act upon their own judgment, but carry out the instuctions given to them." And the continuous flow of operations deprived the worker of control over his work pace. "If you need to turn out a little more," remarked a superintendent at Swift & Co., "you speed up the conveyor a little and the men speed up to keep pace." The United States Industrial Commission (1902) found "that in nearly all occupations an increasing strain and intensity of labor is required by modern methods of production." Life in the textile mills, a union representative told the commission, had become much harder. European weavers entering the woolen mills of Lawrence, Massachusetts, "are apt to find it pretty hard for the first few weeks, because they are not used to such machinery. They call them 'devils' and not machinery." It was, to be sure, always a matter of dispute whether the added burden of work fell on the men or on the machines (as employers invariably claimed in their testimony before the Industrial Commission). But, either way, speed-up meant that control over the pace of the job had passed into the hands of the supervisors.[4]

The workplace dwarfed the workingman. To exploit advancing technology usually meant to expand the scale of production. In steel, for example, where integration of the stages of production became crucial, no basic mill could be built for under $20 million or be capable of economical operation at under 2,500 tons a day. The original Ford plant in Detroit had strained to make an industry record of 10,000 cars in 1909. Five years later the spacious new Highland Park plant, fitted out with assembly lines, was capable of an annual production of 250,000 Model T's. Small shops, employing between six and twenty workers, remained steady in number from 1914 to 1923, but the *proportion* of such jobs was shrinking. In 1923, half of all industrial wage earners worked in factories employing more than 250 people, and over 800 factories employed more than 1,000. The twentieth-century fate of American workers, as a contemporary expert remarked, was to "become members of many armies of employees working under the same roof."[5]

The individual plant was itself becoming subordinate to a vaster system of production. The great depression of the 1890s had touched off a merger movement in American industry. By 1904, experts counted 318 important industrial combinations controlling 5,288 separate plants. Other successful firms were meanwhile building additional plants to reach into new markets. Swift & Co., for example, grew from a single plant with 1,600 hands in 1886 to seven packing houses employing 23,000 in 1903. By 1919, at least a third of the nation's industrial wage earners worked in factories (over 20,000 of them, by the count of the Census Bureau) that were part of multiplant concerns. Much the same had happened to American railroads. In the 1920s the centralizing process extended into such new fields as utilities and retailing. For more and more wage earners, the power over their working lives receded far off into distant central offices and into the hands of men probably unknown to them even by name.

The human scale of nineteenth-century labor thus fell away. For textile workers, the loss had come early. Miners and garment workers, on the other hand, were affected much more slowly. And then there were others—the construction trades, for example—who were entirely bypassed. But ever increasing numbers found themselves in a work environment crushing to any sense of individual mastery or even understanding. "The man working for the United States Steel Corporation," remarked a labor investigator after spending the year 1911 in the Pittsburgh district, "sees on every side evidence of an irresistible power, baffling and intangible. It fixes the conditions of his employment; it tells him what wages he

may expect to receive and where and when he must work."
And any effort to raise his voice would be "either ignored or
rebuked."[6]

The management of labor

At one time, an industrialist remembered, "I knew every
man . . . I could call him by name and shake hands with
him . . . and the [office] door was always open. When I left
the active management . . . we had . . . some thirty thousand employees, and the men who worked . . . would have
stood just about as much chance to get in to see any one with
his grievance as he would to get into the Kingdom of Heaven."
The magnate's tone of regret says something about the
industrial revolution over which he was presiding: the impact
on his workers, profound as he knew it to be, he regarded as
merely a *byproduct* of his entrepreneurial achievement. Only
slowly, and rarely before 1900, did it dawn on American
employers that the management of labor might itself yield the
kind of returns that were being extracted from technology.
One labor-relation expert saluted the pioneering National
Cash Register Company in 1912 for "all-round, lasting efficiency . . . not the efficiency of the tool or the machine, the
thing—but of the man and woman, the workers themselves."[7]
As employers came to that realization, the circle began to
close on what remained of the American workingman's
autonomy.
Inside the nineteenth-century factory, authority had been
highly dispersed. The foreman was the boss of his section,
substantially so for output, cost, and quality, and almost
totally so over the workers. The foreman hired, disciplined,
fired, trained, often set individual wage rates, and always was
the man charged with getting the work out. Where skill
counted heavily, the craft worker held these powers. Glass
blowers, potters, iron puddlers, steel rollers, foundry molders,
and miners hired and paid their own crews, took full charge of

the work, and were paid for their output. David Montgomery's study of rollers and their crews at the Columbus Iron Works in Ohio led him to conclude that "all the boss did was to buy the equipment and raw materials and sell the finished product."[8] Metal-fabricating plants often relied on inside contractors, employees who ran departments autonomously for a set price per unit of output; in the New England machine-tool industry, employee-contractors actually bid on the jobs.

Advancing technology necessarily eroded this decentralized factory system, partly by attacking strategic skills, partly by interjecting factors of production that cut across the jurisdiction of individual foremen. In the setting of the large-scale factory, informal, uncoordinated arrangements took on the appearance of chaos. It was essential, remarked one expert in 1900, "to readjust the balance of responsibility disturbed by the expansion of industrial operations, and to enable central control to be restored in its central operations."[9] Toward the end of the century, systematic record keeping, cost accounting, and inventory and production controls came into widespread use. Systematic management concerned itself rather less with labor proper, and the foreman did not lose his hold over recruitment, training, and discipline. Even so, as formal and orderly procedures reached down from the central office to the shop floor, the workingman found himself increasingly subject to general rules and to standardized terms of work.

The next step was nearly inevitable. Why not devise systematic methods for getting better work out of the men? The question applied especially to those operations either not subject to mechanization, or whose technology did not dictate the pace of work. At the same time, there were increasing doubts about the traditional rough-and-ready techniques of foremen. "The reason why coercive 'drive' methods have prevailed in the past," remarked the industrial-relations expert Sumner H. Slichter, "has been that the central management has been indifferent to the methods pursued by foremen in handling men but has insisted rigidly upon a constantly increasing output and constantly decreasing cost."[10] During the 1890s, companies experimented with wage incentive and profit-sharing schemes. After 1900, the industrial-welfare movement, while springing mainly from philanthropic and public relations motives, began to argue that contented and well-cared-for workers would be more productive. The welfare secretaries, although generally trained as social workers and clergymen, soon turned their attention to shop conditions. They began to claim administrative responsibility over all labor matters, not merely toilets, safety, and recreation. The genesis of the labor-relations expert and the personnel department of the 1920s stemmed directly from the industrial-welfare movement of the prewar years.

But until it could claim the same precision as engineering or accounting, labor management could not come into its own. This was the great achievement of Frederick W. Taylor. Himself an idiosyncratic, upper-class Philadelphian, Taylor was also typical of those engineers (he pioneered mainly in high-speed metal-cutting techniques) who tried to apply their scientific training to the problems of management. Much of what Taylor advocated in the form of central record keeping and planning merely carried to an extreme the methods of earlier management reformers. But in one crucial way Taylor was a true original. He offered a "scientific" method for extracting the maximum efficiency from the individual worker.

To his engineer's eye, the prevailing shop practice was a shocking violation of the industrial progressivism of the modern age. There was a traditional fund of practical knowledge that workers passed on to one another; they performed their tasks unsupervised and by "rule of thumb"; and, what was worse, they customarily worked at a slow pace that conformed to a group-approved norm. In short, "the shop was really run by the workmen, and not by the bosses." To remedy this retrogressive state, Taylor proposed two basic industrial reforms. The first would cut away the brain work inherent in what workers did and place it wholly in the hands of the managers. They would assume "the burden of gathering together all of the traditional knowledge which in the past has been possessed by the workmen and then of classifying, tabulating, and reducing this knowledge to rules, laws, and formulae." The second reform, essentially a function of the first, would deprive workers of the responsibilities they had normally exerted on the shop floor. "Faster work can be assured . . . only through *enforced* standardization of methods, *enforced* adoption of the best implements and working conditions, and *enforced* cooperation. . . . And the duty of enforcing . . . rests with the *management* alone." With the knowledge and the power theirs, management could proceed to put labor on a "scientific" basis—subjecting each task to time-and-motion study, hiring and training the right man for each job, and, what Taylor considered his unique contribution, fixing a differential rate that would give each worker the money incentive to work to the standards of the stopwatch.

In practical application, scientific management was only a modest success. By temperament a root-and-branch man, Taylor insisted on the adoption of his scheme in its entirety. No company ever went through the complete transformation on which Taylor predicated scientific management, and the few that tried paid dearly for the effort. Still, Taylor's influence was enormous. A remarkable proselytizer, Taylor and his disciples spread his scientific-management teachings throughout American industry and beyond.[11] It was a revolutionary event. A new subject had been incorporated into the range of managerial calculation: the workingman himself.

It would take a war crisis, however, to translate the management of labor into a working reality in American industry. An acute labor shortage developed, accompanied by intense industrial unrest. Labor productivity dropped 10 per cent between 1915 and 1918, the first such reversal in the historic upward trend (excepting times of acute depression). Labor turnover, always high in American plants, reached crisis proportions. The war forced employers to ask questions that had not greatly troubled Frederick W. Taylor: how could absenteeism be checked? could men be kept from quitting? why did they go on strike and/or join unions? Clearly, as one expert noted in 1916, the answers required employers to think in terms of "the *human* problem of labor and the wise handling of men." The home-front experience reinforced this approach. Patriotism stirred men and offered a way, as one steel executive remarked, "to stimulate production." Through Americanization programs for immigrants, Liberty bond drives, parades, and rallies, many employers successfully countered the disruptive effects of the war. There was emerging, too, a new school of industrial psychology, and its claims seemed justified by the extensive testing program carried out on war draftees.

The practice of labor management was thus spurred forward and beyond the simplistic economic psychology of Frederick W. Taylor. No longer could an efficiency engineer say that he did not "care a hoot what became of the workman after he left the factory at night, so long as he was able to show up the next morning in fit condition for a hard day's toil." As the manager of the Burgess Sulphite Company put it in 1916: "We employers who feel that management is to become a true science must begin to think less of the science of material things and more of the science of human relationships." Personnel administration, pronounced the National Industrial Conference Board, was "a natural and businesslike method of dealing with the . . . work force to secure results."[12]

So the circle closed on the American worker. With each advance, the quest for efficiency cut further into the prideful autonomy that John Brophy had celebrated in his father's life in the mines. Mechanization, the giant scale of business organization, systematic administration, and, finally, labor management, each in its way diminished the worker and cut him down to fit the productive system. Frederick W. Taylor had not flinched from the consequences. Under scientific management, workers would "do what they are told promptly and without asking questions or making suggestions. . . . It is absolutely necessary for every man in our organization to become one of a train of gear wheels."[13] The industrial-relations people of the 1920s did not deny this vision; on the contrary, theirs was the task of completing it by making the worker a happy—and hence efficient—participant in Taylor's industrial order.

The saving element was, of course, the imperfect success of the efficiency experts. They were often limited to piecemeal activities. The essential administrative base, the industrial-relations department, was absent in most small and medium-sized firms, and even in half the companies employing over 2,000 people during the 1920s. With the most generous of financing and best of the experts, moreover, the practice tended to fall short of industrial-relations theory. The inveterate resistance of workers took many forms, but was always rooted in an informal social order on the shop floor that the most assiduous of managements could not eradicate. Not even the relentless conveyor belt wholly succeeded in defeating the wily tactics of workers to retain some control over their lives in the shop. Still, the thrust of modern management could not be denied: in the name of efficiency, the worker was being reduced to a cog in the great wheel of productive enterprise.

Industrial recruits

Between 1870 and 1929 the physical output of American industry increased fourteen times. Such phenomenal growth generated a demand for workers that could never be satisfied by the country's existing industrial population. So, from the first, labor had to be recruited from other societies. Much of this flow had always come from America's own countryside. During the half-century before 1920, probably half of all rural-born children moved cityward. Immigration was the other source of labor. During the years of prime growth, industry depended heavily on foreign workers. Before World War I, close to 60 per cent of the industrial labor force was foreign born.[14]

Since the 1840s, the country had counted on the brawn of rural immigrants—especially the Irish—to dig the canals, lay the rail tracks, build the cities, and fill the ranks of unskilled factory workers. But much of the overseas migration had come, not from the countryside, but from the industrial districts of northern Europe. English, Welsh, and German artisans brought with them skills crucial for the emergent industrial economy. They also served as the teachers of American labor. Theirs was a shaping influence on working-class culture and institutions, trade unions included, in the nineteenth century.

During the 1890s this northern European migration receded, to be supplanted by an even vaster flow from southern and eastern Europe. In 1900 the numbers annually arriving from Italy and the Austro-Hungarian Empire passed 100,000. Between 1900 and 1914, southeastern Europe sent to America well over 9 million persons. While farming had absorbed one stream of the earlier immigration, the new wave went mostly into the industrial sector. And, unlike their predecessors, the Italian, Yiddish, and Slavic immigrants almost wholly lacked industrial skills. In the tenement districts of New York and Chicago, Jews became the sweated labor of the ready-made clothing shops. Other immigrants, mainly Slavs and Italians, flooded into the bottom ranks of American basic industry. Of the 14,359 common laborers employed at the Carnegie steel mills in Pittsburgh in March 1907, for example, 11,694 were eastern Europeans. The low-paid, heavy work in American factories, outside the South, became the virtual preserve of the recent immigrants. An investigator applying for blast-furnace work was turned away: "Only Hunkies work on those jobs."[15]

These workers saw factory life through peasant eyes. They had been driven from their homes by encroaching forces of modernity—the end of legal limits on the right to sell, subdivide, or mortgage land; the undermining of the village subsistence economy by the spread of manufactured goods and commercial agriculture; and the falling death rate that upset the ancient balance between acreage and population. The peasant, with mortgage payments he could not meet, the younger sons unprovided with land, faced a cruel decline into the dependent, propertyless servant class. The only salvation lay in migration to lands from which men returned with money. First in a seasonal way to neighboring countries, then, as rail and steamship travel became cheap and dependable, in multiplying numbers they went to the United States and other distant lands. The object was always the same: to earn a stake and return to the native village. The immigrants harbored no illusions about America. "There in Pittsburgh, people say, the dear sun never shines brightly, the air is saturated with stench and gas." Letters home warned that "here in America one must work for three horses."

How much could a man expect to earn? In Pittsburgh the going rate for common labor in the steel mills was 16.5 cents an hour in 1910. Two-thirds of the immigrant workers made less than $12.50 a week, one-third less than $10.00, far below the $15.00 that the Pittsburgh Associated Charities set as the weekly minimum for providing the bare necessities to a family of five. Even on the twelve-hour day, seven-day week that many steel workers labored, a family could not be supported.

But the peasant workers did not expect to support families in America. The immigration after 1900 was disproportionately male—upwards of 70 per cent in some peak years. Of immigrant steel workers surveyed in 1907, one-third were single, and of the married men in the country under five years, roughly two-thirds reported their wives abroad. Those with families generally supplemented their incomes by lodging the others in a "boarding boss system." A boarder, paying $2.50 or so a month for his bed and sharing the cost of the food, could reasonably expect to save a third or more of his wage as a common laborer. In return, the boarding boss received a second income and, because of his strategic position, a likely promotion to foreman.

Not wage rates, working conditions, nor living standards figured crucially in the immigrant's calculation, but rather the job itself. "The work is very heavy, but I don't mind it," a brick factory worker wrote his wife, "let it be heavy, but may it last without interruption." A few years' hardship seemed a cheap enough price for the precious savings. America, a Polish worker wrote home, "is a golden land as long as there is work," but "when there is none" the country "is worth nothing." During hard times the immigrant workers flooded back to Europe. In the depression year 1908, more Austro-Hungarians and Italians left than entered the United States.

The disruption of European peasant society produced a labor supply that peculiarly matched the needs of the new industrial order. These preindustrial people adapted to an advanced technological system with little complaint. The innovations so painful to seasoned industrial workers—the undermining of skill and the loss of traditional autonomy—meant little to the immigrants. They entered a modern industrial order assuming that it would be wholly alien to them, and they had compelling reasons for accepting the system stemming from their own Old-World experience. Adaptable and industrious, the numberless immigrants constituted a remarkable windfall for American industry. And, as one scholar shrewdly observed in 1924, employers treated their bounty of immigrant workers "in much the same way that American farmers have used our land supply."[16]

In August 1914 war broke out in Europe. For four years, hostilities interrupted the immigration flow. When the war ended, intensifying nativist sentiment led to restrictive legislation in 1921 and 1924 that effectively closed off the peasant movement into American industry. The accustomed labor recruitment from agrarian peoples, however, did not end.

In the South, the black population was ripe for migration. The boll weavil, low cotton prices, and crop diversification plagued the sharecropper. White repression was unremitting. When labor agents appeared in 1916 with promises of jobs in the North, an exodus began. "You could not rest in your bed at night for Chicago," recalled one migrant from Hattiesburg, Mississippi. By November 1918 upwards of half a million blacks had departed for "the Land of Hope," and another 1.3 million left during the 1920s.

The able-bodied entered American industry in great numbers. The Chicago packing houses, 97 per cent white in 1909, employed 10,000 blacks in 1918—over 20 per cent of the labor force. In 1920 over 10 per cent of the workers in the northern iron and steel mills were black. Only 7 per cent of black males had been employed in industry in 1890; by 1930, 25.2 per cent. The increase partly reflected industrial opportunities in the South, but in the later period mainly the migration northward.

The sharecroppers and farm laborers took the places at the bottom of the ladder vacated by the Slavic and Italian workers. Like the European immigrants, the black migrants perceived their jobs through the eyes of newcomers to the factory world. So much they had in common: an acceptance as given of the modernizing changes that preceded their arrival; the valuation of their jobs in terms of opportunity, and of a kind that their own societies could not have yielded up to them; and finally, the tendency to judge their terms of work against the standards of an impoverished agrarian economy. But there was also one profound difference: the immigrants were products of European society, the black migrants, of Southern racism. Where the immigrant looked back in hopes of a restored place in his native village, the black looked forward to the freedom of the northern city. The resulting calculation of money and time that rendered the immigrant accepting of his industrial situation was unknown to the southern migrant. The same conservatizing effect was accomplished for the black man by his struggle to surmount race prejudice.

His industrial opportunity the black worker tended to see as the gift of his employer. Many black leaders encouraged this idea, and often, as in Henry Ford's hiring record at the River Rouge plant, it was warranted by the facts. From white workers, on the other hand, blacks encountered a wall of hostility. They knew the trade unions to be largely exclusionary or segregationist, and rank-and-file sentiment to be against their employment at any but the most menial and disagreeable of jobs. The wartime conditions under which the black migrants arrived exacerbated racial tensions. In industrial centers, severe housing shortages developed, and blacks and whites jostled each other for living space. The war spirit mixed a brew of anxieties and hopes that inspired frequent racial incidents, many near riots, and several bloody race wars, the worst of them in East St. Louis in July 1917 and in Chicago in July 1919. And the parallel flow of southern whites into northern industry brought into the factories the very notions from which the southern blacks had fled. The racial pressures under which he labored, isolating him from the white workers and attaching him to his employer, dictated to the black worker a logic no less potent than the peasant calculation of the immigrant workers for accepting the factory world as he found it.

The abundant supply of rural migrants from Europe, from the South, and from America's declining rural areas lessened the pressure on other, earlier sources of industrial labor. Prompted by progressive legislation and to some degree by technological advances also, industry began to abandon its traditional use of child labor. Between 1900 and 1930, the portion of children between ten and fifteen years of age who were gainfully employed fell from 18 to 4.7 per cent. The extraordinary educational expansion of these years also took many of the nation's older children off the labor market. Eight times as many young people—half of all those of high-school age—attended high school in 1930 as in 1900. During those years, labor force participation by young people aged 16–19 dropped by 25 per cent, and most of this shrinkage came from the 16 and 17 year olds. Alternative labor supplies, protective legislation, and new technology were to some extent also putting a brake on employment of adult women in factories. The proportion of women in the industrial labor force declined from 17.5 per cent in 1900 to 11 per cent in 1930; after 1910 the absolute number of women in industry remained nearly stationary.

There were, however, compensating gains in other directions. Outside of factories and domestic service (where female employment also leveled off after 1900), dramatic increases occurred: the number of women in clerical jobs jumped eight-fold between 1900 and 1930, and in sales and other service trades it tripled. These gains, more than overbalancing the slowdowns in more traditional areas of women's work, pushed up women's participation in the labor force from 14.5 per cent in 1880 to 21.5 per cent in 1930.

Equally significant was the entry of a new group of women into the labor market in these years. In the nineteenth century, a strong stigma had attached to the outside employment of wives. When they worked, one scholar has remarked, "it was usually a sign that something had gone wrong"—a husband either dead, missing, or unemployable. The social prejudice against working wives was, in fact, solidly grounded in the economy of the nineteenth-century family. After 1900, reliance on wifely labors became less absolute, partly because of the spread of labor-saving conveniences to working-class homes, but equally because of the commercialization of such family chores as canning, baking, and clothes making. World War I had a liberating effect, and so did acculturation among immigrant groups. Among the Italians of Buffalo, for example, less than 2 per cent of the wives in 1905 held regular outside jobs. While this pattern persisted for the first generation, the second generation of Buffalo's Italian wives did begin to move into the labor market. In 1925, 12 per cent were working. Nationwide, married women joined the labor force at twice the rate of women generally after 1900, and the three million at work in 1930 was four times the number in 1900.

Not the earnings of the individual, but the family, constituted the crucial calculation in the working-class economy. Hardly half of all industrial families, an expert estimated in 1912, got along on the earnings of the husband. As the children were pressed into school, as traditional sources of supplementary income from lodgers and homework dried up, the outside earnings of wives took up the slack. A study of Chicago families, based on 1920 census data, revealed that 20.4 per cent of the wives of semiskilled and unskilled men were working. More than half of all the working wives had husbands who were also employed; the portion in this category would have been much smaller two decades before. Two out of every five industrial families in Chicago in 1920 depended on more than one wage earner. The reliance on multiple incomes, especially among the low paid, thus continued to sustain American working-class life.[17]

At the lower end of the employment ladder, strong stabilizing forces were persistently at work in American industry. Managerial prerogative, however, depended ultimately, not on voluntary acquiescence, but rather on the power of employers. After 1900, they put to the test the collective strength of American labor.

The trade-union struggle

The trade unions were built around such workmen as John Brophy's father. For Patrick Brophy, the son recalled, unionism was "taken for granted as a normal part of life." So it was for railroad men, printers, iron workers, carpenters, and a host of other skilled workers.

The union encompassed their working lives. Apprenticeship rules regulated entry into the trade, and the closed shop excluded nonunion men. Incessant policing of jurisdictional lines defended the jobs from rival trades. In the carpenters union, the business agent served as the employment man between the industry and the members. On the job, union rules defined, sometimes in minute detail, the terms of work. The union contract at the Homestead Steel Works contained fifty-eight pages of "footnotes," and this was only a pale imitation of rules and tonnage provisions governing the union puddling mills. For the locomotive engineer, ever on the move and irregularly scheduled, the work rules defined a standard day's work (by hour and/or mileage) and compensation for extra time and lost time, and the engineer's responsibilities and rights while operating his train. In the case of puddlers, machinists, and molders, regulation focused on output; in the case of miners, coal grading and weighing. For craft workers trade unionism was functional, an immediate part of their day-to-day life on the job, and, above all, the protector of traditional skills and prerogatives.

The union influence did not end at the factory gate. There was a potent social component to craft identity. The International Association of Machinists, when it organized in Atlanta in 1888, called together craft workers of "honorable, industrious and sober habits" whose "good reputation" was being injured by the low habits of a minority. The early IAM boasted an elaborate ritual and placed much stock in self-improvement. Similar motives impelled the Brotherhood of Locomotive Engineers, whose constitution directed the local divisions to expel any member who "conducted himself in a manner unbecoming to a man." There also was a desire to provide insurance and mutual aid in the high-risk occupation of train-driving.[18] Despite the general tendency toward bargaining unionism, the fraternal and benevolent impulses remained vigorous within the craft organizations.

Leisure was likely also to center on union activities. Turn-of-the-century union journals are filled with local accounts of baseball leagues, picnics, balls, lectures, and funerals. In Muncie, Indiana, the unions operated an active Workingman's Library and Reading Room. Labor Day was a great event there, given over to parades, orations, sports contests, and dancing, ending in a display of fireworks at the fairground. When Samuel Gompers visited Muncie in 1897, he dined at the mayor's house before addressing a packed opera house.[19] In strong union towns, the local movement was a major force in the community. The local press reported labor affairs fully; commercial interests were respectful and sympathetic; and town officials were reliable allies. On the job and off, the union was an encompassing element in the life of the union working man.

The strengths of craft organization gave rise also to its chief defect: an abiding particularism that made each trade look to itself, and, emphatically, to hold apart from the unskilled and the alien. This tendency the American Federation of Labor legitimized and perpetuated in its basic rules. The handiwork was mostly by the Federation's founder, Samuel Gompers, a man of extraordinary parts—a Jewish cigar-maker schooled in the Marxist debates of the 1870s, a vigorous thinker capable of turning those radical ideas to the purposes of American trade unionism, a crafty and ambitious leader with a sixth sense for the thinking of his followers. The pure-and-simple labor movement that Gompers led for many years reflected the craft worker's view of the world. The limitations of that formulation were not immediately apparent. Hammered out against the structural formlessness and vague reformism of the Knights of Labor, the AFL could present itself as a monument to labor's realism and maturity. The movement, Gompers insisted, was "guided by the history of the past, drawing its lessons from history. It knows the conditions by which working people are surrounded. It works along the line of least resistance and endeavors to accomplish the best results in improving . . . conditions . . . today and tomorrow."[20] At the outset, the AFL's performance matched Gompers's confidence.

In the prosperous years following the depressed 1890s, the labor movement experienced a remarkable period of growth. The building-trades unions grew from 67,000 in 1897 to 391,600 in 1904, the transportation unions from 116,000 to 446,300. Most spectacular was the progress in the coal fields. The bituminous miners struck in 1897 and won the Central Competitive Field Agreement covering virtually the entire industry in Pennsylvania, Ohio, Indiana, and Illinois. The momentous anthracite strike of 1902, skillfully managed by John Mitchell to elicit the aid of the sympathetic Roosevelt administration, brought permanent organization to the hard-coal fields. Between 1897 and 1904 total union membership climbed from 447,000 to over 2 million.

Those were uniquely favorable years for trade unionism. The recent depression had stirred fears of social upheaval, and the conservative message issuing from the AFL was reassuring. Among the corporate giants then emerging there was an eagerness to curry public favor and avoid labor troubles. The National Civic Federation, composed of business magnates, labor leaders, and public figures, endorsed the principles of conservative trade unionism and labor peace, whose "twin foes . . . are the anti-union employers and the Socialists."[21] Among the smaller employers, trade agreements seemed a way to stabilize labor relations and equalize labor costs. With this in mind, often encouraged by the unions, the National Founders' Association, the National Metal Trades Association, the Lake Carriers' Association, and numerous other employer groups sprang up.

A deadly reaction followed. Employers had not counted on a painful period of trial and error, on what seemed to them violations of agreements, on an unremitting flow of fresh demands, on strikes and rank-and-file militancy. "What is the use of wasting time, money, and patience any longer," asked an angry meat packer, "when . . . any agreement into which any of these unions enter is not worth the paper on which it is written?" Union efforts to regulate output and shop practice seemed wholly fatal to the managerial quest for efficiency that was going into high gear after 1900. When the IAM placed limits on apprentices and objected to piece work and doubling up on machines, the National Metal Trades Association adopted a bristling Declaration of Principle asserting that "we will not admit of any interference with the management of our business." One official rendered the damning judgment: the unions had failed "to appreciate the progressivism of the age."

One by one, the trade associations broke with the unions. A host of new organizations, led by the National Association of Manufacturers, joined the battle. The organized employers were formidable enemies. The National Founders' Association provided its members with strike breakers (including a pool of skilled molders and guards to protect them), transferred work to operating mills, and compensated for lost income. The association also maintained industrial spies ("intelligence men") and a central blacklist of known "agitators." The association counseled militant war: try always to settle differences with the men, but after they had gone out "and you have made up your mind to defend yourself, cut off all negotiation and accept nothing but unconditional surrender."[22]

The courts enlisted on management's side. In the Danbury Hatters case (1908), the Supreme Court ruled that trade unions were subject to the Sherman Anti-Trust Act and found the nationwide boycott of the Loewe Company a conspiracy in restraint of trade. The resulting judgment embittered union men everywhere. The 197 members of the Hatters Union were held personally liable for the triple damages claimed by the company and stood to lose their homes and life savings.

Even worse was the legal attack on the strike. No actual violation of law was required. Employers needed only to plead irreparable damages before a sympathetic judge, who would then enjoin the union, in effect, from carrying on an effective strike. So, for example, federal judge Joseph V. Quarles issued a temporary restraining order in June 1906 against Iron Molders Union 125 in its strike against the Allis-Chalmers Company of Milwaukee. In September, despite hundreds of affidavits attesting to the law-abiding behavior of the strikers, Judge Quarles granted a permanent injunction forbidding, among other things, "any interference with the plaintiff's business, peaceful persuasion to induce its employees to stop work, and all picketing." Two years later, after a number of union men had been fined or jailed for contempt, a higher court reversed Judge Quarles. By then, of course, the strike had long since collapsed. Supreme Court Justice Louis D. Brandeis later wrote that the injunction served not so much to protect property as it did to "endow property with active militant power which would be dominant over men."[23]

The justifying rhetoric matched the fury of the attack. "Organized labor . . . does not place its reliance upon reason and justice," NAM president David M. Parry proclaimed. "It is, in all essential features, a mob knowing no master except its own will. Its history is stained with blood and ruin." The defense of the "open shop," moreover, linked the organized employers to traditional national values. Trade unionism, said Parry, "denies to those outside its ranks the individual right to dispose of their labor as they see fit—a right that is one of the most sacred and fundamental of American liberty."[24]

The employer counteroffensive plunged the labor movement into a profound inner crisis. If labor gave in, trade unionism would find itself tightly confined, limited to a narrow segment of its potential constituency, and totally excluded from the heart of the modern economy. Was organized labor prepared to accept so minor a role, and to abandon the vast majority of American working people into the hands of the employers? The answer that came back was deeply ambiguous.

The AFL stood four-square on the principle: it was the movement of all the nation's workers. The authority to speak as labor's voice in the public arena belonged to the Federation alone, and it claimed the sole right to grant jurisdictions and charters to national unions. Any union lacking the mark of legitimacy was branded as a dual and outlaw organization, an enemy to be given no quarter or sympathy. Why a movement rooted as the AFL was in a narrow and particularistic section of the American working class should have developed so abiding a sense of exclusive legitimacy remains one of the great mysteries of American labor history. But having taken this stance, the AFL could never rest easy with its post-1904 status. On the other hand, it lacked the ability to break out of that confined position. The characteristics adopted to meet nineteenth-century conditions proved remarkably inflexible— another of the great puzzles of American labor history—in the face of twentieth-century realities. The force of events did, of course, induce some change, but not nearly enough to make the labor movement a formidable contender against hostile industry and an indifferent state.

Pure-and-simple doctrine had placed the trade unions firmly in the private sector. Workers should never seek, said Gompers, "at the hands of government what they could accomplish by their own initiative and activities." The AFL limited its political objectives to such matters as immigration restriction, convict labor, and seamen's conditions. Even here the Federation restricted its efforts to lobbying within the major parties and explicitly rejected independent or partisan political action.

The massive legal attack forced some moderation of this doctrinaire voluntarism. Prodded by a notorious injunction against the Chicago printers in 1906 ("judicial usurpation and anarchy," Gompers stormed), the AFL stepped up its political work. When Republican leaders rebuffed Labor's Bill of Grievances, the Federation entered the congressional campaign of 1906 to "reward your friends and punish your enemies." Two years later Gompers compromised his cherished nonpartisanship by endorsing the Democratic ticket. Moreover, middle-class progressivism exerted some positive pressure. In practice, a labor movement claiming to speak for the entire working class could not do other than support social legislation that would chiefly benefit working people. At the state level, where most of this activity took place, organized labor could almost invariably be counted on the side of social reform.

Yet the persistence of the voluntaristic orientation was more significant than the points of erosion. No internal reform was undertaken that would have given labor's political arms—the city centrals, the state federations, the AFL itself—the means to do effective political work (not to speak of the formation of the labor party). In neither 1906 nor 1908 had the AFL been able to muster much beyond $8000 in its vaunted electoral campaigns, nor to mobilize the labor vote to any significant degree. Little wonder, then, that its political rewards were modest at best and did not include what labor most required—protection from the equity powers of the courts and genuine immunity from the antitrust laws. As for the positive uses to which government might be put, these seemed simply beyond labor's horizon. The labor movement had not, of course, intended to make its way by political means. The focus was unremittingly economic, and this orientation determined its structure and strategy.

The dominant unit was the national union—the United Brotherhood of Carpenters and Joiners, the United Mine Workers of America, and so on—representing workers of specified occupations everywhere in the United States and often Canada (hence the frequent designation "international"). Theirs was the work of collective bargaining and economic warfare. To them, therefore, went the resources. To them also went the grant of *exclusive* jurisdiction, since overlapping or multiple unions for a given trade would weaken the capacity to bargain and strike. To the national unions, finally, went total authority within their jurisdictions. They had the right, as Gompers said, "to do as they think just and proper in matters of their own trade, without the let or hindrance of any other body of men." Trade autonomy was the ruling principle of the AFL, and it meant that the ultimate choices regarding organizing the unorganized rested with the national unions.

Because they functioned as instruments of collective bargaining, the national unions always came down to this question: were the unorganized a threat to the existing economic position of the union? Clearly they were wherever market competition existed between union and nonunion firms. Thus, the United Mine Workers succeeded brilliantly in the Central Competitive Field because all the producers there came under union contract; the failure to organize the competing West Virginia and Kentucky mines would eventually drive the union out of the Central Competitive Field in the 1920s. Such pressure did not touch the teamsters, construction trades, and other crafts that operated in local product markets. The local unions there moved heaven and earth to organize their own towns, but other places were of no compelling importance (except in a secondary way as a source of nonunion labor).

Technological change provided the other organizing imperative. "Every day our trade is becoming more and more specialized," said President James O'Connell of the Machinists, "and if we hope to . . . protect our craft it is necessary that our qualifications for membership be radically changed." The IAM stopped short of the unskilled. Not so the Butchers Union. After organizing began in the Chicago stockyards in 1900, the union abandoned its craft exclusiveness entirely because "today it is impossible to draw the line where the skilled man leaves off and the unskilled man begins." The division of labor "places the skilled workmen largely at the mercy of common labor and makes it necessary to organize all working in the large plants under one head."[25] As ethnic barriers broke down under this logic, the stockyards experienced a union upsurge between 1901 and 1904 remarkable for the unity it created among native, immigrant, and black workers.

In the needle trades, the workers themselves provided the driving force for organization. America's ready-to-wear clothing derived mostly from a few great urban centers, from the sweated labor of Jewish and Italian immigrants in New York City, Chicago, and elsewhere. The work was seasonal and low-paid, much of it was subcontracted to small shops in tenements, and the less skilled operations were largely in the hands of immigrant girls. When 146 workers, most of them young women, died in the terrible Triangle Fire of March 25, 1911, the exploitative conditions in the industry were at last brought home to the country.

The garment workers had already begun to rise in tumultuous protest. The match was struck at a mass meeting at New York's Cooper Union on November 22, 1909. Angered by the speakers' lengthy pleas for moderation, Clara Lemlich, a young shirtwaist-maker who had earlier taken a savage beating on the picket line, rose and in impassioned Yiddish, demanded a general strike. Shouting its assent, the entire assemblage, arms outstretched, took the Jewish pledge to adhere to the cause or "may this hand wither from the arm I now raise." The next day the shirtwaist workers, young girls predominantly, came out as a body. This "Uprising of the Twenty Thousand" was followed by strikes of the cloakmakers in July 1910, the Chicago men's clothing workers in October 1910, and the fur workers in June 1912. In a dramatic climax the next winter, nearly 150,000 men's and women's garment workers shut down the entire New York industry.

When the dust settled, collective bargaining had come to the needle trades. In women's clothing, the famous Protocol of Peace (1910) put into effect a unique arbitration system, which gave way in 1916 to more conventional collective bargaining. The Hart, Shaffner, and Marx Agreement (1910) became a model for the men's clothing industry. Stable unions were meanwhile emerging. Because the craft-oriented United Garment Workers of America failed to gain the confidence of the immigrant workers in the cities, a dynamic rival union sprang up in the men's clothing field—the Amalgamated Clothing Workers of America, with the brilliant young Sidney Hillman at its head. The fledgling AFL union in women's clothing, on the other hand, was led by men who were themselves recent immigrants, products of the garment shops, and close to the rank-and-file in outlook. They perceived the unrest for the union opportunity that it was and skillfully managed the strikes to build the International Ladies' Garment Workers Union into a powerful organization.

Almost everywhere else, however, the battle went against labor. Corporate employers had grown too large and powerful; they were too unyielding in defense of managerial prerogatives; and craft leverage had weakened too much in technologically advanced fields. Because the issues were so fundamental—on the one hand, the defense of basic and traditional rights, on the other, often the very survival of organization—the trade unions fought back tenaciously. David Montgomery has noted the rise of rank-and-file militancy and "workers' consciousness" in these years.[26] In the metal trades, among the railroad shop crafts, in steel, meat packing, and textiles, bitter strikes were fought against the open shop and the deadly new efficiency systems. Still, the weight of advantage lay with management, and, for all the blood spilled and sacrifices made, the unions mostly went down to defeat. The national unions retreated from the packing houses, the steel mills, the auto plants, the big metal-fabricating factories, and settled for the protected parts of their jurisdictions.

For better (as in the case of the thriving Carpenters' Brotherhood) or worse (as in the case of the 6,500-man Amalgamated
Association of Iron, Steel, and Tin Workers), the labor movement struck a new balance in these years, confining itself to
the economic sector where it could function and, in effect,
letting the rest go. Schooled as they were to deal in hard
realities, union leaders always had to weigh the interests of
their existing organizations against the claims of the unorganized. In an era when the odds ran heavily against success,
there could hardly be any question as to which would be
sacrificed.

Only time would tell whether a more favorable environment might evoke within trade unionism a dynamism not
evident during the hard decade prior to World War I. In the
meantime, these years were providing answers to the related
question: was a genuine alternative open to the American
workingman?

Labor radicalism

Since its founding in 1901, the Socialist Party of America had
developed into a major political force in the country. By 1910
the Socialists boasted a nationwide network of 3,200 branches
and 42 state organizations, a prolific party press, a cadre of
skilled functionaries, and, in Eugene V. Debs, a remarkable
national leader. A spell-binding speaker, a man of enormous
personal warmth, transparently selfless in his identification
with the common man, Debs was a legendary figure even in
his own day. The Socialist record of success mounted up,
primarily at the municipal level, but also nationally in a growing popular vote that reached 897,000 in the 1912 elections.

Socialist sentiment was strong not only among the German
workers of Milwaukee and the Yiddish-speaking garment
workers, but also in such skilled "American" trades as print-
ing, shoe manufacture, and mining. The Massachusetts party
boasted that "in this state [socialism] draws its chief strength

How the Socialist of American tried to remake the Labor movement

from the highest grade of wage-earning labor . . . the aristocracy, as it were, of labor."[27]

The Socialist party was not, however, limited to the working class. There was, first, a strong agrarian element deriving from the defunct populism of the 1890s. In 1912 the largest percentage of the popular vote for Debs came from seven western and mountain states. The Socialist party also drew on substantial middle-class support, strongly augmented in later years by an overflow from progressivism. And, finally, to accommodate the immigrant groups, the party permitted the affiliation of essentially autonomous foreign-language federations.

The fundamental questions thus raised about the Socialist party as a working-class movement were compounded by its performance where it did gain power. In Brockton and Haverhill, Massachusetts, in Schenectady, New York, in Milwaukee, Wisconsin, there was little in practice to distinguish Socialist administrations from reform goverments elsewhere. To vote Socialist could in itself be a meaningful act, and where, as on the East Side of New York City or in the German sections of Milwaukee, party affiliation merged with ethnic and community identity, socialism could be the unifying element in the workingman's life. Still, the future of a socialist movement rooted in the Marxist concept of class struggle depended on its base in the working class.

The key, as party leaders well recognized, lay in the connection with organized labor. While asserting the primacy of political action, they also needed an allied labor movement. The real question was tactical: should they seek to capture the AFL or create a new movement? The Socialist Labor party, under the doctrinaire Daniel DeLeon, had written off the AFL as hopelessly captive to "the labor lieutenants of capital," and had set up in 1895 the rival Socialist Trades and Labor Alliance. It was partly in protest against this action that the moderates had broken from the SLP and joined in forming a broadly based party in 1901.

From the first, the Socialist party officially rejected dual unionism and urged its followers, as a matter of duty, to "assist in building up and unifying the trades and labor organizations." But the party required a reciprocating answer, and when none was forthcoming, initiated a campaign to win over the trade-union movement. The focus of this effort was the AFL convention, where each year the Socialists manfully took up the fight against the Gompers administration. Yet, even if the Socialists had won here, as they very nearly did on occasion, comparatively little would have been gained without an accompanying transformation of the national unions. These would have had to concede a substantial part of their autonomy and income to make the labor movement an effective political force. But beyond political support, the Socialists needed organized labor to provide the mass working-class base that sustained the European movements and that American socialism, despite its popularity, lacked. And this could only be accomplished within the national unions. The Socialists knew, in principle, what they wanted: unions capable of organizing the mass of workers and capable of uncompromising militancy against employers. They had, moreover, ample opportunity to act on their beliefs.

Power and responsibility, however, induced a queer change. Time after time, once they had acceded to office, Socialists begain to act—if they did not always talk—like any other trade unionists. In the Machinists union, for example, the Socialists defeated the conservative James O'Connell in 1912 and installed William H. Johnston as president. Under his administration, the IAM raised dues and extended its benefit system, added regularly to the powers of the national lodge, repudiated the promise for industrial unionism because (as Johnston stated) it would "cause unlimited [jurisdictional] trouble." Further, in 1922 the IAM entered into the Baltimore and Ohio agreement that was the last word in labor-management cooperation. In each instance the union had acted in the name of realism, and in each instance had cast further into

extinction the IAM socialist program.[28] The constant frustration of such efforts prompted the radical Joseph Ettor to
denounce the notion of working inside the trade unions:

> We tried, but the more we fooled with the beast the more it
> *captured us.* . . . We learned at an awful cost particularly this:
> That the most unscrupulous labor fakers now betraying the
> workers were once our . . . comrades, who . . . were not only
> lost, but . . . became the supporters of the old and [the] most
> serious enemies of the new.[29]

Ettor's lament was inadvertent tribute to an enduring fixity
of purpose that derived from labor's basic accommodation to
American life. Voluntary associations in a pluralistic society,
the trade unions necessarily judged men by their performance,
not by their beliefs or other affiliations. But, by the same
token, participants had to adhere to an unyielding code of
priorities: while in the role of trade unionists, their first loyalty could only be to union objectives. Socialist unionists in
fact abided by those terms and thereby rendered themselves
ultimately incapable of remaking the labor movement.

"To talk about reforming these rotten graft infested
unions . . . is as vain and wasteful of time as to spray a cess-
pool with attar of roses," protested Eugene Debs. Socialist
left-wingers sharing Debs's disgust could not but look forward to a new movement. An indigenous radical unionism
had meanwhile developed among the hard-rock miners of the
mountain states. From a decade of bloody industrial war—
Cripple Creek (1894), Leadville (1896), the Coeur d'Alenes
(1899), the disastrous Colorado strikes (1903–05)—the Western Federation of Miners had emerged committed to militant
socialism and to unremitting struggle against the employers.
On June 27, 1905, leaders of these groups, plus a ragtag of
miscellaneous radicals and office-seekers, assembled in Chicago to set up the Industrial Workers of the World. The aim
was "to confederate the workers of this country into a working class movement that shall have for its purpose the emanci-

pation of the working class . . . having in view no compromise and no surrender."

Over the next few years, the IWW went through a remarkable shakedown period, casting out the moderating influences
one by one and producing in the end a homegrown brand of
American syndicalism. First to go was the Western Federation of Miners. Taken over by moderates in 1907, it moved
back into the trade-union mainstream and then back into the
AFL. The WFM left behind not only the heart of a radical
labor ideology, but also such key IWW leaders as the indispensable Vincent St. John and Big Bill Haywood. A giant of a
a man, one-eyed and hard-bitten, a former hard-rock miner,
Haywood seemed to sum up in his own life the experiences
that generated labor radicalism. Next to go were the political
groups. With the "Overall Brigade" providing the margin of
votes, the IWW in 1908 committed itself exclusively to the
industrial field and became more rigidly antipolitical than the
AFL. Daniel DeLeon and his SLP group broke away to form
their own IWW (Detroit). Socialists such as Debs and Algie
M. Simons also dropped out, and the remaining links to the
IWW the Socialist party itself severed by requiring members to
repudiate sabotage.

What remained was a workers' movement committed to the
overthrow of capitalism and advancing direct action at the
point of production as its weapon. Scornful of the state and of
politics in all its forms, the movement counted on the general
strike to make the revolution and perceived the new order as a
stateless society in which industrial unions "take possession of
the industries and run them for the benefit of the workers."
The syndicalism sweeping through European labor in these
years shared a good deal with the American variety, and ideas
crossed the Atlantic in both directions. But the IWW was not
the child of European radicalism. It was, as editor Ben Williams said, "a distinct product of America and American conditions."

The IWW presented itself, as Haywood had boasted at the founding convention, was "an organization broad enough to take in all the working class." In an age of rampant racism and nativism, the IWW was indeed the most open, prejudice-free labor organization in U.S. history. But Haywood had gone on to urge "an uplifting of the fellow that is down in the gutter . . . realizing that society can be no better than its most miserable." This was its real constituency—the most miserable of American workers.[30]

In the East, the IWW acted briefly as a shock force, coming in to lead spontaneous revolts of industrial workers, and content to leave behind no mass organization. This role the IWW played brilliantly in a series of great strikes at McKees Rocks (1909), Lawrence (1912), Patterson (1913), and Akron (1913).

The western workers, however, evoked the IWW's true calling. For the itinerants following the harvest, the lumberjacks on the Pacific slope, the construction men and miners, the IWW tried to build a permanent, ongoing organization. Because the scattered migratory workers gathered there in winter and between jobs, Spokane, Fresno, and other western towns became the strategic points for the IWW. To open these hostile places for organizing work, the IWW was prepared to go through a series of heroic free-speech fights in 1909 and after. More and more of the organizing, however, was done on the job by missionary delegates who were themselves working stiffs. A California investigation in August 1914, prompted by the bloody Wheatland riot, revealed 40 IWW locals in the state, a membership of 5,000, half of them active missionaries, and a wide following of sympathizers. As the IWW progressed, its functional significance began to emerge.

"The final aim . . . is revolution," said a Wobbly organizer, "but for the present let's see if we can get a bed to sleep in, water enough to take a bath in and decent food to eat." No less than the AFL, the IWW concerned itself in practice with immediate, bread-and-butter gains. What trade unionism was to better-situated workers, syndicalism was to the rootless laborers of the West. "We are parasites," Bill Haywood told the U.S. Commission on Industrial Relations.

> The real people . . . are the workers, the productive workers, the ones who make society, who build the railroads, who till the soil, who run the mills. I have done no work for ten or fifteen years, and I am a parasite . . . That is what you are, and that is what the rest of them are that do not labor.

By so glorifying the workingman, the IWW tried to counter the hopelessness and degradation that held the migratory workers in abject bondage. The IWW meeting halls, the IWW press, the songs and heroes provided a sense of community accessible nowhere else. And, not least, the IWW offered a weapon to those lacking in the bargaining power available to other workers. Aggressive syndicalism—the open contempt for law, the advocacy of direct action, the sanctioning of violence—yielded a fairly consistent return of concessions from peace-seeking employers and public authorities.

In 1915–16 the IWW entered a new phase. Beginning with successes among the midwestern harvest workers in 1914, an effective system for the permanent organization of migratory workers seemed to be emerging. With Bill Haywood at the helm, financing was improved and central authority tightened. Dues-paying membership, never above fifty thousand in the first ten years, moved up toward one hundred thousand. The IWW, stated a delegate at the 1916 convention, "is passing out of the purely propaganda stage and is entering the stage of constructive organization."[31]

So, as the nation edged closer to war, this was the sum of labor's collective development. The trade-union movement was strongly rooted, but narrowly confined, in principle encompassing the entire labor force, in fact incapable of reaching the mass of industrial workers. The Socialists had consolidated their political position (notwithstanding a poor showing at the 1916 elections) and retained their hold on a large part of the labor movement, but without substantially affecting its trade-union orientation. The IWW, a bitter and unyielding enemy of the AFL, was building its native-rooted syndicalism into what may best be described as the trade unionism of the dispossessed. No one can know the future these labor developments might have found in the normal course of events. For war arrived in April 1917 and decided labor's future.

World War I: Testing time

Disaster came in full measure to the IWW. Risks there had always been in radical tactics that threatened public order and private property, and, inevitably, a price to be paid in the form of false arrests, beatings, periodic killings, and sometimes crushed campaigns. The IWW never, in practice, lived up to its rhetoric. There is, in fact, a notable lack of evidence of acts of sabotage and violence, certainly nothing comparable to some ninety dynamitings by the AFL's Structural Iron Workers in their bitter war against the National Erectors' Association. Adhering to this line of practical restraint when the country entered the war, the IWW silenced its vociferous antiwar propaganda, declined to counsel its members to resist the draft, and deliberately concentrated on organizing work and concrete issues. Wartime hysteria, however, grievously threw off these cautious calculations.

When the IWW led harvest workers, copper miners, and Pacific timber workers out on strike in the summer of 1917, employers ruthlessly struck back. Loyalty Leagues and vigilantes began to terrorize the IWW throughout the West. In Bisbee, Arizona, 1,200 strikers were rounded up and shipped out in cattle cars to the New Mexico desert. In Butte, Montana, vigilantes brutally lynched IWW organizer Frank Little. On September 5, 1917, the Justice Department staged massive raids on IWW offices and, within a few weeks, began a nationwide roundup of IWW leaders. The aim was, as one U.S. attorney understood it, "very largely to put the IWW out of business."[32]

The IWW had appealed to the Justice Department for protection against the vigilantes. Records were not destroyed nor arrest evaded, and indicted IWW leaders expected the courts to free them. On every score, that faith in American justice was misplaced. With its strikes crushed, its followers terrorized, its veteran leaders jailed, the IWW's promise as a labor movement for the "most miserable" of America's workers died.

The Socialists fared hardly better in the end. On the political front, the Socialist party at first profited from an antiwar stand that attracted dissenters across the country. Party membership jumped substantially, and important successes were registered in the 1917 municipal elections. But within the trade unions, the war undermined the Socialist position. The antiwar stand made the Socialists vulnerable to a skillful patriotic offensive by AFL conservatives. Yet more than patriotism was at work. The Socialist influence had always been predicated on the fact that it would not be a charge on trade-union operations. The war undercut this crucial condition. In the military emergency, Washington was prepared to concede a great deal to organized labor in exchange for labor's enthusiastic cooperation in the war effort. The choice that unions would make could never be doubted, even, as in the needle trades, by those deeply committed to the Socialist cause: they would take the concrete benefits and let the ideological loyalties go.[33] That choice, deeply damaging as it was to the fabric of shared agreement, began a fundamental erosion of the Socialist hold within the labor movement.

At this juncture, American socialism itself encountered a crisis that finished the job. Inspired by the Bolshevik revolution, the left-wingers wanted to reconstitute the Socialist party along Leninist lines and make an American revolution. About to lose control in the summer of 1919, the moderates expelled the opposition and nullified the party election. The desperate maneuver prevented the left-wing take-over of the party, but sacrificed its radical élan plus two-thirds of its membership, and set in motion an irreversible decline. In its later history, as it lost its working-class base, the Socialist party never again constituted a significant force within the American labor movement.

For wholly different reasons, the Communists, who emerged as the new dynamic wing of the American left, had little better success. The crucial distinction amounted to this: that the Communists, unlike the Socialists, were not prepared to operate within the labor movement on trade-union terms. Conservative unionists, indeed, rushed to this conclusion at once. Other unions, especially the needle trades, suffered years of bitter internal strife to resolve the conflict. But always the Communists came finally to be identified as an inimical element lacking a primary loyalty to trade-union ends. Expulsion—the ultimate sanction of voluntary associations—was the acid test. Never at issue in the case of the Socialists, expulsion was almost invariably the fate of defeated Communist factions. In 1928, the Communists abandoned their boring-from-within tactics and began the equally fruitless task of building a rival movement under the aegis of the Trade Union Unity League.

The labor hopes of the American left, hitherto bright, died in World War I and its aftermath. But for trade unionism, too, the war was an extraordinary testing time.

On November 12, 1917, at his own request, Woodrow Wilson came to Buffalo to address the AFL convention. No president had so honored the labor movement before. This was, moreover, the first time Wilson had absented himself from Washington since the declaration of war six months earlier. The plea he made for industrial peace, flanked by a guard of soldiers, underscored labor's strategic place in the war effort.

Realizing labor's opportunity, the wily Gompers cast aside

voluntaristic principles against government interference in union affairs. This event went deeper than appeared on the face of it. For not only did the AFL support the war effort, but it joined the administration's campaign on the antiwar Left. The AFL became a *de facto* instrument of the Wilson administration, accepting money from it (and from industry as well) to fight Socialist influence at home and carrying on at its behest political missions overseas to blunt the peace moves of war-weary European Socialists. This involvement, profoundly at odds with the Federation's voluntaristic philosophy, helped explain the decay of the political tolerence that had so long prevailed within the labor movement, as well as the dismal conservatism of the AFL during the 1920s.

In the short run, of course, Gompers's gambit paid off handsomely. Gradually, the AFL gained a voice in homefront policy. Union men sitting on war agencies not only defended standards against employer pressures, but raised them further, for example, by the imposition of the basic eighthour day. The war also encouraged the idea that workingmen should be free to organize and engage in collective bargaining. By the start of 1918, the AFL was openly demanding government protection of these rights. "No other policy is compatible with the spirit and methods of democracy."[34] The Wilson administration accepted this view, first in a piecemeal way, then, beginning in March 1918, as a matter of national policy. For the first time in the nation's history, American workers could organize without fear of reprisal. This much organized labor gained by its sudden aggressiveness in the public sector. It remained to be seen whether the movement harbored within itself a comparable capacity to seize the opportunity so created and organize the unorganized.

John Fitzpatrick was the veteran head of the Chicago Federation of Labor. This decent, unassuming Irishman represented the best traditions of American labor. A progressive of stature, an incorruptible leader who had driven the racketeers from the Chicago movement, Fitzpatrick had nurtured a life-long dream of bringing trade unionism to the immigrant packinghouse workers. In the summer of 1917, he and others set up the Stockyards Labor Council, recruited an organizing staff mainly of local volunteers, and launched the drive on September 9, 1917. When the unions threatened to strike in December, the President's Mediation Commission negotiated a Christmas Day settlement that gave the unions *de facto* recognition and installed an arbitration system for unresolved issues. The favorable award of March 30, 1918—overtime pay, big rate increases, and other benefits—brought in thousands more and gave the unions a firm hold in the open-shop packing industry.

For the Chicago architects of this triumph, steel was next. At their prompting, the AFL set up on August 1, 1918, a National Committee for Organizing Iron and Steel Workers, with Fitzpatrick in charge. The AFL was putting to the test its ability to organize the basic industries. No one spoke up for industrial unionism. But the Federation had evolved an alternative approach to the mass-production sector: accepting the jurisdictional rights of the craft unions, placing all other workers (including unskilled) in the dominant union holding residual jurisdiction, and achieving common action on a voluntary, cooperative basis. The scheme had worked in the railroad shop crafts, and, on paper, it would work in mass-production industries. In practice, Fitzpatrick's National Committee only half-worked. The twenty-four participating unions gave niggardly financial support (a mere $6,322 in the first five months) and jealously guarded their autonomy and jurisdictional rights. But they did provide organizers, accept standardized recruiting procedures, and permit central guidance of the drive by the National Committee.

The steelworkers came flocking in. They were drawn by two tactics that marked this recruiting drive off from the past: first, by a skillful appeal to the immigrant workers; and, second, by the association of trade unionism with Wilsonian war aims (making the world safe for democracy, as the AFL said, called for "the further spread of industrial democracy in America"). The disillusionment following the Armistice—the crushed hopes for a better world at home—carried the organizing momentum into 1919. By the late spring, the membership stood at 100,000 and was growing.

"The gods," a key steel leader afterward remarked, "were indeed fighting on the side of Labor." And with that help, labor proved willing to fight for itself. The war evoked dynamic qualities unseen in the confined movement of earlier years. The gains in packing and steel were duplicated, even surpassed, in other fields, especially areas essential to the war effort. In all, union membership, doubling in four years, stood at five million in 1920.

But the war had ended, and the Wilson administration immediately reversed course. The wartime controls speedily came off. In 1920, over the bitter objections of the unions, the railroads went back to their owners. The Red Scare had meanwhile boiled up, and, while the witch hunt pursued primarily radicals, the ugly mood was directed at organized labor also. Open-shop employers emerged from the war shaken and bent on reasserting their authority. Across the country, a resurgent movement of organized employers, now calling its program the "American Plan," turned against union labor with renewed fury.

The unions, for their part, could not wait out the storm. A potent rank-and-file insurgency developed and forced union leaders, as those in steel put it, to choose between "undertaking a struggle . . . without adequate preparation" and "standing idly by and allowing the steel movement to drift out of our hands and degenerate into an unorganized uprising."[35] A massive strike wave hit the country. Clothing workers, textile workers, telephone operators, actors, and Boston policemen went out; a general strike shut down Seattle; in late September 365,000 steelworkers staged the biggest strike the country had ever seen; on November 1, the bituminous miners struck for a six-hour day, five-day week, sixty per cent wage increase. In all, over 4 million workers were on strike during 1919—an incredible 20 per cent of the labor force—and as many more in total went out over the next three years.

When the smoke cleared, the labor movement had lost 1.5 million members. The entrenched unions had come through well enough, and some had scored notable gains, but labor's outbreak into open-shop territory had almost everywhere been smashed. The union movement fell back to the confined position it had occupied before the war. The bitter truth was clear: depending on their own economic strength, American workers could not defeat the massed power of open-shop industry. Only public intervention might equalize the battle, and of that there was no hope in the 1920s. Frustration at this turn of events prompted the AFL to support Robert M. LaFollette on the Progressive ticket in 1924. As agitation among labor progressives for a labor party collapsed, the third-party experiment was abandoned, and the AFL returned to political conservatism. This was part of a broader labor retreat during the 1920s. Once again, a hostile environment evoked within American trade unionism the restrictive logic of earlier years.

Something new, however, had been added. At the heart of Gompers's philosophy had stood the notion of power: that labor got only what it was strong enough to command. This tough inner core of pure-and-simple unionism deteriorated sadly during the 1920s. The AFL advanced a new doctrine of labor-management cooperation, expressed industrially in its sudden enthusiasm for efficiency and politically in its eager identification with the standing order. The American Legion and the military became valued allies. Only a few corporate employers actually responded to this conciliatory line, despite encouragement from certain business statesmen and from Herbert Hoover.

The cooperative approach signified labor's deep sense of impotence in the 1920s. The movement might progress only with industry's consent, not by the force of labor's strength.

The doubts went beyond the equations of power. During the New Era, it seemed possible that American trade unionism might have outlived its usefulness and was being readied for history's scrap heap.

Notes

1. John Brophy MSS., Oral History Collection, Columbia University, pp. 94–105, reprinted in Jerold Auerbach, ed., *American Labor: The Twentieth Century* (Indianapolis, 1969), pp. 44–49. An abridged version of Brophy's oral history has been published: John Brophy, *A Miner's Life*, ed. J. O. P. Hall (Madison, 1964).
·2. H. L. Morris, *The Plight of the Bituminous Coal Miner* (Philadelphia, 1934), pp. 28, 29, 83; Anna Rochester, *Labor and Coal* (New York, 1931), pp. 113, 114.
3. Harry Jerome, *Mechanization in Industry* (New York, 1934), pp. 96–108; John W. Kendrick, *Productivity Trends in the United States* (Princeton, 1961), p. 482.
4. Bryan Palmer, "Class, Conception and Conflict: The Thrust for Efficiency . . . , 1903–1922," *Review of Radical Political Economics* 7 (Summer 1975): 37–38; Eli Ginzberg and Hyman Berman, eds., *The American Worker in the Twentieth Century* (Glencoe, Ill., 1963), pp. 91, 95; David Brody, *Steelworkers in America: The Nonunion Era* (Cambridge, Mass., 1960), p. 32; David Brody, *The Butcher Workmen* (Cambridge, Mass., 1964), p. 5; Robert and Helen Lynd, *Middletown* (New York, 1929), p. 76; Auerbach, *American Labor*, pp. 33, 52, 55.
5. *Recent Economic Changes in the United States*, 2 vols. (New York, 1929), 1: 167–68; *Recent Social Changes in the United States*, 2 vols. (New York, 1933), 2: 812.
6. John A. Fitch, *The Steel Workers* (New York, 1911), pp. 11–12.
7. S. J. Scheiner, "The Development of Corporate Labor Policy" (Ph.D. diss., University of Wisconsin, 1965) pp. 54–55, 57.
8. David Montgomery, "Workers' Control of Machine Production in the Nineteenth Century," *Labor History* 17 (Fall 1976): 489.
9. Samuel Haber, *Efficiency and Uplift* (Chicago, 1964), p. 165.
10. Daniel Nelson, *Workers and Managers* (Madison, 1975), p. 34.
11. Frederick W. Taylor, *Principles of Scientific Management* (New York, 1911), pp.· 36, 48–49, 83; Nelson, *Workers and Managers*, chap. 4. For a seminal Marxist analysis of the impact of Taylorism, see Harry Braverman, *Labor and Monopoly Capital: The Degradation of Work in the Twentieth Century* (New York, 1974).
12. Nelson, *Workers and Managers*, p. 22; Palmer, "Class, Conception and Conflict," p. 40; National Industrial Conference Board, *Industrial Relations* (New York, 1931), p. 104.
13. Haber, *Efficiency and Uplift*, p. 24.
14. *Recent Social Trends*, 1: 502; Harold U. Faulkner, *The Decline of Laissez Faire* (New York, 1951), p. 98; John R. Commons *et al.*, *History of Labor in the United States*, 4 vols. (New York, 1918-35), 4: 41.
15. Brody, *Steelworkers in America*, p. 120. Except where otherwise noted, the following discussion is drawn from chaps. 5 and 9 of my book.
16. William M. Leiserson, quoted in David Montgomery, "The Conventional Wisdom," *Labor History* 13 (Winter 1972): 121.

17. *Recent Social Trends,* 1: 714-15, and 2: 779, 825-26; U.S. Department of Commerce, *Historical Statistics of the United States to 1970,* 2 vols. (Washington, 1975), 1: 131-34, 139-40; John W. Smuts, *Women and Work in America* (New York, 1959), p. 55; Day Monroe, *Chicago Families* (Chicago, 1932), chap. 7; Virginia Yans McLaughlin, "Patterns of Work and Family Organization: Buffalo's Italians," *Journal of Interdisciplinary History* 2 (Autumn 1971): 307-13.
18. Mark Perlman, *The Machinists* (Cambridge, Mass., 1961), pp. 5-6; Reed C. Richardson, *The Locomotive Engineer, 1863-1963* (Ann Arbor, 1963), p. 138.
19. Lynd and Lynd, *Middletown,* p. 79.
20. United States Commission on Industrial Relations, *Final Report and Testimony* (Washington, 1916), 2: 1528-29.
21. Commons, *History of Labor,* 4: 48.
22. Brody, *Butcher Workmen,* p. 78; Clarence E. Bonnett, *Employers' Associations in the United States* (New York, 1922), pp. 70, 71, 78, 103.
23. Thomas W. Gavett, *Development of the Labor Movement in Milwaukee* (Madison, 1965), pp. 122-23; Marc Karson, *American Labor Unions and Politics* (Carbondale, Ill., 1958), p. 30.
24. Philip Taft, *Organized Labor in American History* (New York, 1964), pp. 213-14.
25. Perlman, *Machinists,* p. 22; Brody, *Butcher Workmen,* p. 39.
26. David Montgomery, "The 'New Unionism' and the Transformation of Workers' Consciousness in America, 1909-1922," *Journal of Social History* 7 (Summer 1974): 509-29. See also, for example, Palmer, "Class, Conception and Conflict," pp. 41-44.
27. Henry F. Bedford, *Socialism and the Workers in Massachusetts, 1886-1912* (Amherst, Mass., 1966), p. 5.
28. Perlman, *Machinists,* p. 59 and *passim.* For a detailed treatment of this process, see John H. M. Laslett, *Labor and the Left* (New York, 1970).
29. David Brody, "Career Leadership and American Trade Unionism," in Frederic C. Jaher, ed., *The Age of Industrialism in America* (New York, 1968), p. 294.
30. Theodore Draper, *The Roots of American Communism* (New York, 1957), p. 19; Melvyn Dubofsky, *We Shall Be All* (Chicago, 1969), pp. 81, 147-48, 155.
31. Dubofsky, *We Shall Be All,* pp. 155, 343; Auerbach, *American Labor,* pp. 89-90; Philip Taft, "The IWW in the Grain Belt," *Labor History* 1 (Winter 1960): 53-67.
32. Dubofsky, *We Shall Be All,* p. 407.
33. Matthew Josephson, *Sidney Hillman* (New York, 1952), chap. 7.
34. David Brody, *Labor in Crisis* (Philadelphia, 1965), pp. 49-50, 52.
35. Ibid., p. 99.

2
The Rise and Decline
of Welfare Capitalism

"Our job primarily is to make steel," the veteran head of Bethlehem Steel, Charles M. Schwab, told the American Society of Mechanical Engineers in December 1927, "but it is being made under a system which must be justified. If . . . this system does not enable men to live on an increasingly higher plane, if it does not allow them to fulfill their desires and satisfy their reasonable wants, then it is natural that the system itself should fail." Schwab's qualification expressed the key idea of the welfare capitalism of the 1920s. "There has been a change—an enormous change—and within the last ten years," a director of the U.S. Chamber of Commerce said in 1929. "We are acquiring a new industrial philosophy . . . that the fundamentals of decent and right conduct laid down by Jesus of Nazareth constitute the soundest, most sensible, and workable economic system possible to devise." Callousness toward labor was receding into an unlamented past, enlightened businessmen assured themselves. "I have gone through some rather dark chapters in American industry," recollected Schwab (whose brilliant business career went back to the bloody Homestead strike of 1892), "and it is a great joy to me to realize that humanity rules American industrial life today."[1]

From John Braeman et al., eds., Change and Continuity in Twentieth Century America: The 1920's. (Columbus: Ohio State University Press, 1968), p. 147–78. Revised and reprinted with permission.

The new outlook promised to transform the country's labor relations. Many businessmen foresaw a future of "concord and plenty," noted the economist Herbert Feis. "The concord is based chiefly on the expectation of cooperation between workers and management. This cooperation is to show itself in a recognition of the worker's needs and desires. . . . The plenty is to be expected by improving industrial technic, by lessening waste, by the gains of common effort marked by goodwill." Concord and plenty seemed within easy reach in 1928. "Much of American industry," said Feis, "is convinced that it has worked out simple means and policies for insuring steady and peaceful advancement of industrial life."[2]

That confidence proved remarkably ill-founded. Within a few years of the stock market crash in 1929, welfare capitalism collapsed in a burst of unexampled industrial strife. From the bitter 1930s there issued a system of labor relations that rested on collective bargaining, not the benevolence of management. In failure, welfare capitalism has been too casually dismissed. Flawed as it was, it seriously attempted to minimize the human problems raised by industrialization. And it was a more vital phenomenon that it has seemed from the modern perspective.

Welfare capitalism had its roots in the emergence of big business in the early years of the twentieth century. Even before, of course, employers had interested themselves in the welfare of their workmen. Pullman had built his model town near Chicago; Proctor and Gamble had started its profit-sharing plan in 1886; others had provided pensions and encouraged mutual benefit societies. During the industrializing era, however, benevolence had been limited by frantic expansion and ruthless competition. As these moderated, leeway opened for a departure from the hard labor policy ruled by the cost books and the labor supply. The larger scale of business enterprise increased the resources available to progressive employers. Above all, the consolidation movement demanded more enlightened treatment of labor. Less imperative as progressivism subsided, that rationale remained binding in the 1920s.

Consolidationists such as J. P. Morgan intended to restore order to industries "demoralized" by cutthroat competition. Their strategy was, first, to combine warring firms into a giant concern and, second, through its dominance impose "fair" competition on the industry. Business should strive for "cooperation" and "stability," not ruinous warfare. This course would be profitable; it would also be right. Weighty ethics justified fair competition. "From the standpoint of morality," Elbert H. Gary said, the steel industry had been "a shame and a disgrace" before the formation of U.S. Steel. Spreading beyond its original advocates, the doctrine of co-operation dominated American business in the 1920s. "Even the most skeptical devotees of the old dog-eat-dog theory of business competition," said a Chamber of Commerce officer in 1929, "are being gradually persuaded from the sheer, cold pressure of the facts that . . . war doesn't pay in this complicated world of ours." Owen D. Young of General Electric added: "The Golden Rule supplies all that a man of business needs."[3]

This mode of thinking inevitably influenced labor policy. Morgan's partner George W. Perkins told the National Civic Federation in 1909 that if capital and consumers benefited from co-operation, so must the laborer. Ethical standards applied to labor relations no less than to business relations, and would foster the same harmony of interests. "Ruinous competition, the crushing of small companies by monopolistic rivals . . . continual strikes—there is no avoiding the punishment such plagues entail," pronounced a business spokesman in 1929. "Take strikes, for example. . . . Ten years ago it was considered part of the game to cut wages without compunction. . . . Today wage-cutting is the last thing any employer wants to resort to. He knows, from experience, that it is wrong and that it makes trouble." Modern business acted on the "sincere belief that the interests of the employer and employee are mutual and at bottom identical."[4]

These precepts depended on new industrial leadership for implementation. As business grew large and complex, control passed into the hands of lawyers and financial men, and they felt the broader obligation of their high places in the great corporations. General Electric's Owen Young, himself a lawyer, argued that "the new idea in management . . . sprang largely from the fact that lawyers were advanced to high managerial posts. . . . If there is one thing that a lawyer is taught, it is knowledge of trusteeship and the sacredness of that position. Very soon we saw rising a notion that managers were no longer attorneys for stockholders; they were becoming trustees of an institution."[5] And labor was among the beneficiaries of that trusteeship.

Public opinion served as a spur to action. Big-business leaders anxiously cultivated national favor. That alone, Elbert Gary and George Perkins had argued during the progressive era, might protect the vulnerable industrial giants from antitrust action. The legal dangers lifted, if they did not disappear, in the 1920s. But the sensitivity to public opinion remained, sustained as it was by the conviction of business leaders that theirs was an occupation clothed with the public interest. Earlier, muckraking attacks and government investigations had prodded major reforms in industry. U.S. Steel had finally abolished the seven-day week in 1911 after the crusading first vice-president, W. B. Dickson, had threatened to resign and take the fight outside the corporation.[6]

Public relations became less stormy, but not less important, in the 1920s. Businessmen remained sensitive to the country's rising expectations for the treatment of labor. What wants do employees "have a right to see satisfied as far as conditions permit?" asked Charles Schwab in 1927. He listed, among other things, steady employment, a voice in the regulation of their working conditions, opportunity to save and to own stock, and some guarantee of security in old age.[7] This was the measure of national sentiment in the 1920s, so far as business was able to read it.

Initially, welfare work lacked any functional relationship to industrial operations. Businessmen did assert in a vague sort of way that they earned a profitable return on the investment in welfare work, especially in the creation of loyalty and contentment. But the moving impulse came from other than ordinary business considerations. Welfare, said Elbert Gary, was "a simple duty that industry owes to labor"; it was an obligation of the "big, broad employers of labor."[8] In the 1920s that paternal reasoning was joined by a second, more hardheaded argument: employee well-being would increase efficiency.

When Gerard Swope became president of General Electric in 1922, he spread the new gospel in a series of informal talks to plant officials. Their job, he told Schenectady foremen, was threefold: "production, costs, and relations with men. Usually . . . we think of the first two only. . . . The last thing our foremen will remember is the relations with the men who work for him [*sic*] and that, as a matter of fact, is the most important consideration that bears on the results that any executive is to achieve." The workers were not mere adjuncts to the machinery. "And there isn't anything men expect more than fair treatment; they must be dealt with not only fairly and justly, but with sympathy." Swope pressed home his conclusion: "You are constantly being hounded to increase your output. One of the ways of getting it is to have your men cooperate with you."[9]

The intellectual sources for this line of business thinking derived from the scientific-management movement of Frederick W. Taylor and the emerging science of industrial psychology. Many businessmen, too, had seen for themselves during the war how patriotic fervor had stimulated production. Far from being a fixed item, the workers' performance seemed a

THE RISE OF THE PERSONNEL DEPARTMENT—
Human Resources

prime point for improving industrial operations. The war also drew attention to the neglected problem of labor turnover. For the first time, many employers realized the high costs of replacing experienced men. In the 1920s a low turnover rate became an index of the effectiveness of a company's labor program. The handling of labor assumed major importance for American industrialists. Successful management, Charles Schwab told an engineering audience, "is going to depend more and more upon the management of men than upon the organization of machines and other problems of practical engineering." The future engineer would find little challenge in the technical problems. "Industry's most important task in this day of large-scale production is management of men on a human basis."[10]

The industrial-relations movement attempted to place labor policy on a rational, organized basis. It created a professional group of managers (led by such men as Clarence J. Hicks and Arthur H. Young) and experts (such as Industrial Relations Counselors, Inc.) backed by college courses, research and publications, and professional organizations. It centralized labor administration in industrial-relations departments and defined an area of decision-making in the business enterprise comparable to sales, production, and finance. It rationalized the recruitment and handling of labor—above all, by stripping the foremen of the power to hire and fire. The National Industrial Conference Board emphasized "that the individual employee represents a definite investment, and that sound business principles require that the investment be capably handled in order that it may yield a fair return." Advanced businessmen saw personnel administration "not as frill or as a vehicle for the fulfillment of philanthropic impulses, but as a natural and business-like method of dealing with the . . . work force to secure results."[11]

Yet the new approach also buttressed the welfare philosophy of big business. For labor's well-being contributed to industrial-relations objectives. Modern economic life created insecurities among employees, acknowledged E. K. Hall of the American Telephone and Telegraph Company. "We must find ways and means to help our workers get their worries out of their minds so they can get on the job 'rarin to go'." Freed from anxiety over accident and illness, old age and unemployment, men would work with a better will. Many employers placed great faith in stock ownership. "A sense of proprietorship affords a powerful incentive to arouse interest in the performance of work," pronounced Charles Schwab.[12] And the contributing firm would reap further dividends in the form of low turnover, high quality recruits, and labor peace. Welfare found a business justification in the approach of personnel management and, since responsibility for such activities fell to industrial-relations departments, also an administrative home.

The welfare plans proliferating in the 1920s were designed to meet the major hazards of modern industrial life. One group of schemes encouraged men to acquire property. Some companies operated savings plans, often with the incentive of high interest rates or special bonuses. Many firms adopted home-ownership plans that provided employees with various kinds of technical assistance and financial aid. Stock-purchasing plans exerted special appeal in the prosperous 1920s. Most schemes offered special inducements for employees to purchase and hold company stock. By 1927, 800,000 employees had invested over a billion dollars in 315 companies. Other programs protected workmen and their families from losses resulting from accident, illness, old age, and death. Group insurance valued at $7.5 billion covered close to six million workers in 1928. More than 350 companies gave pensions in 1929. Besides granting these basic protections, companies improved plant conditions and safety, provided medical services and visiting nurses, underwrote sports and classes, distributed land for gardening, and assisted workmen in all manner of personal problems. The costs mounted high for major firms: U.S. Steel's expenditures averaged over ten million dollars a year in the

1920s. Such generosity, Judge Gary assured the stockholders in 1923, was justifiable "because it is the way men ought to be treated, and secondly because it pays to treat men in that way."[13]

Both considerations supported employee representation, the most celebrated labor experiment of the decade. The idea had found a small group of advocates before World War I, above all, in John D. Rockefeller, Jr. Overcoming a personal aversion to public speaking, the younger Rockefeller lectured across the country about the plan introduced at his Colorado Fuel and Iron Company in the aftermath of a bloody miners' strike in 1913–14. World War I provided a more forceful influence. Urgently desiring labor peace, many employers became willing to experiment. Simultaneously, the government itself adopted a variant of the idea; in over 125 cases, the War Labor Board ordered companies to install shop committees. Although many smaller firms discarded the arrangement immediately after the Armistice, other employers were won over by employee representation, and a number of large companies—among them, Youngstown Sheet and Tube, International Harvester, Goodyear Tire and Rubber, Yale and Towne Manufacturing—voluntarily introduced the plan in 1918–19. Following the postwar labor crisis, 317 companies joined the movement by which workmen elected fellow workers to speak for them before management.[14]

More than any other item in the program of welfare capitalism, employee representation was couched in idealistic terms. When a strike broke out at the Consolidated Coal Company in Pennsylvania in 1922, the younger Rockefeller, a major stockholder, publicly denounced the operators for denying "their employees all voice and share in determining their working conditions and any adequate machinery for the uncovering and adjustment of grievances. The day has passed when such a position can justly be maintained . . . in a country like ours. . . . Employees in every industrial unit [have] a fundamental right, namely, the right to representation in the determination of those matters which affect their own interests." Rockefeller's letter, widely praised, reflected the thinking of enlightened employers. "Industrial democracy" had become a national byword during World War I. "It would be strange if the people of the United States came out of the War [for democracy in government] without any concessions to the growing demand for more democracy in industry," a steel trade journal had remarked.[15] Bitterly divided on other matters, the President's Industrial Conference of October 1919 was practically unanimous on the proposition that workingmen had a right to representation with employers. Employee representation continued to exert a powerful idealistic appeal throughout the 1920s.

The practical benefits received equal emphasis. The National Industrial Conference Board reported that executives found plant morale significantly improved by employee representation.

> It facilitates quick adaptation to special or changing conditions, when passive opposition would bring about the failure of plans. It engenders greater interest in the job, which leads to the offering of suggestions as to short cuts and improvements that in the aggregate may mean considerable savings for the company. The works council provides a meeting place, where management and working force can consider calmly, on the basis of accurate information rather than rumor, their respective positions and problems. . . . Beyond the settlement of grievances and, better, their prevention, is the broader and more constructive accomplishment of employee representation in welding together management and working force into a single, cohesive productive unit.

Charles Schwab observed that Bethlehem's plan stimulated "constructive cooperation along the lines of increased efficiency, elimination of waste, and improved methods and quality and quantity of products. Along with this development has come a growth in morale and in sympathy and understanding between employees and officials." They had "an unobstructed channel through which their unity of interest may be promoted."[16]

The real aim of welfare capitalism; its problem with unionism

Employers of the 1920s explained their labor policies as an expression of right conduct and as an effort to raise industrial efficiency. But welfare capitalism meant more than that. It sustained a power system that granted management full authority over the terms of employment. Contemporary labor programs, remarked the economist Sumner H. Slichter in 1929, "are one of the most ambitious social experiments of the age, because they aim, among other things, to counteract the effect of modern technique upon the mind of the worker, to prevent him from becoming class conscious and from organizing trade unions." This aim, more than considerations of humanity or efficiency, measured the ultimate value of welfare capitalism to most of its advocates.[17]

When labor trouble threatened U.S. Steel in 1919, Judge Gary told the subsidiary presidents that "there is nothing we can do better than to be sure we are liberal in the protection of our workmen and their families. . . . Make the Steel Corporation a good place for them to work and live." Fair and generous treatment would leave "no just ground for criticism on the part of those who are connected with the movement of unrest." Some benefits—housing, pensions, profit-sharing—gave men a specific stake in their jobs. But the entire welfare effort presumably made workers loyal and contented. Union leaders objected to such programs, a steel trade journal observed, "because they realized that it was resulting in non-union men becoming more closely attached to the companies by which they were employed." Personnel methods reduced the resentments common to industrial employment, guaranteeing equitable, orderly treatment to all and opportunity for training and advancement to the talented few. "To the best men," remarked Sumner Slichter, "promotion thus becomes a more certain and often an easier way of gaining higher wages than is trade union action."[18]

Employee representation hit most directly at the union threat. In 1918 and 1919 many plans had been inaugurated to ward off an imminent danger of unionization. Immediately after the Armistice, Arthur H. Young warned the head of International Harvester that labor agitation was sure to intensify and grow more radical. He urged the quick adoption of his employee representation plan, not only to safeguard the company's open shop, but to serve as an example for American industry generally.[19] In other cases where labor organization had established itself—for instance, the plants of the major meat packers and the shop crafts of the railroads— employee representation replaced the unions as they were driven out. Clearly, the plans were intended to substitute for trade unions, both as a justification to the public and an answer to employee needs.

The difference was, however, fundamental. The American Federation of Labor, said an industry spokesman in 1922, "requires a continuing state of war and the constant preaching of enmity and antagonism." The representation plans, on the other hand, "aimed at the settlement of disputes on a basis of fairness and justice rather than by argument of superior force." Labor and management had mutual, not antagonistic, interests; and employee representation would harmonize those interests. Differing in structure and even in emphasis, the plans agreed on one point: they did not diminish the power of employers. "Management must lead and must accept the responsibility for carrying on industry," said C. B. Seger of the U.S. Rubber Company in discussing employee representation. "Intelligent leadership, however, presupposes that leaders will keep those whom they lead informed and it presupposes also that they will be responsive to those led." Charles Schwab was privately blunt about Bethlehem's widely praised plan: "I will not permit myself to be in a position of having labor dictate to management."[20] Assuredly, labor did not under the company unionism of the 1920s.

Employee representation seemed the capstone of welfare capitalism. Its other activities advanced the material well-being and personal security of workingmen. Employee representation catered to their minds. "The men must be dealt with as thinking men," Gerard Swope lectured to General Electric foremen. Through the representation plans, workers could air their grievances and ideas, and in turn receive an understanding of the policies of their employer. Employee representation, concluded a labor expert, rested on "the citizenship theory of labor relations."[21]

In practice, welfare capitalism fell far short of the boasts of the speechmakers. For all the fine talk, companies failed to act on the most challenging problems. Virtually nothing was done to protect against joblessness, notwithstanding a growing recognition of the spectre of technological unemployment. On the whole, welfare capitalists lacked sympathy for a shorter work week. The steady decline of hours since the 1890s leveled off after 1920. The most notable advance of the decade —the abolition of the twelve-hour day in the steel industry in 1923—was actually forced on Judge Gary and his colleagues by an aroused public opinion and ultimately by the intervention of Secretary of Commerce Herbert Hoover and President Harding. Nor was the "doctrine of high wages," currently in vogue, translated into significant action: while labor productivity was increasing by an extraordinary five per cent a year, lagging wage levels in manufacturing advanced at only half that rate during the decade.

Welfare capitalism was, moreover, a minority phenomenon, limited to the large prosperous firms. The methods of personnel management, widely introduced on a piecemeal basis, frequently lacked the essential administrative base. One survey found industrial-relations departments in 6.5 per cent of companies employing under 500 men, in approximately 30 per cent of companies employing between 500 and 2,000 men, and in 50 per cent of those over 2,000. The National Industrial Conference Board reported that some welfare activities were widespread by the end of the decade: over 90 per cent of the companies surveyed operated safety programs; 70 per cent, group insurance; 60 per cent, mutual aid associations. But only one out of five provided formal pension plans, stock-purchase opportunities, or savings and loan facilities.[22]

Such programs did not always achieve a high level of performance. The vaunted employee-representation plans, for example, were too transparently management's creatures to gain much standing in the shop. At the end of the decade, employee representation covered 1.5 million workers, over 80 per cent of them in some forty companies employing over 5,000 people. Despite the resources and professional help available to such large firms, employee representation rarely, if ever, developed much real meaning. Herbert Feis sat in on one meeting of the Employees Conference Committee at the Ivorydale plant of Proctor and Gamble. No important matters were discussed; no enthusiasm was displayed on either side. "The men are not reaching forward through the plan," concluded Feis; "the management has ceased to attempt any great achievement through it."[23] At International Harvester and Colorado Fuel and Iron, promising plans likewise disappointed their creators.[24] Significantly, all three companies had suffered from an identical betrayal during the severe recession of 1921: wage cuts made either arbitrarily or with the barest pretense of consultation. Other plans, begun hastily and with obvious ulterior purposes, had even less likelihood of achieving any real vitality.

Enthusiasm for welfare programs seems to have been on the wane in the latter part of the decade. Expenditures began to level off, and interest focused increasingly on benefits directly related to the job at the expense of grander community programs. In the view of the most recent student of the subject, Stuart D. Brandes, this was "a direct result of . . . lack of appreciation on the part of the employees," as well as of contemporary social changes that reduced the need for some company activities. It is Brandes's contention that welfare capitalism was a response to one phase of industrialization, that it was bound to be replaced by less paternalistic forms of social services, and that this was already becoming apparent by the end of the 1920s.[25]

At the time, however, the essential vitality of welfare capitalism seemed wholly undiminished. It seemed, above all, the sure guarantee of the existing power system in American industry. In 1929, a business spokesman announced that "the end of the strike era is in sight, and that the next five years will see an unparalleled gain in relationships of mutual understanding and good will between employee and employer."[26] Organized labor was faltering badly, incapable either of recovering the staggering losses it had experienced in the postwar period or of finding new ways of attracting American workers to its banner. "Our trade union movement is going through most extraordinary experiences," John Frey of the AFL wrote in bafflement in 1929. "After business began to revive in 1923, it was found that the former method of organizing did not bring the same results as in previous years. . . . New methods in organizing are required to meet the new conditions in industry which confronts [*sic*] us."[27] The newest condition, for which no improved technique would answer, was the evident satisfaction of the American workingman with the status quo.

The flawed performance of welfare capitalism was not a true measure of its significance. Welfare capitalism exceeded the sum of its parts. It was also an idea: that management accepted an obligation for the well-being of its employees. In May 1929 Charles Schwab reminded the American Iron and Steel Institute of "the responsibilities that repose upon us in the steel industry . . . a real trusteeship . . . for hundreds and thousands of families. We seek to prosper ourselves but above all we seek the welfare, progress and happiness of our people (Applause)."[28] That promise, more than all of its actual programs, constituted the essence of welfare capitalism. What made the promise credible was the performance of American capitalism in the 1920s.

In 1929 John Spargo, a prominent right-wing Socialist who had broken with the Socialist party in 1917 over the war issue, wrote an essay explaining why he had never gone back. American capitalism, Spargo pronounced, had shown Karl Marx to have been grotesquely wrong. Instead of being driven down remorselessly to the level of meanest subsistence, workers "have enjoyed a constantly widening circle of increasing physical comfort and even of luxury . . . which the workers of fifty years ago regarded as unattainable." Inventions never dreamed of by Marx had lifted the life of everyone. Nor were the benefits merely of a material kind. "The recent developments of industrialism," Spargo felt, revealed "a steady progress away from disorder, and from indifference to social consequences, as marked as the technical advance itself." It was Spargo's "deliberate judgement," tempered by years as a critic of free-enterprise capitalism, "that, here in America at least, the industrial system and the economic order resulting from it constitute the best and soundest part of civilization."[29]

Few in the 1920s would have disputed Spargo's euphoric conclusions. They were, indeed, the common currency of the New Era. Real earnings, after slowing under wartime inflationary pressures, now resumed their long-term upward march. Both wages and prices plummeted in the sharp recession of 1921. Wage rates recovered, however, moving from 48 cents an hour for industrial workers in 1922 to 56 cents an hour in 1929, while the price index hovered around the 1922 level for the rest of the decade. Of course, not everyone benefited equally. In the soft coal industry, for instance, the average hourly rates dropped from 90 to 66 cents between 1922 and 1929. Older workers, cast out of American industry in growing numbers, also suffered. Still, on the whole, American workers enjoyed a genuine upward trend: real weekly earnings increased by nearly 15 per cent between 1922 and 1929.[30]

This advance was not in itself so remarkable, neither by comparison to the swifter rise of labor productivity and national income during the 1920s, nor by comparison to earlier spurts in the upward swing of real earnings that characterized the industrializing era prior to World War I. [31] What was extraordinary was the qualitative leap in living standards accompanying the rising real income of the 1920s. A revolution had taken place in household technology. The age of electricity, central heating, and indoor sanitation had arrived. From American industry, too, there now began to flow the consumer durables of modern life—home appliances, the radio and phonograph, and the automobile. All these wonders had come first to the well-to-do, then to the middle class. In the 1920s they became accessible to the workingman. The life that his family thereby achieved truly separated him from the workingman of 1900.

Thanks to the vagaries of Henry Ford, we have an exact record of the living standards of one group of industrial workers at the close of the New Era. The Ford Motor Company, preparatory to establishing a comprehensive wage policy covering its international operations, asked the U.S. Bureau of Labor Statistics to study the expenditures of representative Detroit employees selected by these criteria: earning minimum rates, working full-time, married with two or three children, with no extra people in the household and no second income.

The hundred Ford families chosen earned an average of $1,694 for 1929, slightly above the average for all industrial workers (not unskilled alone). Food constituted 32.3 per cent of their total expenditure, compared to roughly half for workers earning average income in 1900. In some ways, this was the key finding, since a declining share of expenditures for food constitutes a prime index of rising living standards. For the average $556 so spent, the Ford families received an ample and nutritious diet, heavily weighted toward fresh meat, fresh fruits and vegetables, and dairy products. Their housing provided substantial space (an average of one room per person), modern conveniences (electricity in all the houses, central heating in 44), and modern sanitation (inside running water for

97, hot water for 65, inside toilets for 86). Thirty-two families owned their houses. As for the modern consumer goods: 47 families owned cars, 45 phonographs, 36 radios, 19 electric vacuum cleaners, and 49 washing machines.

To achieve this level, the families lived at the very margins of their income. Only 37 saved money, and 44 ran a deficit; on the average, $7.96 more was spent than earned during the year. They generally resorted to the credit buying that became a hallmark of American retailing in the 1920s: 59 families were purchasing items on the "easy installment plan."[32] What would have been undoubted recklessness to the bread-winner of 1900 was in 1929 an expression of confidence in America's bountiful mass-production system.

In their classic study of Middletown (really Muncie, Indiana), the cultural anthropologists Robert and Helen Lynd observed the impact of modern prosperity on the working-man. What struck them most forcibly was the disintegration of the vigorous working-class life that had flourished thirty years before. The primary agency of the labor culture, the local union movement, had greatly declined in power and status, and the key participants, the craft workers, had lost their central place in the Middletown economy. The influence of modernism was pervasive. Leisure time had increased since the 1890s, not so much in the form of vacations, which remained the preserve of the middle-class, but in the work week, which had fallen from sixty hours in the 1890s to fifty hours by the 1920s and included a Saturday half-holiday. This time the Middletown worker no longer spent at the union hall, or at labor picnics and socials, but in activities carried on in isolation from his fellows. His leisure was devoted to the radio, the movie house, and the weekend drive in his prized automobile. The car tended also to disperse residences—45 per cent of the employees in three surveyed plants lived over a mile from their work—so as to destroy the neighborhood basis of labor activity.

The Lynds found virtually no working-class institutional life in Middletown, in contrast to the profusion of social clubs and business organizations catering to the middle class. Nor did they discover any positive working-class identification. For their children, Middletown workers (unlike traditional craft workers) hoped only for an escape into the white-collar world. The extraordinary expansion of secondary-school education put this ambition within reach. In a survey of Middletown high-school boys, over half of them of working-class parentage, only one in five planned to enter manual occupations, and of these only one in three wanted a factory job.

Only the sons might harbor white-collar dreams, not the fathers. It was the material benefits of the here-and-now, the Lynds reported, that reconciled the Middletown worker to the factory grind. "For both working and business class no other accompaniment of getting a living approaches in importance the money received for their work. . . . This . . . rather than the intrinsic satisfactions . . . keeps Middletown working so hard as more and more of the activities of living are coming to be strained through the bars' of the dollar sign."[33] The workingman might have been deprived of pride in, and control over, his job; but he was also granted access to the goods of the productive system beyond the dreams of earlier generations. If his share in making a Chevrolet was the endless repetition of a single task, the assembly-line worker stepped into one of those machines and drove it home at the end of the day.

The age of labor peace seemed at hand. If American enterprise could offer the workingman a share of the nation's abundance and assure his security and well-being, it could expect in return his loyalty and goodwill.

Ralph Easley of the National Civic Federation confidentially polled railroad officials in 1929, seven years after the bitter shopmen's strike: did they detect any revival of interest in trade unionism? Almost invariably (one railroader feared

Communist influence on his immigrant workmen) the answer
came back a confident "no." "In our shops since the strike of
1922, the shop employees have been very quiet," wrote the
head of the Chicago and Alton Railroad. "The employee is
much happier than under the old [union] regime. . . . He is
a peaceful worker and a peaceful citizen and he wants to be let
alone in that state." The statistics confirmed the absence of
discontent. Industrial disputes in 1929 involved less than a
sixth the number of men in 1916, and a seventeenth the
number in the peak year of 1919. The turnover rate had fallen
sharply, according to one 1927 survey running at 40 per cent
of the prewar rate.

To Sumner Slichter in 1929, paternalism unhappily seemed
permanent; he could only suggest that it might better issue
from the government than from private industry. "The desire
for steady employment and higher earnings became more
dominant in the minds of the workers than the feeling for
industrial freedom and independence," admitted another labor expert. The Frenchman Andre Siegfried arrived at a similar conclusion: "The American workman, when he realizes
that society assures him a comfortable income, is ready to
accept the existing organization of industry."[34] But industry
actually could not assure that income. Therein lay the fatal
weakness of welfare capitalism. Employers confidently undertook responsibility for labor's well-being. That obligation, in
the end, they could not fulfil.

"Why work so hard for Mr. Hoover?" General Electric's
Owen Young chided a political friend in September 1928.
"Not that he does not deserve it from his supporters, but
perhaps he does not need it. . . . Worse things can happen
to a country than to have a liberal party in power once in a
while. . . . In any event, nothing very serious is going to
happen to this country however the election turns out."[35] Few
employers of labor had any greater premonition of economic
disaster. Fewer still made any provision to meet it.

A month after the stock market crash in October 1929, President Hoover called into conference Myron Taylor, Owen Young, Walter Teagle, Alfred P. Sloan, Pierre du Pont, and others of the nation's chief industrialists. Confiding his fear that a general depression would follow the Wall Street crisis, the President asked for a pledge against wage-cutting. The magnates readily assented. Actually, they needed no White House prodding. Wage maintenance had become part of the doctrine of "stability" that governed the oligopolistic industries. On October 25, in the midst of the crash, Schwab had lectured the Iron and Steel Institute on the importance of maintaining prices. Noting that the industry's prosperity was unimpaired, Schwab joked about "the smile of uncertainty upon the faces of a few who thought last week they were very rich and not quite so rich this week (laughter)." But, he insisted, steel had a "stabilized price structure" based on manufacturing cost plus a fair rate of return on the investment. The big steel firms would not permit "slight but inevitable fluctuations" to "disturb the healthy balance that has been established." That necessarily held for wages as well. "If you are going to sell your goods and eliminate your profit and expect to get it out of the men in the mills you are greatly mistaken," U.S. Steel's J. A. Farrell sternly admonished those who proposed wage cuts six months after the crash. "Wages are not coming down in the steel industry. . . . We all know that just as soon as they go down, if they should, Mr. Customer gets it."[36] Wage maintenance offered manifold benefits—humanitarian, psychological, and economic (everyone was saying that consumption was the key to prosperity). But the policy depended on industry determination to hold the price line.

Employment lacked that amenability to managerial control. As demand fell, production had to fall and diminish the amount of available work. The depression hit the automobile and textile industries first, and then spread with increasing force to other sectors of the economy. In past depressions

American industry had simply laid off excess men, and so did most smaller firms now. But the proponents of welfare capitalism undertook instead to spread the work. The rubber companies of Akron went on a six-hour day, and many companies shifted to eight hours at this time. The other approach was to rotate men. Using this method, U.S. Steel maintained on its payroll 94 per cent of its regular work force in January 1931, while it was operating below half of capacity. The roll of participating companies included probably every important exponent of welfare capitalism, and then enlisted others as work-spreading gained the support of the National Association of Manufacturers, the Chamber of Commerce, and the Hoover administration, and even spawned an organized Share-the-Work movement. By 1933, according to a Commerce Department survey, work-sharing existed among four-fifths of the country's firms and created one-fourth of all part-time jobs.[37]

Share-the-work naturally evoked the criticism that it merely made "the poor keep the poor." (Only the rarest of employers—the Kellogg Company, for instance—raised wages to compensate for the shorter hours.) Candid employers admitted some validity to the charge. But did critics offer them a better alternative? Business, moreover, did have to pay its share. A Bethlehem Steel executive listed the ways by which the company supplemented work-sharing—extending credit, making work, advancing pensions, providing garden plots and seed. And rotation of men had operational drawbacks. "If low cost production and profits were the only aim of industry in these days," said a business spokesman citing a typical case, "it would probably be wiser for the employer . . . to keep 400 on at full time and let the least efficient 200 join the ranks of the wholly unemployed." That ruthless practice of past depressions "has given way to the belief that the human relationship must be considered." Paul W. Litchfield of Goodyear Tire and Rubber believed "the six hour day in most cases economically unsound . . . but as the rubber industry in Akron employs the bulk of workers engaged in industry, we are permitting social conditions to govern, and are trying to keep as many men at work as possible." Work-sharing in steel seemed to Charles Schwab an "unexampled achievement of management." "Our men have stuck by us through thick and thin, and we are going to stick by them."[38]

To some extent, that responsibility covered even the growing jobless numbers. In October 1930, Schwab urged steel men to care "in part at least for those people who have no jobs at all. . . . We should . . . take such measures as may be necessary to carry everybody connected with the steel industry safely through this depression." And Myron Taylor added inspirationally:

> . . . We shall have to dig deep into our purses to assist those in want . . . and who must be cared for. They shall be cared for! And we of this great industry will do generously our part in this great service to humanity! . . . Let it be said of the steel industry that none of its men is called upon to ask help of the public. (Applause)

When the journalist William Hard visited Braddock, Pennsylvania, the following winter, he found U.S. Steel's Edgar Thomson Works dispensing groceries to 753 jobless employees, and other local plants were doing likewise. "Unemployment is a responsibility of industry very largely," asserted a trade journal, "and industry should take the leadership in practical plans for relief." Some companies established loan funds (General Electric, Goodyear, International Harvester, Standard Oil of New Jersey) or direct relief (Westinghouse) for unemployed men. Some attempted to select workmen for layoffs on a basis of need and number of dependents. Finally, a few firms (Standard Oil of New Jersey, American Rolling Mill, Hills Brothers) acknowledged a kind of property interest of long-term employees in their jobs and made money settlements to those who were permanently let go.[39]

Meanwhile, management thinking turned to reform. Even in the 1920s, unemployment had drawn attention, partly because the problem existed in the midst of prosperity and partly because welfare capitalism emphasized the workingman's security. Concrete results were negligible—only a bare thirteen companies started formal programs—but the main lines of private action did emerge. One avenue was an annual guarantee of work. In 1923 Proctor and Gamble began its famous plan of promising the employees of its soap-making plants 48 weeks of full-time work a year. Essentially, this approach challenged management to stabilize operations and devise labor practices that would regularize employment. Lacking Proctor and Gamble's unusually stable market, few employers dared make guarantees, but General Electric, Bethlehem Steel, and other firms did begin to improve job stability. Once the depression struck, the practices that had been developed were utilized generally in the work-sharing programs—for example, shifting men from department to department, cutting hiring to a minimum, building up inventories, and doing maintenance work in slack seasons. The other approach was to create an insurance reserve, either by the employer alone or on a matching basis with employees, that would provide unemployment benefits of limited duration. General Electric and fourteen Rochester firms, led by Eastman Kodak, introduced insurance plans during the first two depression years. The U.S. Chamber of Commerce thought these confirmed the expectation "that long-range provisions for unemployment are becoming a settled policy of American industry."[40]

Before the National Electrical Manufacturers Association on September 16, 1931, Gerard Swope of General Electric outlined the most ambitious private program to emerge from the crisis. His plan incorporated the two basic concepts of employment stabilization and insurance reserves (as well as provisions for workmen's compensation, life insurance, and pensions), but placed them in an unprecedentedly broad context. Swope argued that the individual firm could not cope effectively with unemployment. Stabilization required industry regulation through trade associations, which in turn would come under some form of federal supervision. Unemployment insurance had to be on a national basis so that coverage continued when a man moved from job to job. The Swope plan evoked tremendous interest, partly because of its controversial features. Whatever the dangers (especially regarding the proto-NRA aspects) he found in the proposals, the enlightened businessman could not question that Swope was right in his urgent concern over unemployment. "That this condition has ever been present in such periods detracts nothing from its wrongness. That industry must . . . first ameliorate and ultimately eliminate it, must be the reaction of every one who has given thought to what is taking place."[41]

Had the economy revived at about the time of Swope's speech, welfare capitalism would have emerged unscathed, indeed, enhanced. "This depression has shown us the extent to which business has become conscious of and accepted its social responsibility," wrote a Chamber of Commerce editorialist. "The employer has learned that labor is something more than a commodity to be bought in the cheapest market." Schwab expected that "the far-sighted and sound handling of our worker's interests . . . will stand out in bold relief as the major accomplishment of American management today." By maintaining wages and spreading employment, business was "keeping our economic organization in orderly condition and guarantee[d] the purchasing power of the public as soon as better conditions resume." But conditions did not improve. They worsened, and worsened further, and bumped down finally to an unimagined bottom of economic stagnation. In 1932 auto production dropped to 20 per cent. After that terrible year, Schwab considered it "a tribute to the sagacity and flexibility" of the steel industry's leaders "that most of our companies are still intact, despite huge losses."[42] But, in the meanwhile, welfare capitalism fell into an irredeemable shambles.

The economic collapse cut short any progress toward private unemployment insurance. Few companies followed the lead of General Electric and the Rochester firms. To supplement General Electric's relief and insurance efforts, Gerard Swope persuaded his board of directors to approve a guarantee of minimum earnings of half of normal for six months beginning November 1931. "Conditions became steadily worse," Swope recalled years later, "and I was very thankful when the six months guarantee period ended. . . . This was too ambitious a plan for any one company to undertake." Nor did he have greater success with his grand plan for industry-wide action. He continued to urge it, but, as he himself admitted, "not with very much effect." While industry remained inactive, sentiment was building up for public unemployment insurance; it gained the support of Governor Roosevelt of New York, was intensively studied by the Ohio Commission on Unemployment Insurance, and even passed into law in Wisconsin. The threat renewed employer support for private insurance in the early months of 1933. Admitting past error, Schwab asserted that the steel industry would build up reserves "to help meet any future depression." If laws were passed, they "should be so drawn as not to affect or impair voluntary activity by forward-looking industries. Otherwise, years of progress and voluntary action would be endangered."[43] As a seasoned businessman, Schwab should have known better than to try to trade on exhausted credit.

The immediate antidepression measures likewise were failing. The wage line could not be held. In steel, prices moved downward despite pleas from industry leaders. The fact was that money was still to be made by a few tightly run, ruthlessly competitive firms like E. T. Weir's National Steel Corporation. And wage rates crept downward as part of the hard

game. "I think it is a pretty cheap sort of business when . . .
men . . . are working three days a week, and then cut that
three days a week another 10 percent," exploded James Farrell of U.S. Steel before the Steel Institute in May 1931. "Now
that . . . is not the idea of the old line companies." But they
were soon obliged to follow. When U.S. Steel announced a 10
per cent cut effective October 1, 1931, wage maintenance died
in steel and in industry generally. A few weeks later, Ford
abandoned the seven-dollar day (which he had dramatically
proclaimed after Hoover's request for wage stability in November, 1929) and by November 1932 had driven the minimum down to four dollars. Average hourly earnings for production workers in manufacturing fell from 51.5 cents in 1931
to 44.2 cents in 1933. The collapse of wage maintenance
revealed the vulnerability of even the largest companies. "None
of us can escape the inexorable law of the balance sheet,"
Schwab admitted after the first reduction in steel. And after a
second in the spring of 1932: "We cannot escape the dictates
of present conditions."[44]

Corporate helplessness had far worse consequences on employment. Work-sharing became hardly more than a cruel
joke as production dried up. In the winter of 1931, Goodyear
employees were working eighteen hours a week. Bethlehem
Steel acknowledged in December 1931 that under its rotation
plan men "are now getting [less] than is necessary to sustain
life." How much worse, then, was their plight ten months later
when the company's operations had fallen nearly 90 per cent
while its regular work force remained only 15 per cent below
normal. Meanwhile, the jobless rolls lengthened alarmingly,
especially in the heavy industries. General Motors had employed an average of 233,286 people in 1929, 116,152 in 1932;
Ford, 101,069 in 1929, 56,277 in 1932. Total jobless estimates
crept upward from eight million in July 1931, to a sickening
fifteen million in March 1933—one out of three in the labor
force.

Long before that, business had ceased to talk about caring for its own, or even to claim that local resources could handle relief. Federal aid, a Chamber of Commerce spokesman had still been telling a radio audience in September 1931, would "paralyze initiative and courage and destroy independence." A poll of Chamber membership went overwhelmingly—more than twelve to one—against federal relief appropriations. By 1932 there was no choice. In June, leading Chicagoans pleaded for federal help for their city: the list included the heads of Armour, Cudahy, Wilson, International Harvester, Inland Steel, Bendix, and U.S. Gypsum. In Washington, business representatives, vocally opposed to relief appropriations in previous years, were conspicuously absent from Senate hearings in early 1933.[45]

The situation was actually worse than it seemed in Chicago and New York corporation offices. Industrial workers were not only losing hope in the promise of welfare capitalism; many were turning actively and fiercely against their employers. They did so despite the patently good intentions of management, for depression had the peculiar effect of spoiling even honest acts of benevolence. The fact was not obvious at a distance; close up, it could be perceived here and there.

In May 1931, 2,000 workers spontaneously walked out of a rubber-goods plant in Mishawaka, Indiana, not far from South Bend. The strike bewildered the management. The plant boasted a long history of good labor relations, first as an independent firm, and now under the control of U.S. Rubber, a leading practitioner of welfare capitalism. When hard times hit the plant in 1930, the company did its best to protect the workers through work sharing. "As a matter of fact," wrote Cyrus S. Ching, the able labor relations chief of U.S. Rubber, "I believe that in our efforts to take care of the situation, the management may have gone further than what might have been considered good business." Making a significant concession to end the strike, the open-shop company agreed to discuss grievances with an employees' committee elected by secret ballot. "We have the extreme desire for the good will of the employees," a company representative assured the committee in September. At that very time a federal conciliator found the workers dangerously angry. Three of "the best type men" warned him that they would kill the superintendent if they went out again. Notwithstanding its best efforts, the company found itself sitting on a powder keg.

The depression had demanded a series of hard decisions. "With a greatly reduced amount of business, and with a reduction in the price of goods, the need of economies has been felt more . . . than ever before," explained the superintendent. To meet the competition, he embarked on a drastic program, introducing new equipment and methods, cutting wages an average 10 per cent after a survey of day and piece rates, hiring an industrial engineer to start time-and-motion studies, and, finally, replacing straight piece work with a task-and-bonus system that figured earnings on an hourly basis plus a bonus for all production over the standard fixed by time-and-motion methods. The new pay plan set off the rebellion in May. The strikers charged that the standards were impossibly high, that many operatives had to start an hour or two early to make an efficiency rating that would keep them on the payroll, and that earnings fell from a third to a half for much more work. Company explanations and assurances did not lessen the hatred for "the heartless and inhuman task and bonus system."

The management faced a bitter predicament. The same depression conditions that called forth humane efforts demanded tough business decisions. What was worse, the benevolent acts themselves compounded the trouble. Had they cut the ranks ruthlessly so as to give the remaining employees full-time work, the Mishawaka managers felt that the task-and-bonus system would have operated better and raised no opposition. Other well-meant measures likewise backfired.

The company had agreed to shift some men to female jobs to keep them employed, and soon came under attack for paying them starvation wages.

> If we had laid those fellows off at the time we didn't have any of their kind of shoes . . . and built up production on Savoys with women, we would have saved ourselves a lot of grief. . . . And we didn't have the work for them, we could have laid them off legitimately.

When the managers reacted accordingly, they merely worsened matters. The second period of labor trouble in September 1931 occurred because of the layoff of fifty men. The employees' committee requested further work spreading and, when the company refused on the ground that it wanted to assure enough work for the remaining workers over the winter, accused the management of discriminating against union men. In May 1932, the firm had to cut wages another 15 per cent, but provided that the reduction would operate only in those weeks when the men had four days' work, doubtless hoping thereby to guarantee a living wage. The men, however, believed it was a trick. Certain that the company would schedule just enough work to effectuate the reduction, they went on strike again. So the bitterness deepened despite company pleas that "we haven't been selfish. We have perfectly clean hands."[46]

This was the terrible irony: just as everything redounded to management's credit in the 1920s, so now to its discredit in the depression. The Mishawaka experience was exceptional only because it resulted in overt trouble (possibly because of the presence of both union and communist sentiment). But everywhere resentment was silently building up. When it burst out under the aegis of the New Deal, the air would be filled with charges of inhuman speed-up, of ruthless rate-cutting, of rampant favoritism in the disposition of work. These grievances sharpened the edge of bitterness over the basic complaint of unemployment.

On January 18, 1933, Goodyear's Paul W. Litchfield confided to a friend "that we are drifting like a rudderless ship into waters that become more and more dangerous. There appears to be an increasing spirit of dejection and disillusionment wherever one goes. . . . The problem of unemployment is underlying all other ills." Litchfield's despair was partly over the intense suffering during the terrible third winter of depression. (The most poignant expression of that sympathy was an earlier outburst by Daniel Willard of the Baltimore and Ohio Railroad that, if he were a jobless worker with a family, he would steal before he would starve.) But it sprang also from a sense of helplessness in the face of economic collapse. Welfare capitalism rested ultimately on confidence in the strength of the big employers. They guaranteed the well-being of their workmen, and in turn received loyalty and goodwill. But the guarantee had not been honored. In August 1932, Myron Taylor observed that U.S. Steel was "at the mercy of business just like any other corporation."[47] It was a fatal admission.

Welfare capitalism had exhausted its credit. "The bankers and industrialists who have been running our country have proved their utter inability, or indifference, to put the country in a better condition," wrote an unemployed machinist who was about to lose his home. In a pathetic letter to Benjamin C. Marsh, head of the People's Lobby, an elderly Ford worker wrote that he had spend a lifetime "helping to create a millionaire." Marsh commented that "if the Ford Company can kick out men like this who have worked 30 years . . . to starve at 65 or 70, obviously the welfare of the wage earners cannot be left to employers."[48]

Careful observers read the signs of the future. Back in June 1929 the labor leader John Frey had felt defeated by "the development of cunningly devised schemes for making trade unionism difficult to maintain." Two years of depression changed Frey's mind about union prospects.

> So many workmen here have been lulled to sleep by the com-
> pany union, the welfare plans, the social organizations fostered by
> the employer . . . that they had come to look upon the employer
> as their protector, and had believed vigorous trade union organi-
> zation unnecessary for their welfare. When we get out of this
> depression . . . I look forward to a period of organizing much
> more extensive than any we have ever had except during the
> period of the war. . . .
> The fact is that the existing banking and industrial system has
> failed to justify the faith people have placed in them. The capitalist
> system as represented by these institutions have [*sic*] broken down
> for the time being.[49]

But Frey, no more than anyone else, estimated the force with
which labor would shortly turn on American industry.

Welfare capitalism could not sustain the management-
dominated system of labor relations. The failure was not inherent in its functioning in the 1920s, but sprang rather from
an extraordinary turn in the business cycle. Scholars have not
tended to treat welfare capitalism in this way; they have
inclined rather to interpret it as a passing and aberrant phase
of American industrialism. Irving Bernstein, for example,
concludes that "the central purpose of welfare capitalism—
avoidance of trade unionism—could be achieved only tem-
porarily because paternalism failed to come to grips with the
main issue: a system of shop government placed in a climate
of political democracy and universal suffrage."[50] Bernstein's
is, of course, a thought congenial to anyone who deplores the
arbitrary control of one man by another. It is comforting to
think that welfare capitalism never was a success, never persuaded workingmen that they were best off as wards of the
employer, and never took deep root in the American industrial order. The facts, however, suggest otherwise. It must
always remain an open question whether welfare capitalism
would not sooner or later have broken down spontaneously.
We do know that it did collapse because of a severe economic
crisis. The paternalistic course of American industrial relations
might well have continued but for the Great Depression.

Notes

1. *Law and Labor* 10 (January 1928): 19; *Nation's Business* 17 (April 1929): 89, and 18 (February 1930): 198.
2. Herbert Feis, *Labor Relations* (New York, 1928), p. 2.
3. David Brody, *Steelworkers in America: The Nonunion Era* (Cambridge, Mass., 1960), p. 149; *Nation's Business* 17 (April 1929): 90, 162.
4. Robert Ozanne, *A Century of Labor-Management Relations* (Madison, 1967), p. 73; *Nation's Business* 17 (April 1929): 90.
5. *Nation's Business* 17 (April 1929): 164; also, *Fortune* 2 (February 1931): 110 ff., and (March 1931): 94.
6. W. B. Dickson to Sidney Hillman, Jan. 27, 1940, Sidney Hillman Papers, Amalgamated Clothing Workers of America.
7. *Law and Labor* 10 (January 1928): 14.
8. Brody, *Steelworkers in America*, p. 117.
9. Quoted, Gerard Swope MSS, Oral History Collection, Columbia University, New York.
10. *Law and Labor* 10 (January 1928): 19.
11. National Industrial Conference Board (NICB), *Industrial Relations* (New York, 1931), p. 104.
12. *Law and Labor* 10 (January 1928): 15, and 11 (March 1929): 53.
13. United States Steel Corporation, *Stockholders' Meeting, April 16, 1923*, p. 9.
14. NICB, *Collective Bargaining Through Employee Representation* (New York, 1933), pp. 12-13.
15. Raymond B. Fosdick, *John D. Rockefeller, Jr.* (New York, 1956), p. 179: Brody, *Steelworkers in America*, pp. 225-26.
16. NICB, *Collective Bargaining*, pp. 39-40; *Law and Labor* 10 (January 1928): 16.
17. Sumner Slichter, "The Current Labor Policies of American Industries," *Quarterly Journal of Economics* 42 (May 1929): 432.
18. United States Steel Corporation, *Meeting of Subsidiary Presidents, January 21, 1919*, pp. 21, 24, 33; *Iron Age*, June 3, 1920, p. 1608; Slichter, "Current Labor Policies," p. 433.
19. Ozanne, *Century of Labor-Management Relations*, pp. 119-20.
20. *Iron Age*, February 2, 1922, p. 356; S. A. Lewisohn and P. T. Moon, eds., "Constructive Experiments in Industrial Cooperation," *Proceedings of the Academy of Political Science* 9 (January 1922): 545-46; A. Pound and S. T. Moore, eds., *They Told Barron* (New York, 1930).
21. Swope MSS, Columbia Oral History Collection; Irving Bernstein, *The Lean Years: A History of the American Worker, 1920-1933* (Boston, 1960), p. 170.
22. NICB, *Effect of Depression on Industrial Relations Programs* (New York, 1934), pp. 4-10; NICB, *Industrial Relations*, p. 54; American Iron and Steel Institute, *Yearbook* (1929), p. 33 (hereafter cited as *AISI Yearbook*).
23. Feis, *Labor Relations*, pp. 60, 71.
24. B. Selekman and M. Van Kleeck, *Employees' Representation in Coal Mines* (New York, 1924), pp. 247 ff.; Ozanne, *Century of Labor-Management Relations*, chap. 7.
25. Stuart D. Brandes, *American Welfare Capitalism, 1880-1940* (Chicago, 1976), pp. 141 ff. Brandes's analysis depends heavily on his claim that there was a swift jettisoning of welfare programs very early in the depression. For doubts on this score, see NICB, *Effect of Depression on Industrial Relations Programs*. A more

serious problem involves Brandes's failure to see welfare capitalism as more than the sum of a collection of welfare activities.

26. *Nation's Business* 17 (April 1929): 90.

27. John Frey to F. Kummer, June 28, 1929, Frey Papers, Library of Congress, Washington, D.C.

28. *Iron Age,* February 2, 1922, p. 356; Lewisohn and Moon, "Experiments in Industrial Cooperation," pp. 545–56; Pound and Moore, *They Told Barron.*

29. John Spargo, "Why I Am No Longer a Socialist," *Nation's Business* 17 (March 1929): 29–31, 168.

30. U.S. Bureau of the Census, *Historical Statistics of the United States: Colonial Times to 1970,* 2 vols. (Washington, D.C., 1975), 1: 164–65, 169–70; President's Research Committee on Social Trends, *Recent Social Trends in the United States,* 2 vols. (New York, 1933), 1: 225–26, 2: 820.

31. Albert Rees, *Real Wages in Manufacturing, 1890–1914* (Princeton, 1961).

32. *Monthly Labor Review* 30 (1930): 11–54.

33. Robert and Helen Lynd, *Middletown* (New York, 1929), pp. 51, 68, 80–81.

34. Bernstein, *Lean Years,* p. 81; William G. Baird to Ralph Easley, November 9, 1929, National Civic Federation Papers, New York Public Library; NICB, *Industrial Relations,* p. 14; Slichter, "Current Labor Policies," pp. 429, 435.

35. Owen D. Young to Marie M. Meloney, September 22, 1928, Meloney Papers, Columbia University Library, New York.

36. Herbert Hoover, *Memoirs. The Great Depression, 1929–1941* (New York, 1952), pp. 43–44; *AISI Yearbook* (1929), pp. 294–97, 302, and (1930), p. 42.

37. Bernstein, *Lean Years,* p. 470.

38. *Nation's Business* 19 (February 1931): 132, and 20 (October 1932): 32; Bernstein, *Lean Years,* p. 478; *AISI Yearbook* (1931), p. 32; *Steel,* December 12, 1932, p. 13.

39. *AISI Yearbook* (1930), pp. 252, 545; *Nation's Business* 19 (February 1939): 128, 129, and 20 (November 1932): 55; *Electrical World,* November 7, 1931, p. 815; William Hard, "Ingots and Doles," *Survey,* February 1, 1932, pp. 453–58.

40. *Nation's Business* 18 (August 1930): 11, and 19 (April 1931): 104. The General Electric plan is printed in *Law and Labor* 12 (August 1930): 180–83. On the Proctor and Gamble plan, see Feis, *Labor Relations,* chap. 10; H. Corey, "Solving the Unemployment Riddle," *Nation's Business* 19 (April 1931): 17–20.

41. The Swope plan is printed in *Law and labor* 13 (October 1931): 217–22. See also Swope MSS, Columbia Oral History Collection; David Loth, *Swope of G.E.* (New York, 1958), chap. 14; J. G. Frederick, ed., *The Swope Plan: Details, Criticisms, Analysis* (New York, 1931).

42. *Nation's Business* 20 (February 1932): 14–15; *AISI Yearbook* (1933), p. 28.

43. Swope MSS, Columbia Oral History Collection; *AISI Yearbook* (1933), p. 36. On the position of the U.S. Chamber of Commerce, see *Nation's Business* 21 (January 1933): 70, and 21 (June 1933): 18. Swope himself came down on the side of public insurance.

44. "National Steel: A Phenomenon," *Fortune* 4 (June 1932): 90 ff.; *AISI Yearbook* (1931), pp. 41, 342, and (1932), pp. 33–34; A. Nevins and F. E. Hill, *Ford: Expansion and Challenge, 1915–33* (New York, 1957), p. 588.

45. *Nation's Business* 20 (June 1932): 24, and (November 1932): 55; Bernstein, *Lean Years,* pp. 317, 467; Nevins and Hill, *Ford,* pp. 587, 588; *Law and Labor* 14 (January 1932): 6; *Electrical World,* December 6, 1930, p. 1031; *Nation,* September 23, 1931, p. 294; U.S., Congress, Senate, Committee on Manufactures, *Federal Relief of Unemployment,* 72nd Cong., 1st sess., 1932, pp. 228, 316.

46. Correspondence, memoranda, and minutes of company meetings with employees' committee, 1931–32, Mishawaka plant, United States Rubber Company, Federal Mediation and Conciliation Service Files, Record Group 174, National Archives.

47. P. W. Litchfield to Ralph Easley, January 18, 1933, National Civic Federation Papers; *Fortune* 13 (June 1936): 113. The formal welfare activities tended to be cut back to only a surprisingly small extent; the stock purchase plans, naturally enough, were the chief victims of the depression. See NICB, *Effect of Depression on Industrial Relations Programs.*

48. V. C. French to William Green, March 29, 1933, International Association of Machinists, National Union File No. 6, AFL-CIO Headquarters, Washington, D.C.; Marsh to James Couzens, December 10, 1932, Benjamin C. Marsh Papers, Library of Congress, Washington, D.C.

49. John Frey to F. Kummer, June 28, 1929, July 28, October 29, 1931, Frey Papers.

50. Bernstein, *Lean Years,* p. 187.

3
The Emergence
of Mass-Production
Unionism

At the coming of the New Deal, American organized labor was an arrested movement. Membership was slightly under three million in 1933. The unionized portion of the nonagricultural labor force—one-tenth—remained unchanged after thirty years. It was not only a matter of numbers. Labor strength was limited to the needle trades, public utilities (excluding communications), coal-mining, building construction, and the railroads. A vacuum existed in manufacturing, above all, in the mass-production sector. Organized labor had not breached the industries characterized by the giant firm; by multiplant operation for a national market; by an advanced technology involving mechanization and division of labor; and by a work force composed primarily of unskilled and semiskilled men. The mass-production core—iron and steel, nonferrous metals, rubber, electrical products, chemicals and petroleum, and food-processing—seemed impervious to trade unionism.

The great breakthrough occurred after 1935. A decade later, most of the mass-production industries had experienced thorough unionization. The consequences were, of course, profound. It was, as Walter Galenson said, "a fundamental,

From John Braeman *et al.,* eds., *Change and Continuity in Twentieth Century America* (Columbus: Ohio State University Press, 1964), pp. 221-62. Reprinted with permission.

almost revolutionary change in the power relationships of American society."[1] The accomplishment had its origin in the 1930s. But the favoring climate of that decade failed to carry the new unionism to its conclusion. Ultimately, permanent success came from the very events that ended the Great Depression and the New Deal.

The unionization of the mass-production industries still requires explanation; that is the purpose of this exploratory essay.[2]

The achievement began within the changing labor movement. The central fact, obviously, was the creation of the Congress of Industrial Organizations (initially, the Committee for Industrial Organization) as the unionizing agency for the basic industries. Several related questions claim our attention here. What was the necessity that split organized labor? What did the CIO bring to bear that had been lacking in the American Federation of Labor approach to the unionizing of mass production? And, finally, was the union effort decisive in accounting for the organization of the mass-production sector?

The irreconcilable issue seemingly was a matter of structure: industrial versus craft unionism. Industrial organization—the inclusion of all workers in an industry within one union—was a choice closed to the AFL for several reasons. Foremost was the numerical dominance of the craft unionists; since theirs were the interests to be injured, industrial-union resolutions had never mustered a majority in AFL conventions. The Federation was also in a constitutional bind. Jurisdiction was exclusive: only one union could hold rights to a given category of workers. And it was absolute: a union did not have to organize its jurisdiction in order to maintain its right. The craft unions had a kind of property interest within the basic industries. Beyond that was the immovable fact of trade autonomy: the locus of power rested with the national unions. The AFL was a voluntary institution, William Green observed, and therefore had "no power to compel any union or person to do anything."[3] Even the passage of an industrial-union resolution, Philip Taft has pointed out, "would not have forced any craft union to surrender its jurisdiction, nor compelled unions to amalgamate with each other."[4] There was, finally, the subtle role of *machtpolitik* within the labor movement. Themselves lacking power, Federation officers respected it in other hands. The power realities ordinarily favored the craft interests, and so, therefore, did the inclination of the AFL leadership. (William Green, agreeing as he did with the viewpoint of the Lewis group, surely displayed that practical quality when the chips came down in 1935 and after.)

These considerations remained binding during the historic debate over structure that took place in the mid-1930s. At the AFL convention of 1934 in San Francisco the issue was joined over the question of chartering national unions in the automobile, cement, aluminum, and other unspecified mass-production fields. Industrial-union sentiment, stimulated by recent events, forced the convention to recognize that "a new condition exists requiring organization upon a different basis to be most effective." But the convention also wanted to "fully protect the jurisdictional rights of all trade unions organized upon craft lines. . . ."[5] This second statement carried more weight. The Executive Council, to which the actual choice was left, excluded tool-, die-, and machine-making workers and parts plants from the jurisdiction of the new United Automobile Workers and maintenance and machine-installing men from the United Rubber Workers. The fateful Atlantic City convention of 1935 ratified the decision against industrial unionism.

It was a choice that John L. Lewis and his supporters could not accept. They insisted, as Charles Howard of the Typographical Union said, that "in the great mass-production industries industrial organization is the only solution." The aftermath of the 1935 convention was independent action that turned rapidly into dual unionism.

It has been hard to hold the momentous events of 1934–35 in perspective. The debate then was couched in the terminology of industrial unionism, and the outcome was the creation of a group of strong industrial unions. So it seemed to follow that the conflict over structure was the key to the formation of the CIO. That conclusion misplaces the emphasis.

The AFL did not lack an alternative arrangement. No less than his critics, Samuel Gompers had seen the inappropriateness of the original craft structure for emerging American industrialism. Over the years, there had developed a response to mass production. Gompers had early accepted the need to organize the unskilled: "With the invention of new machines and the application of new forces, the division and subdivision of labor, many workers who had been employed at skilled trades find themselves with their occupations gone. . . . Thus we see the artisan of yesterday the unskilled laborer of today." The essential device was the federal labor union. Gathered first into these mixed local bodies, the unorganized would be drawn off by occupation into the appropriate national unions or into local trade unions affiliated, as were the federal unions, directly with the AFL. The federal labor unions, said Gompers, were "the recruiting ground for trade union movement."[6]

Besides organizing noncraft workers, the Federation tried to alter the existing structure to make room for them. Charters were granted to national unions covering the unskilled and semiskilled within single industries; for instance, the Hod Carriers in construction and the Tin Plate Workers in tin plate manufacture. But Gompers's preference was for the less skilled to find a place within the "primary unions," that is, national unions covering the occupations specific to an industry.[7] To that end, the AFL urged unions to amalgamate or to accept broader jurisdictions. The optimum result was a national union covering all occupations specific to an industry, irrespective of the skills involved, plus common labor. Such residual jurisdictions in fact were operative at some time in practically every mass-production industry before the 1930s. The craft unions were not victimized thereby. Defining its position in the Scranton Declaration of 1901, the AFL adhered as closely to the "fundamental principle" of craft organization "as the recent great changes in methods of production and employment make possible."[8] Primary jurisdictions would not normally encompass such interindustry occupations as teamsters, carpenters, machinists, and similar trades.

Co-ordination, finally, was encouraged. The primary and craft unions had to act together in the basic industries. As early as the Scranton Declaration, the suggestion had been made of "closely allying the sub-divided crafts" through "the organization of district and national trade councils. . . ." Much of the subsequent co-operation, particularly in joint organizing drives, was on an informal and sporadic basis. During and after World War I, national unions in meatpacking joined together only when faced with the need for common decisions. In steel, on the other hand, twenty-four national unions acted in 1918-20 through the permanent National Committee for Organizing Iron and Steel Workers. At the district level, local unions had formal bodies in the Schenectady plant of General Electric for over a decade after 1911, in meat-packing centers from 1901 to 1904 and again in Chicago from 1917 to 1920, and in steel during the union upsurge of the war period. The departments of the AFL also promoted joint union activity. The Metal Trades Department chartered local councils and mounted co-operative organizing drives, for instance, in the automobile industry in 1914 and 1927. Inadequate though most of these ventures were, they did not show that organizational unity was unattainable under the primary-craft structural arrangement for the mass-production fields.

The AFL was adhering to this established plan in 1935. Its advocates insisted that the formula was workable. The separation of craft workers would not, after all, be numerically important in mass production. The rubber industry was a case in point. Its labor force, according to a breakdown in the census of 1930, was composed of the following:

       559 carpenters
       395 compositors, linotypers, and typesetters
       915 electricians
     1,206 mechanics
     1,148 stationary engineers
       482 millwrights
     4,665 machinists
       805 plumbers
       300 toolmakers
     1,267 truck drivers
       456 painters and glaziers
    80,835 operatives
    29,123 laborers[9]

Jurisdiction over the last two categories would give a rubber workers' union nearly 90 per cent of the labor force in the industry. William Hutcheson of the Carpenters could not see why organization would be impeded by separating "a comparatively small number as compared to the total number employed in the rubber industry." And coordination could surely be made to work. John Frey was convinced that "joint negotiations and joint agreement reached through the [Metal Trades] Department forms the most effective answer to . . . the so-called industrial form of trade union organization . . . enabling an employer to negotiate but one agreement which will cover all his employees. . . ."[10] In September 1934, this policy had been adopted for the metal and building trades. Both AFL departments entered negotiations on this basis with the Anaconda Copper Company.

If not the optimum solution, the AFL alternative nevertheless seemed adequate and reasonable. The primary-craft formula could not be ruled out as unworkable on the basis of past experience. While deprecated by Lewis adherents, it could not by itself drive the breach in the labor movement.

Nor, for that matter, could the appeal of industrial unionism."Much has been said about principles in the war between the C.I.O. and the A.F. of L.," commented the informed labor consultant Chester M. Wright in 1939. "As I see it, the whole dispute is one involving tactics and practices. I fail to find any principles involved at any point."[11] Earlier, industrial unionism had involved fundamental differences. Its advocates had been mainly Socialists and others seeking to make the labor movement a vehicle for political action and/or basic social change. That was not the case in the 1930s. Industrial unionism then was directed only at the mass-production industries, not, as in the amalgamation movement of the early 1920s, at the entire economy. The ideological groundwork was mostly gone. John L. Lewis himself had opposed the amalgamationists of the postwar period. His emergence as industrial-union leader in the early New Deal period presumed that the debate over structure did not reflect basic differences about the role of the trade-union movement.

The antagonists were not doctrinaire even on the narrow structural issue. Bitter opponents of Lewis as they were, the Carpenters, Machinists, and Electrical Workers were themselves asserting industrial jurisdiction over limited areas between 1934 and 1936.[12] For his part, Lewis was not rigid on industrial unionism. When the AFL Executive Council was considering in February 1935 what craft groups to exclude from an auto workers' union, Lewis pleaded that the "cavilling be deferred until in the light of what accomplishment is made in the objective we can take up the question of dividing the members, that contention over the fruits of victory be deferred until we have some of the fruits in our possession." While he retained hope in the AFL, Lewis did not commit himself to industrial unionism.[13]

It was not in itself of importance. Lewis was a pragmatist in the dominant tradition of American trade unionism. Labor leaders responded, as William Green said, to "the fact, not a theory but a situation actually existing. . . ."[14] The formation of the CIO was a drastic measure which, from Lewis's standpoint, had to yield a commensurate return. The structural reform of industrial unionism was not such a return. Nor, in fact, was it absolutely precluded from the pragmatic labor movement. Industrial unions could find a place—as did the United Mine Workers of America itself—within the AFL. The Butcher Workmen had put the fact neatly back in 1922 when the issue over requesting industrial jurisdiction in meat-packing arose. It would be better, the convention decided, first to unionize the industry "and then by reason of the strength that would accompany such an organization, take and retain control over all men of whatever craft employed in the industry."[15] The obstacles to that first point—not the second—were the operative ones in 1935.

What excited Lewis and his adherents was a concrete objective: the organization of the mass-production industries. That accomplished, the structural issue would resolve itself and would, in any case, not be of great moment. "The fundamental obligation is to organize these people," Lewis insisted. The resulting problems should be considered "after we had accomplished organization and not before, after the fact of organization has been accomplished[,] not tie on reservations that will in themselves deter an effective campaign."[16] This revealed the heart of the crisis: would the AFL take the measures necessary for the organization of mass-production workers?

Industrial unionism fitted into this larger context. The immense influence of the idea sprang from the contemporary assessment of the psychology of industrial workers. "I know their state of mind," William Green asserted, speaking of the automobile workers. "If you tell them to go here, you here and you there, you will never get anywhere. They are so closely related and inextricably interwoven they are mass minded."[17] In her perceptive *Industrial Valley,* Ruth McKenney described the problem as she saw it in Akron rubber plants.

> . . . The machinists and the electricians kept coming to the Federal local meetings. [The AFL organizer] could never make them understand they were supposed to stay away, supposed to belong to a separate union. He could never teach them that their interests were different from the common ordinary rubberworker. Stubbornly and stupidly they clung to the Federal locals.[18]

Industrial unionists had here an explanation for the failure to hold the thousands of industrial workers who had flocked into the AFL federal unions in 1933. Sidney Hillman noted, for example, that during the NRA period over 40,000 rubber workers had been organized. Then the AFL "started to divide those workers among the different unions claiming jurisdiction over them. As a result of that procedure, the membership of the rubber workers union fell as low as 3,000."[19]

The problem was *tactical.* Since industrial labor was "mass minded," the first stage of organization had to be on a mass basis. "Vice President Lewis said there is a psychology there among the men . . . ," read the minutes of the February 1935 meeting of the AFL Executive Council. "What he has in mind [is that] the time to quarrel over jurisdiction is after we organize the men rather than before."[20] William Green shared Lewis's view. The mass-production industries should be organized "as best we can, then after they are organized if the question [arises] on the jurisdiction of an international union, perhaps by education we can bring about respect among these workers of the jurisdiction of the national and international unions."[21]

That reasoning explained the hopefulness following the San Francisco convention of 1934. The objectives then enunciated seemed irreconcilable: to protect craft jurisdictions and to organize mass-production fields on "a different basis." But an apparent accommodation had emerged from the many hours of talks off the floor of the convention. The Executive Council was "directed to issue charters for National or International Unions"—the instructions did not specify precise jurisdictions. Second, "for a provisional period" the chartered unions should be under AFL direction "in order to protect and safeguard the members of such National and International Unions as are chartered. . . ." Both these points—temporary AFL control and an undefined jurisdiction—were included in John L. Lewis's seven-point program for an automobile union which was presented to the Executive Council in February 1935. And there was a final point:

> That all questions of overlapping jurisdiction on the automobile parts and special crafts organizations encountered in the administration policy be referred to the Executive Council for consideration at such time as the Council may elect to give these questions consideration.[22]

"This proposal is in strict conformity with the action of the A. F. of L. convention of 1934," Lewis explained, "and in proposing it I intend that if this policy does an injury to any international union that the union thus affected will have the right to take up these questions with the Executive Council of the American Federation of Labor and I assume that judgment will be rendered in conformity with . . . the record of the previous actions of the Council."[23]

Confronting the proposal, the craft leaders could not accept it. Dan Tobin of the Teamsters saw "some merit" in Lewis's view and was willing to permit a "dispensation for six months or so in the hope we will unscramble them later on. . . ."[24] But others, above all Wharton of the Machinists, had higher stakes in the automobile field. They were responding to the realities of the American labor movement: could they successfully exert their jurisdictional rights *after* organization had occurred on an industrial basis? In fact, they had grown critical even of the standard AFL practice of placing skilled recruits in federal unions because these recruits then became reluctant to transfer to the appropriate craft unions.[25] William Hutcheson of the Carpenters thought the jurisdictional question "should be straightened out now to avoid trouble."[26] The Executive Council so decided: specific groups were excluded from the jurisdiction of the Auto Workers and, at the next Council meeting, of the Rubber Workers. In essence, the craft unions were refusing to gamble—at long odds—their vested rights in order to unionize mass-production workers. Tobin put the fact bluntly: "We are not going to desert the fundamental principles on which these organizations have lived and are living to help you organize men who have never been organized."[27]

The jurisdictional problem was only the most visible of the obstacles to effective action. National unions with old-line leadership had primary jurisdiction in a number of basic industries—most importantly, the Amalgamated Association of Iron, Steel and Tin Workers. The industrial bloc agreed with Green's view that "the officers of the Amalgamated cannot organize these workers with their own resources or with the set-up as is. . . .. The change has been taking place but the Amalgamated has been standing committed to its old tradition policy." Lewis urged the chartering of another national union with jurisdiction over steel. The craft unionists refused to abrogate the sacred rights of an autonomous union, as William Hutcheson said, "even if it was in bad straits."[28] They were willing to permit others to mount a steel campaign, but the bulk of the steelworkers would have to go into an organization which had amply proved its incapacity. Exclusive jurisdiction and trade autonomy seemed to be immutable principles.

Finally, the necessary resources were not being directed to the organization of the basic industries. The income of the labor movement accumulated in the national unions, not in the Federation. President Green was able to augment his organizing staff by only fifteen in the critical year 1933. The affiliated unions were unwilling either to raise the per capita going to the AFL or to expend adequate funds directly in the organizing effort. (The response to Green's appeal in March 1936 for funds for a steel drive totaled $8,625 from five unions.) The flabbiness of the financial support could be gauged by the later reaction to the CIO threat: AFL organizing expenses during 1937–39 were triple those of 1933–35.[29] Nor were the unions with jurisdiction in the basic industries roused to a common effort. No joint drives were mounted in 1933–34 that would compare to those of earlier years in steel, autos, textiles, and meat-packing. The AFL convention of 1934 instructed the Executive Council not only to charter national unions in mass-production industries but to inaugurate a union drive in steel. The Council had done nothing beyond passing a resolution by the time of the fateful convention of 1935.

At bottom, the AFL was experiencing a crisis of will. Lewis bitterly commented in May 1935 "that some six months have gone by since we adopted that resolution in San Francisco and there still remains the fact that there has been no administration of that policy, no execution of the promissory note that this Federation held out to the millions of workers in the mass-production industry. . . . Neither do I understand there is any immediate desire to carry out that policy. . . ."[30] The choice rested with the controlling craft unionists. And they were not really committed to organizing the mass-production workers. Dan Tobin of the Teamsters, for instance, spoke contemptuously of "the rubbish that have lately come into other organizations." A widespread feeling was, as Mathew Woll said in 1934, that the industrial workers were "perhaps unorganizable." Tobin was saying in February 1936 that "there isn't a chance in the world at this time to organize the steel-workers."[31]

To John L. Lewis, the basic obstacle was the indifference of the craft leaders. They were the object of his plea at the 1935 convention:

> Why not make a contribution to the well-being of those who are
> not fortunate enough to be members of your organizations? . . .
> The labor movement is organized upon a principle that the strong
> shall help the weak. . . . Is it right, after all, that because some of
> us are capable of forging great and powerful organizations of
> skilled craftsmen in this country that we should lock ourselves up
> in our own domain and say, "I am merely working for those who
> pay me"?

The AFL had to choose between becoming "an instrumental-
ity that will render service to all of the workers" and resting
"content in that comfortable situation that has prevailed
through the years. . . ." Convinced at last that the craft bloc
preferred the second path, Lewis saw independent action as
the only remedy to "twenty-five years of constant, unbroken
failure."[32]

Mass-production unionization merged with industrial unionism only when hope was lost in the AFL. Actually, this
began to happen months before the Atlantic City convention
of 1935. Lewis started to shift his ground after the defeat of his
program for an auto union at the February meeting of the
Executive Council. At the May meeting, he did not try
to apply his compromise formula to the Rubber Workers.
Rather, he wanted "the jurisdiction granted to the organization
to cover all workers employed throughout the rubber industry." Nothing was said at the subsequent convention either in
Lewis's arguments or in the Minority Report about the post-
ponement of jurisdictional questions until after the achievement of mass-production organization (although there were
such intimations in the speeches of Lewis's supporters Charles
Howard and Sidney Hillman).[33] The full commitment to industrial unionism became evident in Lewis's offer of $500,000
toward an AFL steel-organizing fund on February 22, 1936.
One condition was that "all steel workers organized will be
granted the *permanent* right to remain united in one international union."[34]

Having opted for independent action, Lewis had every reason to espouse industrial unionism: it was a desirable structural reform; it would draw in unions such as the Oil Workers and the Mine, Mill and Smelter Workers that were having jurisdictional troubles within the AFL;[35] and, above all, it would serve as a rallying cry in the union rivalry and in the organizing field. But industrial unionism remained a subordinate consideration. When the occasion demanded, it was sacrificed to the necessities of the organizing task and to the inevitable ambitions for the CIO as an institution.[36] Nor did industrial unionism fulfill the expectations of earlier advocates. No real transformation was worked in the objectives of the labor movement. Differing in some ways, the rival federations were, as Chester Wright insisted, "brothers under the skin," and the passage of twenty years was time enough to permit them to join in a merger.

The CIO had been created with the fixed purpose of organizing the mass-production industries. Liberated from past practice and vested interest, the effort could be made with optimum effectiveness. Starting fresh, the CIO thoroughly exploited its opportunity.

The previous restrictions were immediately thrown off. The separation of skilled men no longer, of course, constituted an impediment to organization. Funds in massive amounts were now injected in some areas. The Steel Workers Organizing Committee received in six years $1,619,613 from outside sources, as well as the services of many organizers who remained on the payrolls of other unions.[37] In part, the money came as direct contributions from affluent CIO affiliates. The Mine Workers and the Clothing Workers, frankly anxious for the organization of industries related to them, directed most of their assistance to steel and textiles, respectively. The rest of the CIO income came from a high per capita tax of five cents a month. Proportionately, the investment far surpassed what had been possible within the AFL (although, it should be noted, the latter in response was doing likewise). Finally, the CIO was able to build the new industrial unions, particularly those which first took the form of organizing committees, free from the restricting hand of the past. There were instances, notably in steel and textiles, where AFL unions with old-line leaders came over to the CIO, but they were held to subordinate roles. Able officials were recruited from men rising from the ranks or, as in the case of steel, from experienced unionists elsewhere in the CIO.

The job of organizing was meanwhile changing radically. First, mass-production workers were bursting with militancy. The upsurge of NRA-inspired unionism, for instance, was very largely spontaneous. At the time, it seemed to William Green "a sight that even old, tired veterans of our movement never saw before." Another official believed it would surpass in "numbers, intensity, and duration" the union experience of World War I.[38] Even before the CIO, popular militancy was expressing itself in internal resistance to AFL policies and/or in independent unionism, and in rank-and-file strikes such as that at the Toledo Chevrolet plant in April 1935.[39] The second change followed from the Wagner Act. For the first time, workmen had the legal right to express through majority rule their desires on the question of union representation. On the counts of both rank-and-file sentiment and federal law, success came to depend on the union appeal, hitherto of secondary importance, to the workingmen. To this requirement, the CIO responded brilliantly.

The ingredients of success were unremitting effort and a mastery of the techniques suited to the special conditions of the mass-production industries. A pool of effective organizers for this work could be drawn from CIO affiliates, above all, the Mine Workers; from left-wing groups; and from militants within the industrial ranks. In addition to using the standard methods, CIO organizers emphasized rank-and-file participation. These were the instructions to a group of adherents in Fort Worth on how to organize their Armour plant:

It takes Organizers inside the plant to Organize the plant.

The Committe that organized the Oklahoma City plant was a voluntary committee established inside the plant.

You cannot wait for the National Organizer to do all the work. . . . You people here can have a Union, but you will have to work to build it.

Typically, an intricate network of unpaid posts was established in CIO plants, so that "more men are given responsibility, and our organization becomes more powerful and more closely knit." The aim was to avoid "bureaucratic" rule by putting the leadership, as one organizer said, not in a few hands, but in "the whole body, in one, acting as one."[40]

Another significant CIO tactic arose out of sensitivity to the deep-seated resentments of the workers. At the plant level, grievances characteristically received aggressive support. When the men saw "how the CIO was fighting to protect workers' rights," a Packinghouse Workers' official explained, they flocked into the organization. Direct action was another expression of CIO militancy. Sudden strikes and slowdowns, although often against official policy, were frequently encouraged by local officers. For, as one functionary observed of the stoppages at the Armour Chicago plant, they "demonstrated to all, union members and non-union members, that the CIO had plenty of stuff on the ball and that there was no such thing as waiting for something to happen."[41]

The effectiveness of the CIO had another dimension. The basic industries had drawn the newcomers and underprivileged of American society. Eastern Europeans and then, when the flow of immigrants was stopped by World War I, migrants from the South filled the bottom ranks of mass-production labor. The colored workers had unquestionably been among the chief obstacles to earlier union efforts. William Z. Foster, who had taken a leading part in the AFL drives of World War I, admitted that "we could not win their support. It could not be done. They were constitutionally opposed to unions, and all our forces could not break down that opposition."[42] The problem was of diminishing magnitude in the 1930s. Negro workers, mostly new arrivals from the South fifteen years before, had gone through a lengthy adjustment. In addition, racial tensions had largely abated. There would be no counterpart to the Chicago race riot of 1919, which had disrupted the union drive in the stockyards. Yet the Negro workers still required special treatment.

Here again the CIO capitalized fully on the opportunity. It became an aggressive defender of Negro rights. After a foothold had been gained in the Armour Chicago plant, for example, one of the first union victories was to end the company practice of "tagging", the time cards of colored employees: "the Stars will no longer offend the Negro workers of Armour & Co." The initial informal agreement at the Swift plant included a company pledge to hire Negroes in proportion to their numbers in the Chicago population.[43] The AFL could not match these zealous efforts. From the start, Gompers had insisted on the necessity of organizing the colored workers, not out of concern for "social or even any other kind of equality," but to insure that they would not "frustrate our every effort for economic, social and political improvement."[44] This view prevailed, before as well as during the New Deal, wherever the membership of Negroes was essential to the success of a union. But many craft affiliates could afford to exclude or segregate such workers, and the Federation reluctantly accepted what it could not prevent. Besides being tainted by discrimination, the AFL failed to crusade even where it favored racial equality. Doing so, the CIO swept the Negroes in mass production into its ranks. The same sensitivity to noneconomic factors marked the CIO approach to immigrant and female labor and to the fostering of public support through political work and such communal activities as the "back of the yards" movement in the Chicago packing-house district.

The labor movement thus generated an effective response in the basic industries. A further question remains: Was this the decisive change? It does not seem so. More than the incapacity of organized labor had prevented earlier success. Had everything else remained constant, the CIO effort alone would not have resulted in permanent unionization of the mass-production sector—nor, for that matter, would it even have been attempted.

The sense of urgency was significant. At his last AFL convention, John L. Lewis told Powers Hapgood that a union drive in the basic industries in the past "would have been suicide for organized labor and would have resulted in complete failure. But now, the time is ripe; and now the time to do those things is here. Let us do them."[45] The American system of industrial relations was being profoundly shaken during the mid-1930s. "Conditions as they exist now," Charles Howard told the Atlantic City convention, "make it more necessary, in my opinion, for effective organization activity than at any time during the life of the American Federation of Labor."[46]

In retrospect, employer resistance looms largest in accounting for the long years of union failure in mass production. The sources of that hostility need not be explored here. Suffice it to say that American industrialists found compelling reasons and, more important, adequate means for resisting labor organization. Lewis noted the "great concentration of opposition to the extension and logical expansion of the trade union movement."

> Great combinations of capital have assembled great industrial plants, and they are strong across the borders of our several states from the north to the south and from the west in such a manner that they have assembled to themselves tremendous power and influence. . . .

"There is no corporation in America more powerful than these corporations—General Motors and Ford," William Green said respectfully. "Everybody knows their financial strength. . . . It is a fact we have always recognized."[47] No real possibility of countering the resources and advantages available to industry had earlier existed; the power balance had been overwhelmingly against labor.

In the 1930s, a new legal framework for industrial relations emerged. In the past, the right to organize had fallen outside the law; unionization, like collective bargaining, had been a private affair. Within normal legal limits, employers had freely fought the organization of their employees. Now that liberty was being withdrawn. World War I had first raised the point. The National War Labor Board had protected workers from discrimination for joining unions and thus contributed substantially to the temporary union expansion of the war period. The lesson was inescapable. Unionization in the mass-production industries depended on public protection of the right to organize. The drift of opinion in this direction was discernible in the Railway Labor Act of 1926 and the Norris-LaGuardia Act of 1932. But the real opportunity came with the advent of the New Deal. Then key union spokesmen, notably Green and Lewis, pressed for the insertion of the famous Section 7a in the National Industrial Recovery Act. After an exhilarating start, Section 7a foundered; loopholes developed and enforcement broke down long before the invalidation of the NRA. But the intent of Section 7a was clear, and it soon received effective implementation.

"If the Wagner bill is enacted," John L. Lewis told the AFL Executive Council in May 1935, "there is going to be increasing organization. . . ."[48] The measure, enacted on July 5, 1935, heavily influenced Lewis's decision to take the initiative that led to the CIO. For the Wagner Act did adequately protect the right to organize through a National Labor Relations Board clothed with powers of investigation and enforcement. Employer opposition was at long last neutralized.

The Act made it an unfair labor practice for an employer "to interfere with, restrain, or coerce employees in the exercise" of "the right of self-organization." This protection unquestionably freed workers from fear of employer discrimination. Stipulation cases required the posting of such notices as the following at a Sioux City plant:

> The Cudahy Packing Company wants it definitely understood that . . . no one will be discharged, demoted, transferred, put on less desirable jobs, or laid off because he joins Local No. 70 or any other labor organization. . . . If the company, its officers, or supervisors have in the past made any statements or taken any action to indicate that its employees were not free to join Local No. 70 or any other labor organization, these statements are now repudiated.[49]

Even more persuasive was the reinstatement with back pay of men discharged for union activities. The United Auto Workers' cause at Ford was immensely bolstered in 1941 by the rehiring of twenty-two discharged men as the result of an NLRB decision which the company had fought up to the Supreme Court. By June 30, 1941, nearly twenty-four thousand charges of unfair labor practices—the majority involving discrimination —had been lodged with the NLRB.[50] More important in the long run, vigorous enforcement encouraged obedience of the law among employers. Assured of their safety, workers flocked into the unions.

The law also resolved the knotty problems of determining union representation. During the NRA period, company unions had been widely utilized to combat the efforts of outside organizations. The Wagner Act now prohibited employers from dominating or supporting a labor union. Legal counsel at first held that "inside" unions could be made to conform with the law by changing their structure, that is, by eliminating management participation from the joint representation plans. The NLRB, however, required the complete absence of company interference or assistance. Few company unions could meet this high standard, and large numbers were disestablished by NLRB order or by stipulation. In meat-packing, for instance, the Big Four companies had to withdraw recognition from over fifteen company unions. Only in the case of some Swift plants did such bodies prevail over outside unions in representation elections and become legal bargaining agents.[51] Besides eliminating employer-dominated unions, the law put the selection of bargaining representatives on the basis of majority rule. By mid-1941, the NLRB had held nearly six thousand elections and cross-checks involving nearly two million workers. Given a free choice, they overwhelmingly preferred a union to no union (the latter choice resulting in only 6 per cent of elections in 1937 and, on the average, in less than 20 per cent up to the passage of the Taft-Hartley Act). Having proved its majority in an "appropriate" unit, a union became the certified bargaining agent for all employees in the unit.

An unexpected dividend for union organization flowed from the Wagner Act. In the past, the crisis of mass-production unions had occurred in their first stage. Rank-and-file pressure normally built up for quick action. Union leaders faced the choice of bowing to this sentiment and leading their organizations into suicidal strikes—as happened on the railroads in 1894, in the stockyards in 1904, and in steel in 1919—or of resisting the pressure and seeing the membership melt away or break up in factional conflict—as occurred in meatpacking after World War I. The Wagner Act, while it did not eliminate rank-and-file pressures, eased the problem. A union received NLRB certification on proving its majority in a plant. Certification gave it legal status and rights which could be withdrawn only by formal evidence that it lacked majority support. Defeat in a strike did not in any way affect the status of a bargaining agent. Restraint, on the other hand, became a feasible policy. The CIO unions as a whole were remarkably successful in resisting workers' demands for national strikes in the early years, although not in preventing local trouble. The resulting dissidence could be absorbed. The Packinghouse Workers Organizing Committee, for instance, was in continual turmoil from 1939 to 1941 because of the conservative course of Chairman Van A. Bittner; but internal strife did not lead to organizational collapse there or elsewhere. NLRB certification permitted labor leaders to steer between the twin dangers—external and internal—that earlier had smashed vigorous mass-production unionism.

Years later, the efficacy of the Wagner Act was acknowledged by an officer of the most hostile of the major packing firms: ". . . The unions would not have organized Wilson [and Company] if it had not been for the Act."[52] That judgment was certainly general in open-shop circles.

Yet the Wagner Act was not the whole story. For nearly two years while its constitutionality was uncertain, the law was virtually ignored by antiunion employers. And after the Jones and Laughlin decision in April 1937, the effect was part of a larger favoring situation. John L. Lewis was not reacting to a single piece of legislation. He saw developing in the mid-1930s a general shift toward unionization.

The change was partly in the workers themselves. Their accommodation to the industrial system had broken down under the long stretch of depression. The resulting resentment was evident in the sitdown strikes of 1936–37, which involved almost half a million men. These acts were generally not a calculated tactic of the union leadership; in fact, President Sherman Dalrymple of the Rubber Workers at first opposed the sitdowns. Spontaneous sitdowns within the plants accounted for the initial victories in auto and rubber.[53] Much of Lewis's sense of urgency in 1935 sprang from his awareness of the pressure mounting in the industrial ranks. A local auto-union leader told Lewis in May 1935 of talk about craft unions' taking skilled men from the federal unions. "We say like h— they will and if it is ever ordered and enforced there will be one more independent union."[54] Threats of this kind, Lewis knew, would surely become actions under existing AFL policy, and, as he warned the Executive Council, then "we are facing the merging of these independent unions in some form of national organization."[55] That prophecy, Lewis was determined, should come to pass under his control. The CIO succeeded in large measure because it became the vehicle for channeling the militancy released by the Great Depression.

The second factor that favored union organization was the impact of the depression on the major employers. They had operated on a policy of welfare capitalism: company paternalism and industrial-relations methods were expected to render employees impervious to the blandishments of trade unionism.[56] The depression forced the abandonment of much of this expense and, beyond that, destroyed the workers' faith in the company's omnipotence on which their loyalty rested. Among themselves, as an official of Swift and Company said, industrialists had to admit that grounds existed for "the instances of open dissatisfaction which we see about us, and perhaps with us. . . ."[57]

The depression also tended to undermine the will to fight unionization. Antiunion measures were costly, the La Follette investigation revealed. The resulting labor troubles, in addition, cut deeply into income. The Little Steel companies, Republic in particular, operated significantly less profitably in 1937 than did competitors who were free of strikes. Economic considerations seemed most compelling, not when business was bad, but when it was getting better. Employers then became very reluctant to jeopardize the anticipated return of profitable operations. This apparently influenced the unexpected decision of U.S. Steel to recognize the Steel Workers Organizing Committee. In 1937 the Steel Corporation was earning substantial profits for the first time during the depression; net income before taxes that year ultimately ran to 130 million dollars. And the first British purchases for defense were just then in the offing. During the upswing, moreover, the competitive factor assumed increasing importance. Union firms had the advantage of avoiding the disruptions incident to conflict over unionization. Certainly a decline of 15 per cent in its share of the automobile market from 1939 to 1940 contributed to the Ford Company's retreat of the following year.[58]

Finally, the political situation—the Wagner Act aside—was heavily weighted on the side of labor. Management could no longer assume governmental neutrality or, under stress, assistance in the labor arena. The benefits accruing to organized labor took a variety of forms. The Norris-LaGuardia Act limited the use of injunctions that had in the past hindered union tactics. A federal law prohibited the transportation of strikebreakers across state lines. The *Thornhill* decision (1940) declared that antipicketing laws curbed the constitutional right of free speech. Detrimental governmental action, standard in earlier times of labor trouble, was largely precluded now by the emergence of sympathetic officeholders on all levels, from the municipal to the national. Indeed, the inclination was in the opposite direction. The response to the sitdown strike illustrated the change. "Well, it is illegal," Roosevelt commented. "But shooting it out and killing a lot of people because they have violated the law of trespass . . . [is not] the answer. . . . There must be another way. Why can't those fellows in General Motors meet with the committee of workers?"[59] This tolerance of unlawful labor acts, as sitdowns were generally acknowledged to be, could not have happened at any earlier period of American history. These were negative means of forwarding the labor cause.

But political power was also applied in positive ways. The La Follette investigation undermined antiunion tactics by exposure and, among other ways, by feeding information on spies to the unions.[60] At critical junctures, there was intercession by public officials ranging from President Roosevelt and Labor Secretary Perkins down to Mayor Kelly of Chicago. Governor Frank Murphy's role in the General Motors controversy is only the best known of a number of such mediating contributions to the union cause.[61] At the start of the CIO steel drive Pennsylvania's Lieutenant-Governor Thomas

Kennedy, a Mine Workers' officer, announced that organizers were free to move into steel towns and that state relief funds would be available in the event of a steel strike. The re-election of Roosevelt in 1936 no doubt cast out lingering hopes; many employers bowed to the inevitable after FDR's smashing victory with labor support.

These broader circumstances—rank-and-file enthusiasm, economic pressures on management, and the political condition—substantially augmented the specific benefits flowing from the Wagner Act. In fact, the great breakthroughs at U.S. Steel and General Motors in early 1937 did not result from the law. The question of constitutionality was resolved only some weeks later. And the agreements themselves did not accord with the provisions of the Wagner Act. The unions dared not utilize procedures for achieving certification as bargaining agents in the auto and steel plants. Lee Pressman, counsel for the SWOC, later admitted that recognition could not then have been won "without Lewis' brilliant move" in his secret talks with U.S. Steel's Myron C. Taylor.

> There is no question that [the SWOC] could not have filed a petition through the National Labor Relations Board . . . for an election. We could not have won an election for collective bargaining on the basis of our own membership or the results of the organizing campaign to date. This certainly applied not only to Little Steel but also to Big Steel.[62]

Similarly, the *New York Times* reported on April 4, 1937: "Since the General Motors settlement, the union has been spreading its organization rapidly in General Motors plants, which were weakly organized at the time of the strike." The NLRB could not require either U.S. Steel or General Motors to make agreements with unions under those circumstances. Nor did the companies grant the form of recognition contemplated in the Wagner Act, that is, as *exclusive* bargaining agents. (This would have been illegal under the circumstances.) Only employees who were union members were covered by the two agreements. These initial CIO victories, opening the path as they did for the general advance of mass-production unionism, stemmed primarily from the wider pressures favorable to organized labor.

The Wagner Act proved indecisive for one whole stage of unionization. More than the enrollment of workers and the attainment of certification as bargaining agent was needed in unionization. The process was completed only when employers and unions entered bona fide collective bargaining. But this could not be enforced by law. Meaningful collective bargaining was achievable ultimately only through the interplay of nonlegislative forces.

The tactics of major employers had shifted significantly by the 1920s. Their open-shop doctrine had as its declared purpose the protection of workingmen's liberties. "We do not believe it to be the wish of the people of this country," a U.S. Steel official had said, "that a man's right to work shall be made dependent upon his membership in any organization."[63] Since the closed shop was assumed to follow inevitably from collective bargaining, the refusal to recognize unions was the fixed corollary of the open shop. The argument, of course, cut both ways. Open-shop employers insisted that their employees were free to join unions (whether or not this was so). The important fact, however, was that the resistance to unionism was drawn tight at the line of recognition and collective bargaining. That position had frustrated the attempt of the President's Industrial Conference of October 1919 to formulate principles for "genuine and lasting cooperation between capital and labor." The union spokesmen had withdrawn in protest against the insistence of the employer group that the obligation to engage in collective bargaining referred only to shop committees, not to trade unions.[64] In effect, the strategy was to fight organized labor by withholding its primary function.

Federal regulation of labor relations gradually came to grips with the question of recognition and collective bargaining. During World War I, the NWLB only required employers to deal with shop committees. Going further, the NRA granted employees the right to "bargain collectively through representatives of their own choosing. . . ." This was interpreted to imply an obligation of employers to deal with such representatives. The major failing of Section 7a was that the NRA did not implement the interpretation. In practice, determined employers were able, as earlier, to escape meaningful negotiation with trade unions.[65] It seems significant that the permanent union gains of the NRA period came in those areas—the coal and garment industries—where collective bargaining did not constitute a line of employer resistance. Profiting by the NRA experience, the Wagner Act established the procedure for determining bargaining agents and the policy of exclusive representation and, by the device of certification, withdrew recognition from the option of an employer.

But recognition did not mean collective bargaining. Section 8 (5) did require employers to bargain with unions chosen in accordance with the law. Compliance, however, was another matter. In the first years, hostile employers attempted to withhold the normal attributes of collective bargaining. When a strike ended at the Goodyear Akron plant in November 1937, for example, the company insisted that the agreement take the form of a "memorandum" signed by the mediating NLRB regional director, not by company and union, and added that "in no event could the company predict or discuss the situation beyond the first of the year."[66] (Although the Rubber Workers' local had already received certification, it would not secure a contract for another four years.) Westinghouse took the position that collective bargaining "was simply an opportunity for representatives of the employees to bring up and discuss problems affecting the working force, with the final decision reserved to the company. It rejected the notion of a signed agreement because business conditions were too uncertain. . . ."[67] Some companies—for instance, Armour in April 1941—unilaterally raised wages while in union negotiations.

The contractual forms were resisted: agreements had to be verbal, or take the form of a "statement of policy," or, if in contractual terms, certainly with no signatures. These blatant evasions of the intent of Section 8 (5) were gradually eliminated: a series of NLRB and court rulings prohibited the refusal to negotiate or make counteroffers, the unilateral alteration of the terms of employment, and opposition to incorporating agreements into written and signed contracts.

The substance proved more elusive than the externals of collective bargaining. "We have no trouble negotiating with Goodyear," a local union president observed, "but we can never bargain. The company stands firmly against anything which does not give them the absolute final decision on any question."[68] The law, as it was interpreted, required employers to bargain "in good faith." How was lack of good faith to be proved? The NLRB tried to consider the specific circumstances and acts, rather than the words, of the employer in each case. That cumbersome procedure was almost useless from the union standpoint. Delay was easy during the case, and further evasion possible afterward. Barring contempt proceedings after a final court order, moreover, the employer suffered no penalties for his obstruction; there was no counterpart here for the back-pay provisions in dismissal cases. The union weakness was illustrated at Wilson & Co. The Cedar Rapids packing plant had been well organized since the NRA period, but no agreement was forthcoming from the hostile management. In 1938 the union filed charges with the NLRB. Its decision came in January 1940, and another year was consumed by the company's unsuccessful appeal to the Circuit Court. The negotiations that followed (interrupted by a strike which the union lost) led nowhere because, a union official reported, Wilson "as always . . . tried to force the Union to accept the Company's agreement or none at all."[69] The contract which was finally consummated in 1943 resulted neither from an NLRB ruling nor from the free collective bargaining that was the aim of the Wagner Act. Clearly, "good faith" was not to be extracted from recalcitrant employers by government fiat.

The collective-bargaining problem had a deeper dimension. The bitter-enders themselves constituted a minority group in American industry. For every Westinghouse, Goodyear, Ford, and Republic Steel there were several major competitors prepared to abide by the intent of the law and enter "sincere negotiations with the representatives of employees." But, from the union standpoint, collective bargaining was important for the results it could yield. Here the Wagner Act stopped. As the Supreme Court noted in the Sands case, "from the duty of the employer to bargain collectively . . . there does not flow any duty . . . to accede to the demands of the employees."[70] No legal force sustained the objectives of unions either in improving wages, hours, and conditions or in strengthening their position through the union shop, master contracts, and arbitration of grievances.

The small utility of the law in collective bargaining was quickly perceived by labor leaders. The CIO packing-house union, for instance, did not invoke the Wagner Act at all in its three-year struggle with Armour. The company, in fact, objected to the intercession of Secretary of Labor Perkins in 1939 on the ground that the union had not exhausted, or even utilized, the remedies available through the NLRB.[71] The dispute actually did involve issues which fell within the scope of the Wagner Act. But the union clearly was seeking more effective ways—federal pressure in this case—of countering Armour's reluctance to negotiate and sign contracts. For the prime union objective was a master contract covering all the plants of the company organized by the union, a concession which could only be granted voluntarily by the company. Collective bargaining, both the process itself and the fruits, depended on the working of the other advantages open to the unions in the New Deal era.

Where negotiation was undertaken in "good faith," there were modest initial gains. The year 1937, marking the general beginning of collective bargaining in mass production, saw substantial wage increases as the result of negotiations and/or union pressure. In steel, the advances of November 1936 and March 1937 moved the unskilled hourly rate from 47 cents to 62.5 cents. In rubber, average hourly earnings rose from 69.8 cents to 76.8 cents; in automobiles, from 80 to 93 cents. Other gains tended to be slender. The U.S. Steel agreement, for instance, provided the two major benefits of time-and-a-half after eight hours and a grievance procedure with arbitration. The vacation provision, on the other hand, merely continued an existing arrangement, and silence prevailed on many other questions. The contracts were, in contrast to later ones, very thin documents.[72] Still, the first fruits of collective bargaining were encouraging to labor.

Then the economy faltered again. In 1938 industrial unions had to fight to stave off wage cuts. They succeeded in most, but not all, cases. Rates were reduced 15 per cent at Philco after a four months' strike. Less visible concessions had to be granted in some cases. For example, the SWOC and UAW accepted changes which weakened the grievance procedure at U.S. Steel and General Motors.[73] The mass-production unions were, in addition, hard hit by the recession. Employment fell sharply. The UAW estimated that at the end of January 1938, 320,000 auto production workers were totally unemployed and most of the remainder of the normal complement of 517,000 were on short time. The union's membership was soon down to 90,000. It was the same story elsewhere. In the Chicago district of the SWOC, dues payments fell by two-thirds in the twelve months after July 1937 (that is, after absorbing the setback in Little Steel).[74] Declining membership and, in some cases, internal dissension rendered uncertain the organizational viability of the industrial unions. And their weakness in turn further undermined their effectiveness in collective bargaining. They faced a fearful choice. If they became quiescent, they would sacrifice the support of the membership. If they pressed for further concessions, they would unavoidably become involved in strikes. By so doing, they would expose their weakened ranks in the one area in which labor legislation permitted the full expression of employer hostility—and in this period few even of the law-abiding employers were fully reconciled to trade unionism.

Collective bargaining was proving a severe obstacle to the new mass-production unions. The Wagner Act had little value here; and the other favoring circumstances had declining effectiveness after mid-1937. Hostile employers were evading the requirement of negotiating in good faith. For the larger part, the industrial unions achieved the first approximation of collective bargaining. But from 1937 to 1940 very little more was forthcoming. The vital function of collective bargaining seemed stalled. The situation was, in sum, still precarious five years after the formation of the CIO.

John L. Lewis had made something of a miscalculation. The promise of the New Deal era left mass-production union-ism short of permanent success. Ultimately, two fortuitous circumstances rescued the industrial unions.

The outbreak of World War II finally ended the American depression. By 1941, the economy was becoming fully engaged in defense production. Corporate profits before taxes leaped from 6½ billion dollars in 1939 to 17 billion in 1941. The number of unemployed fell from 8½ million in June 1940 to under 4 million in December 1941. It was this eighteen-month period that marked the turning point for the CIO. Industry's desire to capitalize on a business upswing, noted earlier, was particularly acute now; and rising job opportunities and prices created a new militancy in the laboring ranks. The open-shop strongholds began to crumble. Organization came to the four Little Steel companies, to Ford, and to their lesser counterparts. The resistance to collective bargaining, where it had been the line of conflict, was also breaking down. First contracts were finally being signed by such companies as Goodyear, Armour, Cudahy, Westinghouse, Union Switch and

Signal. Above all, collective bargaining after a three-year gap began to produce positive results. On April 14, 1941, U.S. Steel set the pattern for its industry with an increase of ten cents an hour. For manufacturing generally, average hourly earnings from 1940 to 1941 increased over 10 per cent and weekly earnings 17 per cent; living costs rose only 5 per cent. More than wages was involved. Generally, initial contracts were thoroughly renegotiated for the first time, and this produced a wide range of improvements in vacation, holiday, and seniority provisions and in grievance procedure. Mass-production workers could now see the tangible benefits flowing from their union membership. These results of the defense prosperity were reflected in union growth: CIO membership jumped from 1,350,000 in 1940 to 2,850,000 in 1941.[75]

The industrial unions were arriving at a solid basis. That achievement was insured by the second fortuitous change. American entry in the war necessitated a major expansion of the federal role in labor-management relations. To prevent strikes and inflation, the federal government had to enter the hitherto private sphere of collective bargaining. The National War Labor Board largely determined the wartime terms of employment in American industry. This emergency circumstance, temporary although it was, had permanent consequences for mass-production unionism. The wartime experience disposed of the last barriers to viable collective bargaining.

For one thing, the remaining vestiges of antiunionism were largely eliminated. The hard core of resistance could now be handled summarily. In meat-packing, for instance, Wilson & Co. had not followed Armour, Swift, and Cudahy in accepting collective bargaining. In 1942 the NWLB ordered the recalcitrant firm to negotiate a master contract (Wilson was holding to the earlier Big Four resistance to company-wide bargaining). Years later in 1955, a company official was still insisting that Wilson would not have accepted "a master agreement if it had not been for the war. Such an agreement is an unsatisfactory arrangement; today or yesterday."[76] Subsequent negotiations having yielded no results, a Board panel itself actually wrote the first Wilson contract.[77]

Beyond such flagrant cases, the NWLB set to rest an issue deeply troubling to the labor-management relationship in mass production. With few exceptions, the open shop remained dogma even after the acceptance of unionism. "John, it's just as wrong to make a man join a union," Benjamin Fairless of U.S. Steel insisted to Lewis, ". . . as it is to dictate what church he should belong to."[78] The union shop had been granted in auto by Ford only; in rubber, by the employers of a tenth of the men under contract;[79] in steel, by none of the major producers (although they had succumbed under pressure in the "captive mines"). The issue was profoundly important to the new unions. The union shop meant membership stability and, equally significant, the full acceptance of trade unionism by employers. The NWLB compromised the charged issue on the basis of a precedent set by the prewar National Defense Mediation Board. Maintenance-of-membership prevented members from withdrawing from a union during the life of a contract. Adding an escape period and often the dues checkoff, the NWLB had granted this form of union security in 271 of 291 cases by February 1944. The CIO regarded maintenance-of-membership as a substantial triumph. And, conversely, some employers took the measure, as Bethlehem and Republic Steel asserted, to be a "camouflaged closed shop." Among the expressions of resentment was the indication in contracts, following the example of Montgomery Ward, that maintenance-of-membership was being granted "over protest."[80] This resistance, however, was losing its force by the end of the war. The union shop then generally grew from maintenance-of-membership.

The war experience also served a vital educational function. A measure of collective bargaining remained under wartime government regulation. Both before and after submission of cases to the NWLB, the parties involved were obliged to negotiate, and their representatives had to participate in the lengthy hearings. From this limited kind of confrontation, there grew the consensus and experience essential to the labor-management relationship. Wartime education had another aspect. The wage-stabilization policy, implemented through the Little Steel formula by the NWLB, tended to extend the issues open to negotiation. Abnormal restraint on wages convinced labor, as one CIO man said, that "full advantage must be taken of what leeway is afforded" to achieve "the greatest possible gains. . . ."[81] As a result the unions began to include in their demands a variety of new kinds of issues (some merely disguised wage increases) such as premium pay, geographical differentials, wage-rate inequalities, piece-rate computation, and a host of "fringe" payments. Thus were guidelines as to what was negotiable fixed for use after the war and a precedent set that would help further to expand the scope of collective bargaining. The collapse of economic stabilization then also would encourage the successive wage increases of the postwar rounds of negotiation. However illusory these gains were in terms of real income, they endowed the industrial unions with a reputation for effectiveness.

Finally, the wartime restrictions permitted the groping advance toward stable relations to take place in safety. The danger of strikes that might have pushed the parties back to an earlier stage of hostilities was eliminated. Strikes there were in abundance in the postwar period, but these could then be held to the objective of the terms of employment, not the issue of unionism itself. Nothing revealed more of the new state of affairs than the first major defeat of an industrial union. The packinghouse strike of 1948 was a thorough union disaster in an industry traditionally opposed to trade unionism. Yet the United Packinghouse Workers of America recovered and prospered. As one of its officials noted with relief, it was the first time in the history of the industry that a "'lost' strike did not mean a lost union."[82]

Unionization thus ran its full course in mass production. The way had been opened by the New Deal and the Great

Depression. The legal right to organize was granted, and its utilization was favored by contemporary circumstances. John L. Lewis seized the unequalled opportunity. Breaking from the bounds of the labor establishment, he created in the CIO an optimum instrument for organizing the mass-production workers. These developments did not carry unionization to completion. There was, in particular, a failure in collective bargaining. In the end, the vital progress here sprang fortuitously from the defense prosperity and then the wartime impact on labor relations. From the half-decade of war, the industrial unions advanced to their central place in the American economy.

Notes

1. Walter Galenson, *The CIO Challenge to the AFL* (Cambridge, 1960), p. xvii, and for growth of union membership, pp. 583–93.
2. Important recent research based on new sources has added much information on this subject, and the documentation will reveal my debts. But no satisfying analysis has emerged from this scholarship. It was this conclusion that led to the undertaking of the present essay.
3. James O. Morris, *Conflict within the AFL: A Study of Craft Versus Industrial Unionism, 1901-1938* (Ithaca, N.Y., 1958), p. 8.
4. Philip Taft, *The A.F. of L. in the Time of Gompers* (New York, 1957), p. 200.
5. AFL, *Proceedings, 1934*, pp. 586–87.
6. Ibid., 1897, pp. 6, 15.
7. For lack of an apt term in the literature, I have coined the phrase "primary union" to describe organizations with residual jurisdiction in mass-production fields. It should be noted that the local unions of these nationals tended to be organized around trades or departments rather than plants, as would be the case with industrial unions.
8. AFL, *Proceedings, 1901*, p. 240. AFL organizing assistance, for instance, required prior agreement, as the Butcher Workmen were informed in 1915, "that when the employees of the meat trust are organized, they shall be assigned to their respective organizations" (AFL Executive Council Minutes, February 21–26, 1916, p. 5 [hereafter cited as AFL ECM]).
9. Harold S. Roberts, *The Rubber Workers: Labor Organization and Collective Bargaining in the Rubber Industry* (New York, 1944), p. 98.
10. Philip Taft, *The A.F. of L. from the Death of Gompers to the Merger* (New York, 1959), pp. 86, 91.
11. Chester M. Wright, *Here Comes Labor* (New York, 1939), p. 47.
12. Morris, *Conflict within the AFL*, p. 177; Robert A. Christie, *Empire in Wood: A History of the Carpenters' Union* (Ithaca, N.Y., 1956), chap. 9; Mark Perlman, *The Machinists: A New Study in American Trade Unionism* (Cambridge, 1961), pp. 90-91.

13. Taft, *A.F. of L. from the Death of Gompers,* pp. 105, 107; AFL, *Proceedings,* 1934, p. 588.
14. Taft, *A.F. of L. from the Death of Gompers,* p. 106.
15. Amalgamated Meat Cutters and Butcher Workmen of North America, *Proceedings,* 1922, pp. 18, 35, 81–82.
16. Taft, *A.F. of L. from the Death of Gompers,* p. 107.
17. Ibid.; AFL, *Proceedings,* 1934, p. 592.
18. Ruth McKenney, *Industrial Valley* (New York, 1939), p. 109.
19. Mathew Josephson, *Sidney Hillman: Statesman of American Labor* (New York, 1952), p. 385.
20. AFL ECM, January 29–February 14, 1935, p. 213. I have utilized the Council minutes in this account. I have, however, thought it more helpful to give references to Taft or Galenson except in instances in which selections from the minutes do not appear in those secondary sources.
21. Taft, *A.F. of L. from the Death of Gompers,* p. 91.
22. Ibid., p. 105; AFL, *Proceedings,* 1935, pp. 94–96, 538. At the San Francisco convention of 1934, Lewis's explanation of the industrial union resolution was thoroughly unrevealing, no doubt for good tactical reasons. The most he would say, when pressed, was that the jurisdictional decisions rested with the Executive Council (to which he and his supporter David Dubinsky were being added). But see the speech of Mathew Woll, in AFL, *Proceedings,* 1934, pp. 593–94; also, the editorial in the *American Federationist* 41 (November 1934): 1177.
23. AFL ECM, January 29–February 14, 1935, pp. 68–69, 218–19.
24. Ibid., pp. 214–15.
25. See Morris, *Conflict within the AFL,* pp. 152–58; Sidney Fine, "The Origins of the United Automobile Workers, 1933–35," *Journal of Economic History* 18 (September 1958): 254–55.
26. AFL ECM, January 20–February 14, 1935, p. 213.
27. Ibid., April 30–May 7, 1935, p. 124.
28. Taft, *A.F. of L. from the Death of Gompers,* p. 116.
29. Morris, *Conflict within the AFL,* p. 162.
30. AFL ECM, April 30–May 7, 1935, p. 115.
31. Ibid., p. 174; Taft, *A.F. of L. from the Death of Gompers,* p. 118; Edward Levinson, *Labor on the March* (New York, 1938), p. 84; also, the speech of A. O. Wharton, in AFL, *Proceedings,* 1935, pp. 569–72.
32. AFL, *Proceedings,* 1935, pp. 534, 536, 541.
33. Ibid., pp. 526, 746; AFL ECM, April 13–May 7, 1935, pp. 113–16. At the May meeting of the Council a resolution was offered to postpone the jurisdictional decision on the Rubber Workers until after they had formed an international and drawn up a constitution with a proposed jurisdiction. This compromise came not from Lewis but, significantly, from AFL Secretary Morison, probably with Green's backing. The craft majority refused this alternative, as well as Lewis's offer to exclude "those engaged in new construction work" (Ibid., pp. 135–39).
34. Galenson, *CIO Challenge to AFL,* p. 79 (italics mine).
35. See, for example, Vernon H. Jensen, *Nonferrous Metals Industry Unionism, 1932–1954: A Story of Leadership Controversy* (Ithaca, N.Y., 1954), chap. 3; Lowell E. Gallaway, "The Origin and Early Years of the Federation of Flat Glass Workers of America," *Labor History* 2 (Winter 1962): 100–02.
36. In some instances, for example, CIO unions attempted to keep groups out of bargaining units if a close election was forthcoming or in order to avoid trouble with the strategic Teamsters. (11 NLRB 950 [1939], 14 NLRB 287 [1939], 16 NLRB 334 [1939], 21 NLRB 1189 [1940].)

37. Galenson, *CIO Challenge to AFL,* p. 110.
38. Morris, *Conflict within the AFL,* p. 147.
39. On the experience in automobiles, see Fine, "Origins of the United Automobile Workers," *passim,* and Sidney Fine, "The Toledo Chevrolet Strike of 1935," *Ohio Historical Quarterly* 67 (1958): 326-56.
40. Joint Executive Board Minutes, Oklahoma City and Ft. Worth Locals, Packinghouse Workers Organizing Committee (PWOC), August 9, 1942; District 2 Conference Minutes, PWOC, January 14, 1940, Files of United Packinghouse Workers of America (UPWA); *People's Press,* July 23, 1938.
41. Arthur Kampfert, "History of Unionism in Meat Packing," in UPWA Files; *CIO News. Packinghouse Edition,* November 5, 1938, p. 8.
42. Chicago Commission on Race Relations, *The Negro in Chicago* (Chicago, 1922), p. 429.
43. *CIO News. Packinghouse Edition,* January 2, 1939, p. 2; Kampfert, "History of Unionism in Meat Packing."
44. Gerald N. Grob, "Organized Labor and the Negro Worker, 1865-1900," *Labor History* 1 (Spring 1961): 168.
45. Hapgood quoting Lewis, in Saul Alinsky, *John L. Lewis: An Unauthorized Biography* (New York, 1949), p. 80.
46. Ibid., p. 70; AFL, *Proceedings,* 1935, p. 525.
47. AFL, *Proceedings,* 1935, p. 535; AFL ECM, January 29-February 14, 1935, p. 64, also, for example, p. 213.
48. Taft, *A.F. of L. from the Death of Gompers,* pp. 89-90.
49. 31 NLRB 967-68 (1941).
50. Harry A. Millis and Emily Clark Brown, *From the Wagner Act to Taft-Hartley* (Chicago, 1950), p. 77.
51. James R. Holcomb, "Union Policies of Meat Packers, 1929-1943" (M.A. thesis, University of Illinois, 1957), pp. 101-02, 124, 139, 161-62.
52. James D. Cooney quoted in Ibid., p. 173.
53. Galenson, *CIO Challenge to AFL,* pp. 185 ff., 269 ff.; Roberts, *Rubber Workers,* pp. 144 ff.; McKenney, *Industrial Valley,* part 3. On the spontaneous character of the decisive shutdown at the Ford River Rouge complex, see Irving Howe and B. J. Widick, *The UAW and Walter Reuther* (New York, 1949), pp. 100-01.
54. Fine, "Origins of the United Automobile Workers," p. 280.
55. Taft, *A.F. of L. from the Death of Gompers,* pp. 89-90. See also, for example, Howard's speech, in AFL, *Proceedings,* 1935, p. 525.
56. See, for example, Irving Bernstein, *The Lean Years: A History of the American Worker, 1920-1933* (Boston, 1960), chap. 3.
57. F. I. Badgeley, in *National Provisioner,* October 28, 1933, pp. 82-84.
58. Galenson, *CIO Challenge to AFL,* pp. 93-94, 108-09, 182.
59. Frances Perkins, *The Roosevelt I Knew* (New York, 1946), p. 322.
60. Robert R. R. Brooks, *When Labor Organizes* (New Haven, 1937), p. 72.
61. J. Woodford Howard, "Frank Murphy and the Sit-Down Strikes of 1937," *Labor History* 1 (Spring 1960): 103-04; Barbara W. Newell, *Chicago and the Labor Movement: Metropolitan Unionism in the 1930's* (Urbana, 1961), pp. 178-79; George Mayer, *Floyd B. Olson* (Minneapolis, 1951), pp. 159-60. For a summary of New Deal "sensitivity" to labor, see Milon Derber and Edwin Young, eds., *Labor and the New Deal* (Madison, 1957), chap. 5.
62. Alinsky, *Lewis,* p. 149.
63. David Brody, *Steelworkers in America: The Non-Union Era* (Cambridge, 1960), p. 176.

64. Lewis L. Lorwin and Arthur Wubnig, *Labor Relations Boards: The Regulation of Collective Bargaining under the National Industrial Recovery Act* (Washington, D.C., 1935), pp. 13–18.
65. On the difficulties over this question in the automobile industry, see Sidney Fine, "Proportional Representation of Workers in the Automobile Industry," *Industrial and Labor Relations Review* 12 (January 1959): 182–205.
66. Roberts, *Rubber Workers,* p. 223.
67. Twentieth Century Fund, *How Collective Bargaining Works: A Survey of Experience in Leading American Industries* (New York, 1945), pp. 763–64.
68. Roberts, *Rubber Workers,* p. 247.
69. National Wilson Conference Minutes, PWOC, February 14, 1942, UPWA Files. See also, 19 NLRB 990 (1940).
70. Quoted in Joseph Rosenfarb, *The National Labor Policy and How It Works* (New York, 1940), p. 197.
71. *New York Times,* September 12, 1939.
72. For an analysis of the U.S. Steel agreement, see Robert R. R. Brooks, *As Steel Goes. . . : Unionism in a Basic Industry* (New Haven, 1940), chap. 8.
73. Ibid., p. 211; Galenson, *CIO Challenge to AFL,* p. 158.
74. Galenson, *CIO Challenge to AFL,* p. 157; Newell, *Chicago and the Labor Movement,* p. 144.
75. Joel Seidman, *American Labor from Defense to Reconversion* (Chicago, 1953), pp. 27, 31, 32; Galenson, *CIO Challenge to AFL,* p. 587; on contract terms, see Twentieth Century Fund, *How Collective Bargaining Works.*
76. Holcomb, "Union Policies of Meat Packers," p. 172.
77. 6 War Labor Reports 436–41 (1943).
78. Benjamin F. Fairless, *It Could Only Happen in the United States* (New York, 1957), p. 38.
79. Roberts, *Rubber Workers,* p. 310.
80. Seidman, *American Labor from Defense to Reconversion,* chap. 6.
81. Officers' Report, 2nd Wage and Policy Conference, July 8–10, 1943, PWOC, UPWA Files.
82. *Packinghouse Worker,* August 20, 1948, p. 7.

4
Thinking about
Industrial Unionism

The New Deal and the
Labor Movement [1973]

The question before us here is: How did the New Deal change America? My assignment is to apply the question specifically to the American labor movement and to what was its chief development during the 1930s, namely, the rise of industrial unionism. I began to wonder, as I thought about it, whether whoever it was who formulated the question did so by design or (as seems more likely) merely to delineate an area of discussion and chose the question because it had a nice ring to it. For the fact is that the question—certainly as it applies to the labor movement—is a tough one indeed to answer.

Given the volume of work done on the New Deal and on the labor history of this period, it may come as a surprise that no one has actually attempted a comprehensive and systematic exploration of the question: How did the New Deal change the American labor movement? In part, I suppose, this is because the political historians tend not to have much interest in the labor side, and the labor historians (myself included) tend to treat the political factor only as they see it

This essay was read before the British Association of American Studies, Canterbury, England, in June 1973.

acting on the events they are studying. I suspect also that the question is skirted because of the inherent difficulties of analysis. These arise partly from the ambiguous nature of the New Deal; partly from the problems of isolating and weighing the political as against other factors; and partly even from uncertainty about defining the changes that the American labor movement underwent during the New Deal era.

At the start, the labor movement had under 3 million members—no more than a tenth of the nonagricultural work force—and was entirely excluded from the mass-production sector of the economy. The corporate industries—steel, auto, rubber, electrical equipment, food processing—had developed on open-shop lines and had successfully resisted the unionization of their properties for many years. The struggle for organization is one of the distinctive features of the American labor experience: no less than half the strikes of the mid-1930s were fought over basic rights of organization rather than over wages, hours, and conditions. This kind of industrial struggle would certainly provide one of the principal starting points in any comparative study with, say, British labor. The advantage finally shifted to American labor's side in the mid-1930s: in 1935, 10.2 per cent of the production workers in metal manufacturing were organized; in 1939, 51 per cent. The great mass-production industries were by then well on the way to complete unionization. By the end of World War II, there were over 14 million union members, and the movement had become, so Walter Reuther proclaimed in 1947, "the vanguard in America . . . the architects of the future."

Of the contributing political factors, first in importance clearly was the development of public protection for the right to organize and engage in collective bargaining, ineffectually at first in Section 7a, then most successfully in the Wagner Act of 1935. Once the Supreme Court validated the act in 1937, unionization really became a matter of free choice for American workers. By the end of 1941, nearly 6,000 representation elections had been held and 2 million votes had been cast. Related to this was the work of the LaFollette Civil Liberties Investigating Committee, which filled the gap before the Wagner Act became operative and which, through exposure, largely neutralized the repressive weapons hitherto used in the fight against trade unionism.

The Democratic revolution also was important. It put a number of industrial states, such as Pennsylvania and Michigan, in the hands of the political friends of labor and opened company towns that had always been closed to organizers. At many key points, open-shop employers lost allies in state and local government who had performed yeoman service in earlier industrial wars. The massive shift of the labor vote into the Democratic party, and especially the enormous enthusiasm for President Roosevelt, was shrewdly exploited by the CIO. In the mill towns of Pennsylvania in 1936, the CIO steel drive and the presidential campaign were united into a single movement. Immediately after the election, a union circular went out with this heading: "Steel Workers Win: Labor Vote Defeats Steel Barons at Polls: Roosevelt Re-elected." This was the heart of the message: "You beat the Steel Barons by re-electing Roosevelt. You can beat them again by organizing your own union."

Political considerations had also helped to revitalize the labor movement. From their NRA experiences, John L. Lewis and Sidney Hillman drew these lessons: first, that the public sector was going to be increasingly important to labor; and, second, that what labor gained there would depend on how strong it was. So it was crucial to bring in the mass-production workers, even if this meant overriding the craft majority in the AFL. In the autumn of 1936 high political expectations helped push CIO leaders at the decisive point into taking the independent line transforming the industrial-union movement into a genuine rival to the AFL. Finally, public intervention during the war period helped assure the permanence of the union gains made in the Depression: first, by breaking the resistance of the hard-core open-shop employers; second, by establishing a functioning relationship between sides only recently engaged in industrial war; and, finally, by imposing a system of union security—maintenance-of-membership—that strengthened the internal stability of the new unions.

Taken together, these contributions from the political sector probably amounted to a necessary condition for the growth of industrial unionism. It is hard to see how such expansion could otherwise have taken place. The New Deal impact on the character of the labor movement, on the other hand, seems less clear. The early CIO clearly did have some radical potential: a strong element of rank-and-file militancy; a willingness to use such forms of direct action as sit-downs and mass picketing; an influential cadre of left-wing leaders; political activism, not excluding the formation of a labor party; an aggressively advanced position on social issues, including racial equality; and advocacy of a form of industrial democracy by such leaders as Philip Murray and Walter Reuther. The radical possibilities in all of this faded more or less quickly. A significant residue did continue to distinguish the CIO from the AFL, especially in politics, but the differences after a decade meant far less than the common ground they shared as agencies for collective bargaining within the existing economic order. That course, it seems to me, was set primarily by forces inherent in American labor. From the very first the CIO operated within essentially conventional terms of American trade unionism that would have prevailed over contrary tendencies even in the absence of the New Deal. But neither can there be much doubt that the political influence speeded the conservative outcome.

Consider, for example, the rank-and-file militancy on which New Left historians quite rightly place great store. Pressure from below alone might have counteracted a CIO leadership dominated by professionals drawn from the mining and garment unions. But listen to Bob Travis, a UAW militant and the key man in the General Motors sit-down strike. After a graphic account of how he had engineered the capture of the transmission plant Chevy 4, the decisive blow against the company, Travis says:

> We had not asked for it. We had been content to allow reason and common sense to rule in our relationship with the company. But when pressed to the issue, we had to answer blow with blow to convince General Motors of our rights under the law. . . . We hope that the letter and spirit of the settlement will be adhered to. . . . We are prepared to co-operate fully toward the efficient functioning of the industry. (*United Automobile Worker*, February 25 1937, reprinted in J. S. Auerbach, *American Labor: The Twentieth Century* [Indianapolis, 1969], pp. 328–31).

This daring physical attack on company property aimed at nothing more than extracting collective bargaining from General Motors. The sit-down strikers perceived of themselves as fighting for legal rights already theirs: the company stood outside the law, not they. The focus on collective bargaining in wholly traditional terms would probably have prevailed anyway, but the spirit of legitimacy with which it was pursued clearly derived from the political sector. Even in the great rank-and-file movements of 1934, the militants thought of the Roosevelt administration as labor's friend and made their fight over no more than the rights presumably granted under Section 7a. After 1935 they could, with far greater justification, identify their struggle as one congruent with established national policy. The deadly effect of such an identification on labor radicalism is all too obvious. And if New Deal labor policy helped draw any radical potential from the militancy of the early CIO, the day-to-day implementation of that policy—rounds of NLRB hearings and appeals, representation elections and certification of bargaining agents—inexorably stifled the spirit of militancy, not to say any genuine labor radicalism.

The other primary New Deal influence is just where one would expect to find it, namely, on the political role of

American labor. Political calculations, I have said, helped stimulate the CIO into life and then helped assure that it would take an independent course. For a time the CIO leaned toward the formation of a labor party. President Roosevelt stood athwart that path. He could hardly be bypassed, given the New Deal's preemption of the left-of-center position and FDR's own hold on the labor vote. Nor could he be carried along. Although FDR sometimes toyed with the notion of revamping the two-party system along conservative–progressive lines, he could never in practice extricate himself from traditional coalition politics, not to speak of rebuilding on the basis of labor partisanship. Roosevelt's inability to see the CIO in the political terms in which it was attempting to cast itself was evident in a variety of ways—for example, in his uncomprehending rejection of John L. Lewis's claim that the CIO stood in a special relationship to the administration and could demand favored treatment from it; in his eagerness to see the CIO patch up its differences with the old-line AFL; and in his slowness, surprising in one so politically astute, to see the political uses of the new unionism. The formation of Labor's Nonpartisan League came entirely at the initiative of CIO leaders and was coolly received by Democratic party chiefs. Once the league proved itself in the 1936 campaign, of course, Roosevelt embraced the alliance with the CIO, but only on his own terms. Labor's Nonpartisan League evolved, not into the labor party its founders had hoped for, but, especially in its reincarnation as the Political Action Committee of the 1940s, into an appendage of the Democratic party. Sidney Hillman became Roosevelt's labor lieutenant, and the embittered John L. Lewis drifted out into the curious limbo of his later career.

All of this, of course, spelled a real departure from the voluntarism of Samuel Gompers. No longer could the labor movement claim that it operated wholly within the private sector. The price of government protection for the right to organize and engage in collective bargaining was public accountability. Although that bill was not presented at once (thereby lulling traditional unionists into a false sense of security), it would come soon enough in the form of accumulating legislative constraints on labor's freedom to handle its internal affairs and its relations with employers as it saw fit. Neither could organized labor any longer deny its large concern with social policy, nor expect to advance its political interests save by a generous investment of resources and by an essentially partisan connection with the Democratic party. For this degree of movement from the voluntarism of the past, the New Deal bears a large responsibility. But it is equally true that the New Deal helped hold in check any potential for more far-reaching change inherent in the labor upheaval of the 1930s.

How did the New Deal come to have the effects that it did on American trade unionism? On the matter of labor's orientation, the answer seems entirely straightforward. The New Deal was merely expressing its own essential conservatism. Roosevelt's unreflective acceptance of America's basic institutions guided him wherever he had a choice to make—as he did, for example, on the question of labor's political role and, even more decisively during the war period, in response to CIO proposals for industrial democracy.

But the New Deal stimulus to labor organization is more puzzling. Only during World War II can it be said that the Roosevelt administration pursued labor policies that deliberately promoted union growth, but even conservatives understood that this had nothing to do with reform, and everything to do with carrying on an efficient war effort. Otherwise, Roosevelt's part was entirely problematic. The public men who carried labor's fight occupied state houses, mayors' offices, and congressional seats, and what they did on behalf of labor they did independently of the New Deal administration. Senator Wagner introduced his National Labor Relations bill in 1935 entirely on his own. The administration had torpedoed his efforts the previous year and withheld support from the second version until the Senate was about to pass it. Senator LaFollette launched his investigation into the violations of civil liberties without administration backing. Always inadequately financed, the investigation would hardly have made its initial impact but for the aid of the idle staff of the NLRB.

Nor can it be said that the Roosevelt administration led either in formulating or advocating the ideas that sustained the new public policies favoring labor organization. The notion that labor should have the right to organize and engage in collective bargaining had long preceded the coming of the New Deal. Those rights had already been granted to railway workers in 1926. They were stated as public policy (but with no provision for enforcement) in the Norris-LaGuardia Act of 1932, which gave potent expression to the view that the legal deck had been unfairly stacked against labor. (For many unions, in fact, the resulting freedom to picket and boycott was far more useful for organizing purposes than any benefits deriving from the Wagner Act.) The new direction of labor legislation actually reflected a massive shift of American opinion. The most that can be said for the New Deal administration was that it followed in the wake of this change, finally acquiescent, but never innovative. We have it on the authority of his Secretary of Labor, Frances Perkins, that Roosevelt never fully grasped the crucial issues involved in the Wagner Act. One carries away a distinct impression of *inadvertency* in the role the New Deal played in the expansion of the labor movement.

Anyone pondering the New Deal will at some point probably conclude that it was somehow more than the sum of its parts. Certainly this was so in its impact on the struggle for labor organization. It is easy to explain why the New Deal did not take a more positive line, and why it was, indeed, down-right obstructive in the battles over Section 7a during the NRA period. But why should the consequences have been so consistently favorable to the union cause? The answer I think lies in an extra dimension to the New Deal, clearer perhaps to contemporaries than it is to us, of open possibilities and basic labor sympathies that touched virtually the entire range of political factors advancing industrial organization: in recruiting labor sympathizers into places of power at every level; in giving them confidence to act on their own; in spurring on the progressive elements within the labor movement; and, especially after 1935, even in disheartening the defenders of the open shop. A touchstone can perhaps be found in John L. Lewis's famous slogan in the Mine Workers' drive of 1933: The President Wants You To Organize. There was "more drama than truth" in this claim, Frances Perkins remarked gently in *The Roosevelt I Knew*. When the CIO revived the slogan in 1936, the infuriated Secretary of Commerce Daniel Roper wanted to take legal action. But, as CIO publicist Len DeCaux said, could the president say he didn't want the workers to organize? In fact, FDR resisted heavy pressure in early 1937 to protest the use of the slogan. The point was, of course, that industrial workers believed it was true; they thought the president did want them to organize. Its underlying labor sympathy was the New Deal's special contribution to making the conditions for organizing America's industrial workers.

John L. Lewis [1978]

When the miners were voting down the first contract during the prolonged coal strike of 1977–78, CBS News showed a film clip of John L. Lewis in his prime, hurling defiance at

Review essay of Melvyn Dubofsky and Warren Van Tine, *John L. Lewis: A Biography* (New York: Quadrangle/The New York Times Book Co., 1977). Reprinted from *Reviews in American History* 6 (September 1978): 410–14, with permission from the Johns Hopkins University Press.

operators and government alike in one of the great strikes of the 1940s. It is hard to think of another American labor leader who, nearly ten years after his death and out of the public eye for a much longer time, might still command this kind of attention from the nation. In part, of course, this bespeaks the enormous impact coal strikes used to have on the nation's life, as well as the suspicion that what Lewis did in his long career at the head of the miners is now coming back to haunt the country in the form of a new cycle of disruptive coal strikes. But Lewis's place in American memory derives even more from his remarkable part in the history of the 1930s and 1940s, when he led the industrial-union movement, cut a wide swath through the New Deal, and ended in notorious defiance of public opinion during World War II.

Biography has not served American labor leaders well in general, but the absence of a good book on Lewis has been particularly unfortunate. The one biography on which we have relied—Saul Alinsky's *John L. Lewis: An Unauthorized Biography* (1949)—now stands exposed as a thoroughly unreliable and flimsy account. So it is a great event for all students of recent American history to have this major biography of John L. Lewis by Melvyn Dubofsky and Warren Van Tine.

Lewis presents the biographer with formidable problems. For all the relish with which he played his public role, Lewis was in fact an intensely private person, always shielding his family life from view and unwilling (or unable) to expose his inner feelings and motives even to his closest associates. And he was equally adept at concealing the inside record of his trade-union career. Almost invariably, and always deliberately, he did business on the telephone or face to face. In retirement he fended off all appeals from historians and others to fill in the record (although, in the process, usually having some fun at their expense).

Dubofsky and Van Tine have done exceedingly well under

these adverse conditions. They wisely chose not to try to penetrate Lewis's psyche. They were assiduous at collecting all the bits and pieces we are likely to get about his obscure early life, and by so doing exploding the romantic myths surrounding his origins and young days (including some cultivated by Lewis himself). Dubofsky and Van Tine scoured the records of Lewis's associates, of his political allies and rivals, and of the public agencies with which he dealt. This probing research has yielded rich materials that largely make up for the barrenness of Lewis's own records. And on the many points for which the evidence cannot provide definitive answers—why Lewis ran against Gompers for the AFL presidency in 1921, why he countenanced Communist support, how he reached the secret U.S. Steel agreement in 1937, why he split with Roosevelt, and so on—Dubofsky and Van Tine engage in productive speculation. This they do with the utmost candor, explaining the nature of the problem, assessing what others have said about it, and then proceeding to lay out their explanations for what Lewis did on the basis of the known facts and reasonable surmise. They generally make good sense of it, at the very least sweeping away the doubtful assertions of earlier writers, and always giving the reader a lesson in vigorous and provocative historical conjecture.

Where Lewis does tend to defeat his biographers is not where they know too little, but too much. The history of collective bargaining in coal is voluminous. Even in the hands of a master practitioner, as Lewis was, most of the details lose their significance when a given struggle is over and the new contract signed. It is a major problem for the trade-union biographer to be able to delineate the main trends in a collective-bargaining history without overburdening the reader with the record of day-to-day events in an ongoing and largely repetitive cycle. Dubofsky and Van Tine have not wholly avoided this trap, and it will take a quite determined reader to stay with them through all the twists and turns of Lewis's long career as strike leader and contract negotiator.

In some ways, the most provocative findings of the book have to do with the personal side of Lewis's life. He was born into a family of Welsh miners. He worked in the coal mines of Lucas, Iowa, as a young man—for precisely how long remains unclear—but he never had any thought of spending his life in the mines. He nearly finished high school in an age when few sons of workers went beyond grade school, studied acting and elocution, tried local politics, went into the feed grain business, and married the daughter of the local doctor and town elder. After his political and business ventures failed, he and the entire Lewis clan moved in 1908 to the booming coal town of Panama, Illinois. Inside of a year, John L. was president of the local union (his brothers were also getting along) and launched on his meteoric climb from appointive office to appointive office up to the national presidency of the UMWA in 1920. A trade-union career had long since become a common avenue of upward mobility for American workers, but few probably seized the opportunity with so deliberate and clear-eyed a determination, and fewer still used their rise as Lewis did to separate himself from the class from which he had sprung. Lewis never associated socially with fellow union leaders once he had made his way, preferring instead the company of businessmen and the socially prominent. His passport described him as an executive, not a union official. His children attended exclusive private schools and then Bryn Mawr and Princeton. After the UMWA headquarters were moved to Washington, D.C., in 1934, Lewis purchased the historic Lee house in Alexandria, a fitting setting for the superb collection of antiques his wife was amassing. At the very time that he was launching the CIO and leading America's industrial workers in their climactic struggle against the open shop, Lewis was hectoring his economic advisor W. Jett Lauck to get him an invitation to join the prestigious Cosmos Club of Washington!

There is much to ponder in this personal history of John L. Lewis. It seems clear enough why, unlike nearly all his predecessors, he never chose to move on to a government post or a lucrative business career: nothing there could have given him the kind of power and public standing he acquired as UMWA president. Nor can there be much question of his identification with the miners or his determination to advance their interests. Nothing else can explain the loyalty he inspired among coal miners for more than thirty years. But his personal values probably tell a good deal about the way he served them and about the ruthless control he exerted over the union. He made no bones about his contempt for democratic processes that he considered injurious to the efficient operation of the union as a "business proposition." And the lack of any working-class philosophy surely helped account for the remarkable opportunism he displayed in politics and in his relations with ideological enemies. With John L. Lewis as the heroic figure of the 1930s, it is not any wonder that those great days did not transform American trade unionism into a social movement.

From Dubofsky and Van Tine's biography we can perceive more clearly also the constraints acting on a trade-union leader even of Lewis's enormous talents. What he might accomplish depended ultimately on the industry, and coal was a troubled and declining field during most of Lewis's union presidency. Fully cognizant of these intractable realities and a keen student of the coal business, Lewis played a part exceptionally activist by the lights of American trade unionism to advance the interests of his industry. But the basic market forces were largely beyond his control, and even what fell within his reach—the unionization of the low-wage southern competition, for example—resisted his best efforts for long stretches. And there were also the claims of a union membership whose short-term interests could not be reconciled to those of the industry—hence Lewis's disastrous policy of "no backward step" during the 1920s that led to the collapse of collective bargaining in the Central Competitive Field. Only after World War II did Lewis manage to bring into precarious balance the economic and labor factors in the coal industry, but at the price of displacing hundreds of thousands of coal miners and with the achievement of a health and pension system that has not withstood the tests of time.

The union problems in coal led to another kind of dilemma. Lewis was quick to realize that the salvation of the miners depended on government action, and during the 1920s he became an avid lobbyist for a public program of coal stabilization linked to federal protection of miners' right to organize. This advocacy helped bring about the National Industrial Recovery Act of 1933 and, through Section 7a, the Wagner Act of 1935. But if Lewis welcomed the benefits to miners (and industrial workers generally), he also shared Gompers's suspicion of government, a feeling much sharpened by Lewis's experiences during World War I. It was his deep resentment of political control over labor's affairs that partly explained his recalcitrance during World War II and his furious opposition to the Taft-Hartley Act of 1947. By the early 1950s Lewis was advocating the repeal of the Wagner Act and a return to the unfettered labor relations of the pre-New Deal era. No one probably ever heard Lewis say he had brought it on himself, but he could not have failed to recognize the cruel dilemma that he and his miners faced—of both requiring the aid of the government and of suffocating in its embrace. The trade-union stage was too confining for Lewis, hemmed in as he was by forces beyond his mastery. Much that is arresting and puzzling in Lewis's career may be explained by this basic predicament, which Lewis did not escape even when he briefly held the center of a broader stage than the UMWA.

No man ever made so swift a leap to national eminence as did John L. Lewis after 1932 from his discredited presidency of the moribund Mine Workers. The account of Lewis's rise to the leadership of the industrial-union movement is in some ways the least satisfactory part of Dubofsky and Van Tine's book. The facts are there, certainly, but not the dynamics. Dubofsky and Van Tine are right to say Lewis did not foresee what would happen; in fact, he was a little slow getting on the bandwagon. But once on he played a truly remarkable role, especially during the uncertain launching of the CIO. It is surprising that his biographers somehow understate Lewis's enormous contribution in 1935–36. He provided not only the indispensable funds and the charismatic presence, but, above all, the determination to push forward. At key points throughout 1936 it was his will alone, and the initiatives he took on his own, that carried his reluctant partners along the path that led to the break with the AFL. Without Lewis, it is hard to see how the CIO would have emerged as an independent industrial-union movement.

Dubofsky and Van Tine are much better at explaining Lewis's fall from the heights. They trace with great skill the complex circumstances pushing Lewis, step by step, into a position of dissidence and finally of isolation, both as a political influence and within the labor movement. Dubofsky and Van Tine stress the fundamental differences over economic and diplomatic policy that led to the break with Roosevelt. They even make sense out of Lewis's decision to gamble his CIO chairmanship on the outcome of the 1940 presidential election. In the end, Lewis fell victim to the very same kind of fate that in a smaller way had befallen him as leader of the Mine Workers. Despite his triumph on the national stage, he found that he could not control events, surely not in the political arena dominated by Roosevelt, nor even in the industrial-union movement he had done so much to build. His fury at the inherent limitations of his situation accounts for much that was self-destructive and wrongheaded in his behavior from 1939 onward. It was Lewis's misfortune to be incapable of settling easily for the restricted role that is the fate of the labor leader in American society.

No book is ever likely to do full justice to John L. Lewis. (Certainly this was his own view of the matter.) But Dubofsky and Van Tine's biography has laid the solid groundwork for whatever will be said about Lewis in the future. They have made a splendid contribution that will earn the thanks of all students of modern American history.

The CIO after Fifty Years
A Historical Reckoning [1985]

> Lewis did most of the talking. His voice was low, and he spoke with passion. He outlined the conditions in all of the major industries of the country. He emphasized that thousands upon thousands of workers were waiting with outstretched arms for unionization to come to them. Lewis then said, "And it can only come from you and you and you," as he dramatically punctuated his statement by stabbing his finger at each man seated around the table. He painted the breathtaking potentialities of a great labor movement embracing almost every workingman in the country. . . .
>
> As Lewis spoke, most of the food on the table went untouched and grew cold; but the men around the table were on fire. They too had caught the vision, and it became their gospel.

This is Saul Alinsky's account of the first meeting of industrial-union advocates the morning after the adjournment of the AFL convention at Atlantic City. Two weeks later, on November 9, 1935, John L. Lewis and his confederates formed the Committee for Industrial Organization. Never mind whether Alinsky's words are strictly accurate; they cast the founding of the CIO in the proper heroic mold. In the months that followed, America's industrial workers rose up against their corporate employers; those great bastions of the open shop—General Motors and United States Steel—caved in during early 1937, and industrial unionism swept the mass-

Reprinted, with permission, from *Dissent* (Fall 1985): 457–72.

production sector. In his on-the-spot history, Edward Levinson concluded triumphantly: "Labor was on the march as it had never been before in the history of the Republic."

Fifty years of history have passed since John L. Lewis launched the CIO, and so have nearly fifty years of historical writing about those events that Levinson first chronicled in *Labor on the March* (1937). Ongoing research has vastly increased our fund of information: in their definitive 1977 biography of John L. Lewis, Melvyn Dubofsky and Warren Van Tine call Alinsky's version of that first breakfast meeting "overly dramatic" and, indeed, they dismiss Alinsky's widely read 1949 biography (*John L. Lewis: An Unauthorized Biography*) as largely fiction.

New directions in the discipline, especially the rise of social history, have prompted labor historians to explore well beyond the political/institutional boundaries that first defined the events of the 1930s. More important yet has been the impact of a new generation of historians whose ideological roots go back to the New Left. And, finally, historical judgments have been tempered by the unfolding history of the industrial-union movement, as it consolidated itself within the trade-union mainstream and then, in our own day, fell increasingly on hard times. If the CIO has not proved to be the transforming event that Edward Levinson anticipated, neither can later historians cast that history in the heroic terms of Edward Levinson's *Labor on the March*.

With all this by way of preface, let us proceed to some reckoning of where we stand today on what *Fortune* in 1937 called "one of the greatest mass movements in our history."

Current scholarship, in fact, hinges very largely on the treatment of the CIO as a "mass movement." This is a subject by no means ignored by such leading CIO scholars of the older generation as Walter Galenson, Sidney Fine, and Irving Bernstein. No one, indeed, has written—or is likely to write— a more complete account of industrial struggle than Fine's

Sit-Down (1969) on the great General Motors strike of 1936–37. And Bernstein's *Turbulent Years* (1970) contains the best narrative history we have of the labor battles of the 1930s.

But consider the scene with which Bernstein concludes his book. President Roosevelt is meeting with a group of worried publishers in April 1937 at the height of the sit-down wave. He reassures them that the new unions are going through "growing pains." Collective bargaining, a difficult process in the best of times, can be learned "only by experience." Ultimately, "we are going to get a workable system." In Bernstein's schema, perfectly captured in the book's ending, the central history of *Turbulent Years* is about the institutionalization of the CIO. This also is Sidney Fine's view. He quotes approvingly Jay Lovestone's remark after the GM sit-down strike that "rarely does a single event of and by itself mean so much"—but with this qualification: "insofar as it applies to the growth of unionism in the automobile and other mass-production industries."

A rival generation of younger historians would have struck out Fine's qualification. "Recent historians associated with the Left," Staughton Lynd wrote in 1972,

> . . . have declined to join in the liberal celebration of [the] results [of] industrial union organizing in the 1930s. . . . We have dwelt on happenings which for liberal historians are merely preliminary or transitory, such as the mass strikes in Toledo, Minneapolis, and San Francisco in 1934, the improvisation from below of local industrial unions and rank-and-file action committees. . . .[1]

In Lynd's formulation, the rank and file becomes the true subject of New Deal labor history, and the logic of that history resides not—as Fine or Bernstein would have it—in how militancy progressed to stable collective bargaining but rather in how that process killed the rank-and-file character of industrial-union organization.

History does not readily shift in its moorings. This was one of those moments. Lynd's conception of industrial-union history drew its inspiration from the syndicalist streak in New Left thinking. The mainspring of revolution, as George Rawick had seen it in 1969, was "working-class self-activity," by which, as Rawick said of the sit-down strikes of the 1930s, "the genuine advances of the working class were made by the struggle from below, by the natural organization of the working class, rather than by the bureaucratic elaboration of the administration of the working class from above."[2]

Rawick thought he was witnessing in 1969 the next phase in that struggle from below. He and others of the New Left glimpsed revolution in the factory unrest of the Vietnam era and, on a grander scale, in the Paris spring of 1968. That heady moment passed. But it implanted a syndicalist enthusiasm that, transmuted and refined, has to a considerable degree redefined the terms on which the historical study of industrial unionism has proceeded ever since.

II

That history turns on the theme of *containment*—of rank-and-file radical potential held in check and ultimately defeated. But who did the containing? A logical question, of course, and one that instantly established a fresh reference point for thinking about the institutional history of industrial unionism. No agency could claim exemption from this question and, given its syndicalist presuppositions, none passed muster—not the CIO, not the New Deal, not even the left.

Communist trade-union work, wrote Martin Glaberman, was best described as "'bureaucratic'—the tendency to substitute the power of officials and institutions for the direct power of the rank and file." For an anti-Stalinist like Glaberman, this tendency was fundamental in nature, stemming from a conception of "the motive power of historical development as being the Party rather than the class."[3]

Even writers basically sympathetic to the CP role, once they fell within the containment mode, defined party history in terms of "mistakes" in the relation to the rank-and-file struggle. On this basis, James R. Prickett constructed a re-periodization of party history no longer pegged to the swings in Comintern policy. For Prickett, the decisive moment came when the CP shifted from the United Front from Below—from the rank-and-file work of the early 1930s—to the Popular Front—to integration into the industrial-union structure, a period lasting until the expulsions of the cold-war era.[4]

As for the CIO, listen to how Staughton Lynd concludes his case study of the steelworkers' movements of the early 1930s: "The rank and file dream passed into the hands of [John L.] Lewis in the bastardized form of an organizing committee [SWOC] none of whose national or regional officers were steelworkers, an organizing committee so centralized that it paid even local phone calls from a national office. . . ."

The New Deal itself, however, has been designated the key agency of containment. Its potency here derived not so much from FDR's broad political appeal to the working class—a familiar complaint of the Old Left—as from the specific impact of the organizing and bargaining protections granted by the Wagner Act (1935) on the self-activity of industrial workers. Thus, in a characteristic statement, Rick Hurd writes:

> The tendency was to eschew direct action and to opt instead for NLRB elections, or where capital was obstinate to file unfair labor practice complaints with the NLRB. As a result the working class was taught to rely on the protection of the law rather than on their own strength. Although the New Deal contributed only marginally to the unionization of the working class, it did help shape the movement which evolved. It furthered the expansion of unions which worked within the economic system. . . .[5]

An institutional configuration emerged altogether different from that of the liberal historiography: instead of agencies ranged for or against the unionization of industrial workers, all institutions found themselves grouped on one side as more or less hostile to the radical self-activity of the rank and file. With New Deal labor policy installed as the centerpiece in this alignment, a focus existed for thinking about intriguing questions of intention and design. Whose hand was behind a strategy so ingeniously constructed to forestall radical change?

The answer most confounding to liberal assumptions would have granted industry that role. This was an expectation already well certified in New Left thinking before the advent of the syndicalist phase. The group centering around *Studies on the Left* (1959–67), with William Appleman Williams as mentor, had advanced the thesis of corporate liberalism, which, first, identified America's corporate leaders as the key actors in the modern capitalist order, and, second, identified moderate reform as their principal method for stabilizing the system. "It is precisely this flexibility and sophistication on the part of American businessmen," wrote James Weinstein in 1965, "that has given the system its strength and durability."[6]

The corporate-liberal thesis was tested out mainly on Progressivism, but it was presumed to apply equally well to the New Deal. Organized labor served as a kind of junior partner in the corporate-liberal enterprise, accepting—to use Ronald Radosh's phrase—a "corporate ideology" and working actively during the New Deal for "the integration of organized labor into the corporate order."[7]

Unfortunately, the facts have run too stubbornly against applying the corporate-liberal thesis to industrial-union history. Although they spoke a reformist idiom and encouraged other New Deal welfare measures, corporate liberals drew the line (as indeed had their precursors in Weinstein's account of corporate liberalism in the Progressive era) against entering any genuine bargaining relationship with trade unions. It was precisely at the point when Section 7a pushed them on this issue, as Kim McQuaid has shown, that labor-business collaboration within the National Recovery Administration broke down.[8]

From that time in 1934 until the Supreme Court ruled in favor of the Wagner Act in 1937, organized business presented virtually a united front against New Deal labor policy. The program, concluded one sympathetic writer after a careful assessment of the known facts, "had very little to do indeed with the manipulative ingenuity of a politically sophisticated *corporatist* element of the American business elite."[9]

If not corporate business, then the best candidate as the guiding hand of containment would seem to have been the New Deal itself. This view has been strongly underwritten by a theory of the state in capitalist societies advanced in the 1970s by such neo-Marxist writers as Nicos Poulantzis and Fred Block. They posited a capitalist state relatively autonomous of private capital, capable even of overriding its wishes in defense of the social order. (So that, in the case at hand, the New Deal might impose the Wagner Act on an industrial business class too short-sighted to recognize its own long-term interests). The theory presumed, however, a sureness of state purpose that poorly described how the New Deal labor policy came about.

The events leading to the Wagner Act were circuitous and contradictory, heavily affected by the unexpected struggles over Section 7a during the NRA period. What seems clear is that the Roosevelt administration never had a blueprint for such legislation and indeed mostly resisted it until its imminent passage. The guiding hand clearly was Senator Robert Wagner's. It depends, of course, on how one defines the state. With a sufficiently broad conception—one accommodating substantial internal conflict and uncertainty and stressing the *enabling* aspects of reform regimes (that is, that the New Deal created the conditions making the Wagner Act possible)—the New Deal doubtless can be made to fit the neo-Marxian mold.[10]

Other routes, too, can be found to that end. The legal scholar Karl Klare, for example, saw the Wagner Act at its birth as "indeterminate," and "susceptible to an overtly anti-capitalist interpretation." That the outcome was otherwise Klare put down to deep-rooted judicial reasoning processes that rested on "assumptions of liberal capitalism and fore-closed those potential paths of development most threatening to the established order."[11] So the capitalist state need not be entirely purposive: its very processes assured a properly conservative outcome.

The difficulties in the New Left assault on liberal institutional history should not blind us to the very real benefits likely to result from breaking out of a unilinear approach to the labor movement, the New Deal, and industry. One sees this, for example, in Steve Fraser's current work on Sidney Hillman, who best fits the model of the labor leader well-connected to government and industry and actively pursuing a reconstructed labor-relations system.[12] The connections do not, however, run to the old corporate liberals but rather to early advocates in business and professional circles of the Keynesian state. Fraser has assimilated the New Left perspective, but the outcome is both more sophisticated and less pejorative than, say, Radosh's earlier work on Hillman. Nor should one underestimate the extent to which that perspective has taken hold among historians.* Thus a seasoned practitioner such as David Montgomery speaks of a "New Deal formula" that was "simultaneously liberating and co-optive for the workers." Governmental intervention freed them from employer control, yes, but "also opened a new avenue through which the rank and file could in time be tamed and the newly powerful unions be subjected to tight legal and political control."[13]

---

*Including this author. Readers will note that the next chapter, "The Uses of Power I: Industrial Battleground" (which was written in 1978–79), takes "containment" as its theme in the discussion of the impact of the workplace rule of law on the self-activity of industrial workers after World War II.

III

As institutional analysis, the New Left approach redefined the terms, but not the terrain of industrial-union history. But if the rank-and-file upsurge was the core event in this history—the event that gave it a logic of containment—then historical inquiry had to proceed on an entirely different plane as well. Lynd's call to arms demanded nothing less than a rank-and-file history of industrial unionism.

It happened (not entirely by chance) at roughly the same time that larger changes within the historical discipline strongly reinforced the hand of the radical historians. Social history began to preoccupy the profession. For labor historians, this meant a shift in attention from union institutions to the workers themselves. Some students, strongly influenced by Edward P. Thompson and Herbert Gutman, explored working-class culture. Others, following the lead of Harry Braverman and David Montgomery, concerned themselves with the shop-floor experience of American workers. And much other social-history scholarship led by a variety of avenues—ethnicity, race, family, urbanism, and gender—into the study of working-class life. Little of this activity dealt with the modern period; nineteenth-century materials lent themselves much more readily to what social historians were trying to do. But once radical historians placed the rank and file at the center of New Deal labor history, it followed that social history would be enlisted in the effort to understand the mobilization of industrial workers during the 1930s.

Thus Peter Friedlander subtitled his book, *The Emergence of a UAW Local, 1936–1939* (1975), *A Study in Class and Culture.* His point of departure was primarily the conception put forward in Thompson's *The Making of the English Working Class* (1963), and adopted by his American disciples, that working-class consciousness was the product of preindustrial worker cultures transformed in the crucible of industrial capitalism. "The crux of the problem of labor history in the

thirties," so it seemed to Friedlander, was "the historic emergence of specific structures of personality and culture out of
the collapse and/or transformation of a complex and variegated collection of prebourgeois cultures. . . ."

Friedlander undertook, in effect, a labor ethnography—
arranging the workers partly by occupational categories but
mainly by ethnic and generational groupings—of an auto-
parts plant located in the Polish Hamtramck district of Detroit. Friedlander's methodology also was drawn from the
social-history scholarship that aimed at capturing concretely
and in depth the experience of nineteenth-century workers.
The unit of study remained local but was defined by a single
factory rather than by a nineteenth-century industrial town,
and the local evidence came not from census records, town
directories, and newspapers but almost entirely from the
intensive interviewing of surviving participants.

Friedlander wrote social history, but in service to Lynd's
conception of the labor history of the 1930s as the self-
mobilization of workers for collective action. His story was
about how UAW Local 229 became organized. What has
proved notable, even remarkable, about his pioneering little
book on a minor auto-parts plant is that its findings very
largely prefigured an entire decade of further research on the
rank-and-file history of the 1930s.

From the time union activity began in December 1936,
triggered by the wave of sit-down strikes in the area, three
years passed before the auto-parts plant became fully organized. Only step by step, as the union demonstrated its growing power in a series of confrontations with management, did
the body of workers sign on. There was nothing random
about this slow process. On the contrary, Friedlander was
able to map quite precisely how the social groupings he had
identified—the second-generation Poles, the low-skilled first-
generation immigrants, the Appalachians and, last of all, the
Yankee toolmakers and inspectors—joined the union and the
kinds of union men they became. The social-history analysis

Friedlander had undertaken suggested that their sociocultural characteristics inhibited the class development of his auto workers.

Not all subsequent research of this kind fits Friedlander's findings. The ethnic identity of French-Canadian workers, for example, was forged into a notably militant industrial unionism in the carpet industry of Woonsocket, Rhode Island.[14] In a particularly keen analysis, Bruce Nelson has linked the militancy of West Coast maritime unionism—for which the San Francisco general strike of 1934 was the exemplary event—to the subcultures of the seamen and longshoremen.[15] But, on balance, the ethnocultural influences seem to have run counter to rank-and-file militancy. The leading historian of Slavic-American workers during the Great Depression, John Bodnar, has stressed their "realism," the high value they placed on job security, the insulating effect of their familial and community ties.[16] They became loyal union men (as did the immigrant workers in Friedlander's study), but they were not on the barricades in the great industrial battles of the 1930s.

Still less active were the black workers, for whom the CIO cause seemed less a hopeful event than a threat to their precarious place in American industry. August Meier and Elliott Rudwick's *Black Detroit and the Rise of the UAW* (1979), in fact, puts an odd gloss on the New Left conception of industrial-union history. For in a racially divided labor force, fair play for the oppressed minority may translate itself into containment of the white rank-and-file majority. The agent of this process, Meier and Rudwick argue, was the UAW leadership. And, by its success, this union bureaucracy laid the groundwork for the transformation of a quiescent black labor force in 1935 into a militant union group a decade later.

IV

The search for the rank-and-file activists that Staughton Lynd had in mind narrows down to a small band of industrial workers. Friedlander identified the four key men who launched the union struggle at his plant: the most important (and Friedlander's main informant) was Edmund Kord, an anticlerical Polish-American socialist and night student at Wayne University; his ally in the torch-welding department had been a union miner; of the two leaders in front-welding, one was self-educated and probably of radical background, the other a devout Catholic active in church affairs. Around these four, a handful of activists coalesced to undertake the uphill mobilization of the other workers. What impressed Friedlander was "the narrowness of the base of active involvement and . . . the breadth of the more passive mass. . . ."

Other research has turned up variations on Friedlander's theme. The French-Canadian carpet weavers of Woonsocket were led by highly skilled Franco-Belgian anarcho-syndicalists. Among the mostly Irish transit workers of New York City, the key leaders were veterans of the IRA who, as Joshua Freeman remarked, differed from their fellow Irishmen in "matters of personality, politics, and ideology."[17]

To this mix, Ronald Schatz's systematic study of the electrical workers has added an occupational factor. To an unexpected degree, the industrial-union movement seems to have been sparked by craft workers. At General Electric and Westinghouse, the union pioneers were Anglo-Saxon long-service employees activated in many instances by demotions from high-status jobs during the Depression. "We were skilled men on unskilled work! . . . We were just part of the common mass, you might say. And that's what got us really thinking a lot about unionism." The speaker was vice-president of the UE Erie local, where most of the members were low-skilled immigrant workers. The women leaders were more closely representative of female electrical workers in job terms— short-service, young, semiskilled—but they differed crucially in their personal lives: they lived independent lives while their sister workers mostly were dutiful daughters living at home and turning over their pay to their parents.[18] So, consistently, these rank-and-file leaders were unrepresentative workers, and unrepresentative, as Friedlander said, in ways that gave them "more profound ideals of a broadly democratic nature. . . . They shared a 'resentment of injustice'. . . ."

Members of this group made up what there was of a radical American working class. Edmund Kord was a socialist, and he recruited his entire secondary leadership into the Socialist party. To what purpose? Friedlander stresses the instrumental benefits. The Kord people gained confidence, a sense of direction and purpose, and practical training in the arts of organizing and running a local union. Much the same logic, one presumes, applied to the Socialist leadership of the aluminum workers in Kensington, Pennsylvania, and of the Lynn, Massachusetts, electrical workers; to the Musteites in the Toledo Auto-Lite strike; to Trotskyists among the Minneapolis teamsters; to the IWW at the South Philadelphia Westinghouse works.

Did that instrumental logic apply as well to the Communists? Schatz's study of UE pioneers suggests that it did. They did not go from communism to unionism. "Most radical workers traveled in the opposite direction: they were union activists who joined the party for support in organizing." Their indigenous character emerges increasingly in recent scholarship as the key to understanding the CP unionists. It helps, for one thing, to account for the durable support they enjoyed among a noncommunist rank and file. And it throws into a rather different light their relationship to the CP apparatus. They cannot be seen any longer simply as foot soldiers, so to speak, in the march and countermarch from the Third Period to Popular Front to Cold War. The point need not be pushed too far and, in any case, is likely to resist precise resolution. That ways could be found for evading or reconciling conflicting claims can certainly be demonstrated, as has been done, for example, by Ronald Filippelli's ingenious explanation of the success of the UE's CP leadership: it struck an implicit bargain with the membership, whereby the party line could be followed on the editorial page and in convention, but at the bargaining table primacy went strictly to bread-and-butter issues.[19]

The New Left/social-history orientation thus has had the effect of disengaging CP labor history from the formal party history (just as, on the flip side, it has had the effect of treating the Communist party as an agent of rank-and-file containment). The need for relative independence was of a piece with the need for the party connection in the first place. Radical the rank-and-file leadership may have been—but radical in service to the cause of industrial unionism.

V

What of the shop-floor actions that swept the industrial plants in the first stages of unionization? Here, too, Friedlander's findings have proved prescient. The wildcats and slowdowns in his parts plant sprang not from any class perspective or even from a strongly felt sense of grievance. They were the work of young "new hires" who had little interest in the union and whose activities Friedlander considered "nihilistic." There is a similar, if more variegated, drift to much of the subsequent research into shop-floor militancy.

The sit-downs at Akron's rubber plants, Daniel Nelson found, included after the first wave many that were called for frivolous or nonexistent reasons. "'We didn't care' is a common recollection of the sit-down veterans." Factionalism also contributed. Firestone, lacking the shop-floor turbulence of the Goodyear plant, exhibited a higher degree of solidarity, as measured, for example, by the vote given to labor candidates in the 1937 municipal elections. "Militancy and union power were inversely correlated," Daniel Nelson concluded.[20]

In his study of auto plants during this period, Nelson Lichtenstein found "an inherently parochial and localistic focus" to shop-floor actions.[21] They were mostly limited to strategically placed work groups (not on assembly-line work); they were called over grievances specific to those groups; and they occurred with little regard for the interests of other workers. That shop-floor actions might take a reactionary turn became evident in the wartime wildcats in Detroit auto plants, culminating in the week-long "hate" strike at Packard in 1943, called against the hiring or upgrading of black workers.

As a measure of emergent working-class consciousness, shop-floor militancy becomes increasingly cloudy and problematic. Might it not, however, have signified a more limited kind of struggle—one directed against the collective-bargaining system that was then taking shape under industrial unionism? This notion certainly runs as an undercurrent through the syndicalist visions of New Left scholars. Thus Karl Klare's analysis of the "deradicalization" of the Wagner Act turned on just those cases that gave primacy to the contract and "responsible" collective bargaining, culminating in the *Fansteel* decision (1939), which denied NLRB protection to sit-down strikers:

> *Fansteel* . . . bolstered the forces of union bureaucracy in their efforts to quell the spontaneity of the rank and file. As such . . . it marked the outer limits of disruption of the established industrial order that the law would tolerate. The utopian aspirations for a radical restructuring of the workplace . . . were symbolically thwarted by *Fansteel*, which erected labor law reform as a roadblock in their path.

How strong a case can be made for the proposition that the shop-floor struggles of the 1930s aimed at "a radical restructuring of the workplace" or, more precisely, at a bargaining system that might result in such a restructuring? There was, first of all, a historical context for such a struggle. Nowhere else, recent scholarship suggests, was the conflict between labor traditions of autonomous work and the

Taylorist demand by management for control so sharply joined and so endemic as under American industrialism. The workplace was, in Richard Edward's nice phrase, "contested terrain."

That mass-production workers seized every chance for shop-floor control seems clear from Nelson Lichtenstein's study of the auto industry during the sit-down era and during World War II and from postwar industrial-relations research into shop-level resistance to the formal contractual system. What has not been demonstrated is the existence of any rank-and-file conception of an alternative—say, of the shop-steward system that existed in England, or the even less structured shop-floor relations in Australia.

In their recent *Second Industrial Divide* (1984), Michael Piore and Charles Sabel make a strong case for technologically determined labor relations. The American mass-production system, based on special-purpose machinery and line assembly, called for narrowly defined job structures (in which the job, not the worker, carried the wage rate), orderly job allocation, and hierarchical control. It does not appear that industrial workers challenged these basic, determining elements. One of their earliest demands was for seniority, that is, for a *more* formalized system of job allocation. Grievance procedures were installed in the first GM and U.S. Steel agreements. And narrow job structures very quickly became the framework for wage determination under collective bargaining. The very logic of their work environment would seem (if one follows Piore and Sabel) to have compelled industrial workers to opt for a rule-bound system that militated against shop-floor self-activity.

The farther we probe, the more intractable becomes the social history of the CIO. Consider two very recent studies at the far ends of the working-class spectrum. One deals with the success of Endicott-Johnson's welfare policy in forestalling unionization at its extensive upstate New York shoe plants. Gerald Zahavi's point is not, however, that employer paternalism purchased labor quiescence but, on the contrary, that it inadvertently gave to workers considerable leverage in bargaining informally with management. That is, rank-and-file activism could occur in settings outside, and resistant to, union development.[22]

The second study deals with a climactic moment in CIO power at Akron in 1937. Newly triumphant in the rubber plants, the CIO seemed invincible. A labor ticket was fielded for the 1937 city elections and was roundly defeated. "Akron unionists, who more than most industrial workers might have been expected to conform to [a monolithic CIO] image, nevertheless defied it," concluded Daniel Nelson in a detailed study of the Akron election. CIO leaders "assumed a unity of purpose and outlook that did not exist and overlooked forces that restricted the workers' willingness to act in concert."[23]

Worker resistance to paternalistic control at Endicott-Johnson does not lead to (in fact, evades the need for) unionism; labor militancy in Akron does not translate into class-conscious politics. And, to draw things to a conclusion, neither can the complex reality that is emerging be reduced to the New Left conception of a rank and file potentially revolutionary but somehow contained by external forces.[24]

VI

"It could have been otherwise." Staughton Lynd's words are a kind of touchstone to the new scholarship on industrial unionism. From that thought flowed a host of new questions about the known history of the CIO and about the unknown history of America's industrial workers. But that research must in the end be able to show that indeed "it could have been otherwise." Rich though the scholarly findings have been, they have not brought forth the one essential for historical reformulation: they have not revealed the alternative that rivaled the union course that was actually taken. So the field must ultimately be yielded to the liberal conception of industrial-union history.

Liberal historiography, however, is no longer what is was when it came under New Left assault fifteen or so years ago. Bernstein's and Fine's central assumption had been the durability of the industrial-union achievement. (This was equally true of the New Left: the dividing line at bottom was whether one valued or deplored the stable collective-bargaining system.) That assumption has fallen increasingly into question in recent years.

Today industrial unionism is in crisis. Its bargaining structure, constructed painstakingly over many years, has begun to unravel. (The latest—May 6, 1985—the major steel firms announce they are ending industry-wide bargaining.) The political strategy pioneered by the industrial unions is also in shambles. (The latest—May 4, 1985—Lane Kirkland denounces the Democratic party for seeking, in the aftermath of the 1984 elections, to distance itself from the labor movement.) Nor have the industrial unions held their own within the labor movement. As a group, they have shrunk by at least a quarter since 1955, and today they constitute scarcely 15 per cent of the AFL-CIO. For a labor movement under siege, the industrial unions constitute a weakening battalion in the order of battle.

A perceptible change has overtaken the liberal interpretation of industrial unionism. Early on, in fact, as the AFL showed itself to be the more dynamic unionizing force over the longer term, historians began to downgrade the craft versus the industrial issue over which the CIO had been launched.[25] The heroes of industrial unionism also have lost much of their earlier luster. In Dubofsky and Van Tine's biography, John L. Lewis emerges as a deeply flawed figure, briefly remarkable as the founder of the CIO but incapable of providing it with sustained leadership and incapable even of keeping political faith with his followers (he plotted for Herbert Hoover's nomination in 1940 before settling for Wendell

Willkie). A sad undercurrent runs through the later chapters of John Barnard's fine brief biography of Walter Reuther. For all his social vision and boundless energy, the UAW leader was inexorably defeated by the environment in which he operated.

More telling yet has been the recent treatment of New Deal labor policy. In liberal historiography, the Wagner Act occupied a place of honor: it liberated workers from employer control and paved the way for collective bargaining. Now fifty years of legal evolution have made the National Labor Relations Act seem a straitjacket for the labor movement and increasingly also a tool of modern antiunion employers. (Lane Kirkland speaks of repealing the law; some unions are boycotting the NLRB.) One would expect that shadow to be cast back on the formative history of the Wagner Act. So we find James A. Gross's detailed account of the early NLRB devoted to describing the political counterattack that transformed a vigorous, independent NLRB "into a conservative, insecure, politically sensitive agency preoccupied with its own survival and reduced to deciding essentially marginal legal issues using legal tools of analysis exclusively."[26] By 1940, Gross's analysis suggests, we were already on course to the Reagan NLRB.

Christopher Tomlins's new history goes Gross one better. The heart of the matter for Tomlins is not the emasculation of the Wagner Act, but the fact that it was in inherent opposition to the voluntaristic basis of the labor movement. Tomlins's hero is not Robert Wagner or John L. Lewis but Samuel Gompers, for Gompers at least understood—in Tomlins's words—that "a counterfeit liberty is the most that American workers and their organizations [could] gain through the state. Its reality they must create for themselves."[27] Perhaps it is time to coin a new historiographical designation, say, along the lines of postliberal revisionism.

And what of the future? Readers will doubtless have been struck by how strongly the unfolding history of industrial unionism has shaped our thinking about the opening struggles for that movement. At some point, past and present begin to disengage. The historian's own world becomes too remote from past events to dictate, in any direct sense, his or her conception of those events. The past can then be understood on its own terms, a lost world to be recaptured in the historian's imagination. That would apply, for example, to the nineteenth-century Knights of Labor, which was the expression of a long-gone small-producer economy. But the manufacturing economy on which industrial unionism was built seems today also on its way to extinction. (The latest— June 8, 1985—the U.S. Commissioner of Labor Statistics reports that 2 million manufacturing jobs have disappeared since 1980, and that nearly all the 7 million jobs created since the 1981 recession have been in services and construction.) Are we coming to the time when the CIO—at least in its original incarnation—will become the kind of historical subject that the Knights of Labor is today?

Notes

1. Staughton Lynd, "The Possibility of Radicalism in the Early 1930s: The Case of Steel," reprinted in James Green, ed., *Workers' Struggles Past and Present: A "Radical America" Reader* (Philadelphia, 1983), p. 190.
2. George Rawick, "Working-Class Self Activity," in Green, *"Radical America" Reader*, p. 147. James Green's introduction to this useful collection of *Radical America* essays sketches in the ideological background and further evolution of Rawick's worker self-activity thesis.
3. Martin Glaberman, "Vanguard to Rearguard," *Political Power and Social Theory: A Research Annual* 4 (1984): 44, 59.
4. James R. Prickett, "New Perspectives on American Communism and the Labor Movement," in *Political Power and Social Theory: A Research Annual* 4 (1984): 3–36.
5. Rick Hurd, "New Deal Labor Policy and the Containment of Radical Union Activity," *Review of Radical Political Economics* 8 (Fall 1976): 40.
6. James Weinstein, "Gompers and the New Liberalism," reprinted in James Weinstein and David W. Eakins, eds., *For a New America: Essays . . . from "Studies on the Left"* (New York, 1970), p. 111.

7. Ronald Radosh, "The Corporate Ideology of American Labor from Gompers to Hillman," reprinted in Weinstein and Eakins, *For a New America*, p. 138.

8. Kim McQuaid, "The Frustration of Corporate Revival during the Early New Deal," *Historian* 41 (August 1979): 682–704.

9. Stanley Vittoz, "The Economic Foundations of Industrial Politics in the United States and the Emerging Structural Theory of the State in Capitalist Society: The Case of New Deal Labor Policy," *Amerikastudien* 27, no. 4 (1982): 365. Vittoz's emphasis.

10. For a brilliant attempt at this, see Theda Skocpol, "Political Response to Capitalist Crisis: Neo-Marxist Theories of the State and the Case of the New Deal," *Politics and Society* 10 (1980): 155–201.

11. Karl E. Klare, "Judicial Deradicalization of the Wagner Act and the Origins of Modern Legal Consciousness, 1937–1941," *Minnesota Law Review* 62 (March 1978): 291–92.

12. Steve Fraser, "From the 'New Unionism' to the New Deal," *Labor History* 25 (Summer 1984): 405–30.

13. David Montgomery, *Workers' Control in America* (New York, 1979), p. 165.

14. Gary Gerstle, "The Mobilization of the Working Class Community: The Independent Textile Union in Woonsocket, 1931–1946," *Radical History Review* 17 (Spring 1978): 161–67.

15. Bruce Nelson, "'Pentecost' on the Pacific: Maritime Workers and Working-Class Consciousnes in the 1930s," *Political Power and Social Theory: A Research Annual* 4 (1984): 141–82.

16. John Bodnar, *Immigration and Industrialization: Ethnicity in an American Mill Town, 1870–1940* (Pittsburgh, 1977); Bodnar, "Immigration, Kinship, and the Rise of Working-Class Realism in Industrial America," *Journal of Social History* 14 (Fall 1980): 45–59.

17. Joshua B. Freeman, "Catholics, Communists, and Republicans: Irish Workers and the Organization of the Transport Workers Union," in Michael H. Frisch and Daniel J. Walkowitz, eds., *Working-Class America: Essays . . .* (Urbana, Ill., 1983), p. 263.

18. Ronald Schatz, "Union Pioneers: The Founders of Local Unions at General Electric and Westinghouse, 1933–1937," *Journal of American History* 66 (December 1979): 586–602.

19. Ronald Filippelli, "UE: An Uncertain Legacy," *Political Power and Social Theory: A Research Annual* 4 (1984): 217–52.

20. Daniel Nelson, "Origins of the Sit-Down Era: Worker Militancy and Innovation in the Rubber Industry, 1934–1938," *Labor History* 23 (Spring 1982): 198–225; Nelson, "The CIO at Bay: Labor Militancy and Politics in Akron, 1936–1938," *Journal of American History* 71 (December 1984): 583.

21. Nelson Lichtenstein, "Auto Worker Militancy and the Structure of Factory Life, 1937–1955," *Journal of American History* 67 (September 1980): 353.

22. Gerald Zahavi, "Negotiated Loyalty: Welfare Capitalism and the Shoeworkers of Endicott-Johnson, 1920–1940," *Journal of American History* 70 (December 1983): 602–20.

23. Nelson, "The CIO at Bay," pp. 565–86.

24. There also were scholars who were quick to voice their doubts about the rank-and-file formulation. See especially Robert Zieger, "The Limits of Militancy: Organizing Paper Workers, 1933–1935," *Journal of American History* 63 (December 1976): 638–57; and Melvyn Dubofsky, "Not so 'Turbu-

lent Years': Another Look at the American 1930s," *Amerikastudien* 24 (1979): 5-20.

25. The best summary of this reassessment is in Christopher L. Tomlins, "AFL Unions in the 1930's: Their Performance in Historical Perspective," *Journal of American History* 65 (March 1979): 1021-42.

26. James A. Gross, *The Reshaping of the National Labor Relations Board . . . 1937-1947* (Albany, 1981), p. 267.

27. Christopher L. Tomlins, *The State and the Unions . . . 1880-1960* (New York, 1985), p. 328.

5
The Uses of Power I:
Industrial Battleground

On New Year's Day, 1950, the historian Arthur M. Schlesinger assessed the ten events "that profoundly shaped and shook history" in the first half of the twentieth century. Second only to the two world wars, Schlesinger placed the "upsurge of labor." Its rise to power had occurred on the European continent, in Britian, Australia, and New Zealand, well before the American movement "firmly entrenched itself in law, industry and political life." Yes, interjected J. B. S. Hardman, American labor "was late[,] but well nigh phenomenal for the speedy headway it made. . . . In a matter of only a few years, American labor unionism emerged organized, invigorated. . . . The amazingly rapid growth of unionism and of its power potential . . . goes beyond anything ever known."[1]

A distinguished labor intellectual, long-time educational director for the Amalgamated Clothing Workers, Hardman had observed the American movement at close range for over thirty years. He enumerated the main facts as they appeared at mid-century. After World War II, union membership stood at fifteen million, a five-fold increase since 1933. Among production workers in manufacturing, over two-thirds came under collective bargaining. In transportation, coal and metal mining, steel, automobiles, meat packing, rubber and other basic industries, union coverage was complete or nearly so (80–100 per cent organized). What was more, the first years of peace confirmed the durability of labor's gains. After V-J

Day, a great strike wave swept the country, causing 4,630 work stoppages in a single year, bringing out 4.9 million workers, and costing the nation 119.8 million man-days of lost production. Only the labor upheaval of 1919 was comparable, but with this difference: after World War I, government and industry had crushed the unions. Witness both to 1919 and 1946, Hardman noted the change. "One was determined and ruthless, the other circumspect and mindful of a kind of 'protocol' of civilized behavior." Strikebreaking had fallen out of favor. Nor would labor's strength be confined to its traditional sphere. The old days had fostered "an inbred, socially isolated, doghouse philosophy." That no longer held. *"American labor unions have become a social power in the nation and are conscious of their new import."*[2]

Many others echoed Hardman's words. "Measured in numbers, political influence, economic weight, or by any other yardstick," conceded the president of the U.S. Chamber of Commerce in 1944, "labor is a power in our land." The eminent economist John Maurice Clark remarked two years later that "the balance of power has shifted radically in a generation, culminating at an almost revolutionary rate in the past fifteen years." The surge of trade unionism, added the labor-relations scholar Sumner H. Slichter, "means far more than the substitution of collective bargaining for individual bargaining. It means that the United States is gradually shifting from a capitalistic community to a laboristic one—that is, to a community in which employees rather than businessmen are the strongest single influence."[3]

These voices of the 1940s offer us a useable perspective on the contemporary history of American labor. The earlier history had a compelling logic of its own. As Professor Clark remarked in 1946: "So far, the story of the labor movement has started with groups who did not have the power to get what they wanted, and has been concerned with the means by which they might gain that power."[4] With that accomplished, however, the story lost its clear focus. We have, in fact, no coherent history for the years since World War II at all comparable to that for the years when labor was struggling for recognition. The uses of power may well constitute inherently the more ambiguous, complex theme. But if we keep firmly in mind that at the end of World War II labor at last had become "a power in our land," and that the scope of that power seemed endless at the time, then we have a beginning point for thinking about the labor history of the past thirty-five years.

On November 5, 1945, notables from the principal wings of the labor movement (AFL, CIO, Mine Workers, Railroad Brotherhoods) and organized business (NAM, U.S. Chamber of Commerce) gathered in Washington, D.C., to "lay the basis for peace with justice on the home front." The brainchild of Senator Arthur H. Vandenberg, the President's National Labor-Management Conference was intended to do for industrial peace what the United Nations conference in San Francisco had presumably just accomplished for world peace. "Responsible management knows that free collective bargaining is here to stay . . . and that it must be wholeheartedly accepted," the Republican senator had said in suggesting the conference to President Truman. No one openly doubted this view at the Washington conference. But if it certified the new status of trade unionism in postwar America, the conference was equally significant for the anxieties that it revealed, above all, over the "Right to Manage." The committee entrusted with this issue reached a stalemate, and the two sides submitted separate reports. The sticking point was labor's refusal to agree to any listing of specific functions that were exclusively management's. Industry people could only "conclude, therefore, that the labor members are convinced that the field of collective bargaining will, in all probability, continue to expand into the field of management. The only possible end of such a philosophy would be joint management of enterprise." Nor was the threat merely speculative. "Even today," charged the industry members, "efforts are continuing on the part of certain unions to extend the scope of collective bargaining to include matters and functions that are clearly the responsibility of management."[5]

What they doubtless had in mind was the General Motors strike that broke out before the conference adjourned. On August 18, 1945, Walter Reuther had demanded a 30 per cent wage increase with no rise in the price of GM products. Reuther then challenged the company to "open the books," so as to permit the union to ascertain GM's ability to pay higher wages at existing price levels. This was, responded GM, "an opening wedge whereby the unions hope to pry their way into the whole field of management. It leads surely to the day when union bosses, under threat of strike, will seek to tell us *what* we can make, *when* we can make it." The strike that began on November 21, 1945, seemed, as one of Reuther's aides later said, "the first act of a new and significant era in American unionism, an era in which labor might break away from the bonds of business unionism, to wage an economic struggle planned to advance the welfare of the community as a whole, and to lay the foundations for new economic mechanisms designed to win security without sacrificing liberty."[6]

The struggle to organize the mass-production industries had generated an authentic thrust that went beyond pure-and-simple unionism. From among old labor progressives such as John Brophy, from union intellectuals such as Clinton Golden of the Steelworkers, from young leaders such as the Reuther brothers and James Carey, came a keen sense that the CIO was destined for more than business unionism. In the early stages of the war, they had advanced the notion of industrial councils by which management and labor would jointly run war industries. If the immediate purpose was to streamline the defense effort, ultimately industrial councils would lead to "industrial democracy." CIO progressives advocated "a national planning effort" that would make organized labor "a coequal with management, with the government acting as the arbiter between these two relatively independent groups in a free society."[7]

Among the vocal advocates of industrial councils was the young Reuther, who gave the idea a dramatic twist by linking it to his novel plan for converting the auto industry to aircraft production. As the war progressed, he put forward fresh proposals, always responsive to wartime exigencies, always carving out a major place for labor. His initial postwar thinking, prompted by contract cancellations in 1944–45, envisaged a national-planning program that would convert government-owned war plants to the mass production of rail equipment and low-cost housing. When inflation, not the expected depression, began to grip the postwar economy, Reuther shifted gears and launched his wage-price assault on General Motors.

In taking this audacious step, Reuther was acting within the mainstream of CIO progressivism. Nor was his economic reasoning considered idiosyncratic. So long as high profits could be made at low levels of production, Reuther argued, corporate industry would never generate enough jobs for American workers.

> It is *desirable* to raise wage rates without raising prices, because a stabilization program that aims to stabilize the economy must be geared to a plan for achieving capacity operation at the earliest possible moment, and must refrain from making low-level operations profitable by holding wages too low in relation to prices, as they are now.

Within the CIO, a Wage Research Committee arrived at the same conclusion as Reuther's on the wage-price policy needed, as Philip Murray said, "to lay the groundwork for an era of full employment." The very creation of the CIO research committee, whose purpose was to advise affiliated unions on bargaining policy, signified a notable departure from a reliance on independent, freewheeling collective bargaining. Even the AFL officially acknowledged labor's need for a voice in "over-all economic policies." The point was not lost on management, evident in its protests "that we . . . aren't managing the country as a whole. We're responsible for showing a profit to *our* stockholders." Industry ought not be surprised by labor's impatience with a narrowly confined form of collective bargaining, said Professor Slichter. "A laboristic community must be expected to re-examine the value judgments reached when property owners were the dominant influence in the country. No area of capitalist thought is likely to be examined more thoroughly and critically than that pertaining to profits . . . in particular . . . excess profits."[8]

The postwar threat to management rights went beyond labor's ambitions for injecting large policy issues into the collective-bargaining arena. To most managers, in fact, the assault seemed more real and more pervasive in the ordinary practice of negotiations within the individual firm. After interviewing sixty major executives during the winter of 1945–46, Professor E. Wight Bakke of Yale reported that collective bargaining so far had left them with "anxiety . . . about the future; uncertainty as to where the process will end; a fear that it will eventually culminate in such stringent impairment of management's freedom that it will not be able to do its job satisfactorily."[9]

Inevitably, the newness of the experience provoked uneasiness. The existing generation of managers had grown up believing in the inherent prerogatives of management. Nor had collective bargaining fairly begun before the war; in the early years, the depression had kept the industrial unions on the defensive. The first contracts had been thin affairs, largely codifying existing conditions and limited to wages, hours, vacations, and weakly drawn grievance and seniority provisions. Now, with the war over, industrial management confronted aggressive bargaining from the new unions, and was taken aback by the sweeping scope of the assault.

The challenge was felt most acutely on personnel actions. Committed to the principle of seniority, the industrial unions persistently tried to restrict managerial discretion regarding promotion, layoff, transfer, and rehire. By 1946 they had largely succeeded in rubber, meat-packing, and some public utilities. In auto, steel, and electrical goods, managers retained the right to take account of merit and ability, but they normally were obliged to justify actions that violated seniority. By pressing always for uniform standards and well-defined rules, unions hemmed in management in many other ways. Often the first step involved no more than the inclusion of existing company practice in a contract, but, as the NAM warned, it then became a bargainable issue in the next negotiations. Another favored approach was to demand the right of prior agreement by a union representative on such matters as discipline, bonus changes, and job assignments. If these advances were characteristically piecemeal, sweeping change might also occur in a single stroke, as happened, for example, in steel and meat packing as a result of wartime directives to end wage inequalities (i.e., different rates for comparable work). Unions and companies renegotiated over many months the entire wage structure, with every job studied and placed in the appropriate classification.

While union penetration was "deepest and widest" on personnel matters, encroachment extended to job content, operation rates, and other production issues, and then more tenuously out to the farthest reaches of managerial decision-making. In the automobile industry, the union wanted to discuss seasonal demand; in electrical goods, contracting out of work; in steel, technologial change; in rubber, the opening of new plants; and almost everywhere, financial policies as these bore on wage determination. It was the union's responsibility, one labor leader said, to regulate the employer "at every point where his action affects the welfare of the men." This absence of defined limits gave to collective bargaining its sinister edge. "Sometimes there's a particular restriction that gets your goat," one manager told Professor Bakke, "but on the whole it's the overall sense of being closed in on . . . that gets you. . . . You wonder how long it can go on and leave you able to meet your responsibilities."[10]

Management could at least come to grips with the union challenge at the bargaining table. An insidious erosion of its authority was meanwhile taking place on the shop floor. The roots of this problem went back to the organizing years when shop-steward systems had sprung up and job actions had disrupted the mass-production industries. That initial surge of rank-and-file militancy subsided in the sharp recession of 1937–38, only to revive in a more sustained way with the advent of World War II. Conversion to war production undermined factory discipline and production standards, partly because of uncertainty about the costs for new products being rushed into production, even more because of the easy cost-plus provisions of government contracts. On the other hand, wartime conditions produced a spirit of truculent independence among industrial workers. Labor was in desperately short supply, especially among seasoned workers. The wage-freeze generated a corrosive sense of grievance. An influx of black workers triggered wildcat strikes among whites in Detroit and elsewhere. And local organizations turned rebellious against the higher echelons of union leadership that supported the no-strike pledge and urged maximum production.

Trouble at the first line of supervision meanwhile cast doubt on management's capacity to keep the upper hand. The coming of collective bargaining, as one handbook for foremen pointed out, was bound to clip "the wings of many foremen. . . . The union contract sets forth certain rules of the game which we all have to follow . . . [on] many subjects which you and I once considered to be the sole concern of management. And those of you who were once accustomed to driving your men have had to change your methods." The war further undercut the foreman's authority. Rank-and-file militancy commonly elevated the shop steward to co-equal status. The caliber of foremen meanwhile fell sharply. Compounding management's problems was a union movement that swept through the foremen's ranks after 1941, involving mainly the Foremen's Association of America, but also production unions in meat packing and electrical utilities. So exercised were employers that they injected the issue into the National Labor-Management Conference: they considered it "fundamental that there be no unionization of any part of management." There was, a foremen's study reported in January 1946, "deep anxiety in American industry about the future status of its foremen."[11]

The outcome remained doubtful in the immediate postwar period. When Professor Neil Chamberlain of Yale conducted extensive interviews in six principal industries during 1946, he found virtually all major firms convinced that more authority had been lost than had been formally conceded in the union contracts. "We recognize that in some of our shops the union committeeman exercises greater authority than the foreman," acknowledged the industrial-relations director of a big rubber firm. For automobiles, Chamberlain heard this unqualified claim: "If any manager in this industry tells you he has control of his plant he is a damn liar."[12]

From ambitious demands for a share in basic policy-making down to day-to-day struggles on the shop floor, American industry felt itself embattled on every level in the postwar period. "The question how far employees should have a voice in dictating to management is at present one of the hottest issues before the country," pronounced the *Washington Post* on January 10, 1946. No answer clearly offered itself. But, for the moment, anything seemed possible. Only by legally confining collective bargaining to "its proper sphere," GM President Charles E. Wilson warned the Senate committee considering amendments to the Wagner Act, could "what we have come to know as our American system" be saved from a social revolution "imported from east of the Rhine. Unless this is done, the border area of collective bargaining will be a constant battleground . . . as the unions continuously attempt to press the boundary farther and farther into the area of managerial functions." For their part, labor leaders would have been inclined to deny only the ominous conclusions Wilson had drawn. In the end, one CIO national official confided to Professor Chamberlain, unions "must be conceded the right to bargain respecting all functions of management."[13]

That day has not come. Reuther's large conception of labor negotiation did not lead to the kind of co-determination that prevails, for example, in West Germany. The union contract did not end with labor on an equal footing with management inside the firm. Rank-and-file militancy did not bring the shop-floor control such as exists under the shop-steward system in England. Charlie Wilson need not have feared for the "American system."

In 1960 Sumner Slichter and two Harvard colleagues published the results of a three-year field study of contemporary labor relations in America. *The Impact of Collective Bargaining on Management* offered massive testimony to the expanding scope of the union agreement since World War II. As Slichter wrote: "The American workman is more richly endowed with self-determined rights than the workman of any other country, and American managements must conduct their operations within an elaborate framework of rules and policies." But these constraints had not gone in the direction so feared by the employers of the 1940s. On decision-making remote from the immediate interest of workers (such as prices), the threat to managerial prerogative had long since evaporated. And while great diversity still existed on operational matters—"some unions are in fact only a slight check on management; other unions run the shop"—the persistent tendency sustained the authority of management. Slichter considered it "a fact of greatest importance . . . that in most plants . . . appeasement by management [was] dying out." Instead, "a balanced relationship" was emerging, by which Slichter meant well-matched unions and managements, vigorous in representing their constituencies, but also responsive to economic realities, not excluding even "restoring plant efficiency" and "removing the effects of excessive past concessions." Since World War II, moreover, the distinction between "legal" strikes and "illegal" strikes (those in violation of an agreement) had so sharpened as to be in "almost unconscious use today." The labor relations of 1960, concluded Sumner Slichter, "represents substantial progress compared with the state of affairs in 1940 or 1950."[14]

Of firms that had mastered the union challenge, General Motors was the exemplar. Its top officers, said Slichter, "saw clearly from the start . . . that the rise of unions threatened the freedom of management."[15] And just as clearly they saw how to quash that threat.

Singled out for special attack in 1945, General Motors responded implacably. It would not discuss prices. It would not open its books. It would not submit anything to arbitration. General Motors was prepared to face down the government as well as the UAW. In the fourth week of the strike, on December 14, 1945, President Truman appointed a fact-finding board. When it secured authority to examine the company's books and ruled for taking into account ability to pay, General Motors walked out. When the board in early January 1946 recommended an increase of 17.5 per cent (19.5 cents an hour on the base rate), General Motors rejected the finding outright. It was the government that gave way. To settle the nationwide steel strike, the Truman administration scuttled its price-stabilization program. In exchange for an 18.5 cent an hour increase, the industry was permitted five dollars more a ton for steel. Forced thus to abandon the price issue, Reuther demanded at least the 19.5 cents recommended by Truman's fact-finding board. Over that penny, General Motors let the strike drag on for another month, and when it ended on March 13, 1946, the penny had not been surrendered. To preserve what it considered to be management prerogatives, GM had taken a 113-day strike, accepted losses of nearly $89 million (of which $52.9 million was recovered through tax credits), and, most important, conceded its headstart to competitors in the race for postwar markets.

Having driven home the point, General Motors unveiled the liberal side of its labor strategy. Even in the heat of the 1945–46 battle, the company had shown notable restraint. No effort had been made to resume operations or break the strike. And while, for bargaining purposes the company had cancelled the entire contract and demanded sweeping concessions, the final settlement essentially restored the status quo on nonmonetary issues. In 1948, GM's President Wilson seized the bargaining initiative with two proposals: first, pegging wage rates to the cost of living; and, second, relating further increases to productivity, so as to assure the GM worker "a higher living standard over the years." The two-year agreement called for eight cents an hour to cover recent price increases, a cost-of-living adjustment every three months, and an additional three cents an hour each year as labor's share of higher productivity. By agreeing on "the right thing to do," GM hoped the two sides might "prevent another round of disastrous strikes" and build a relationship that could "be stabilized over a substantial period of years." The 1950 contract improved on the established formula, granted a modified union shop requiring new employees to join the union but permitting withdrawals after one year, and lengthened the term to five years. In 1953 Reuther sought to reopen the contract on the theory that long-term agreements were "living documents" subject to reconsideration under changing conditions. Conscious of considerable rank-and-file restiveness, General Motors did renegotiate the agreement, fusing nineteen cents of the cost-of-living increases of the Korean War period into the base rates, increasing the productivity factor by a penny to five cents an hour, granting an additional ten cents an hour to skilled workers, and improving the benefits under the pension plan.[16]

The company thus defined the terms for dealing with the UAW. The union was accepted as a permanent presence. Benefits would be forthcoming at regular intervals and in decent increments. The essentials of managerial authority had to be left alone. On that subject, the toughness displayed on the price issue characterized GM policy at every level. The company would not bargain on matters designated as within the sphere of management. It opposed any form of labor-management cooperation that gave the union a place, however minor or advisory, on management's side of the line. It policed the agreement like a hawk. On handling grievances, the labor-relations vice president remarked in 1949, "we have been making every reasonable effort to settle picayune cases . . . but have conceded no ground whatsoever on fundamental principle matters which would have the tendency of watering down management's responsibility to manage the business." On matters of discipline, above all, the company enforced its authority rigorously. To do otherwise "means giving away another finger, another part of your management responsibility." General Motors, noted one investigator, was always "willing to have entire plants shut down completely rather than back water on disciplinary action taken against a handful of union members." Enormous resources, of course, backed up GM's labor policies. And, by common consent, it was among the best managed corporations in the country. "General Motors is tough, but it does have policies," Reuther acknowledged respectfully.[17] Exceptional as GM was, however, its approach did represent the central tendency of American industry.

The right to manage was deeply rooted in American entrepreneurial thought, going back to nineteenth-century notions of property and to the imperatives of scientific management. Hardly less fundamental was the liberal side of GM's strategy, reflecting as it did the welfare capitalism of the 1920s and, in a deeper way, the corporate-liberal philosophy originating in the Progressive era. Only the object changed. Instead of seeking an accommodation that would forestall organization, now the purpose shifted to confining the unions within acceptable limits.[18]

Not even the mighty General Motors, however, was immune to the force of events. Originally, it had reserved from collective bargaining those benefits—pensions, health and welfare—traditionally provided by great corporations. Distinguishing sharply between "union relations" and "employee relations," GM intended to preserve as much as it could of its earlier welfare system. Collective bargaining pushed in the opposite direction. It only took a breakthrough with one major firm to force a new item on the bargaining table everywhere. When Chrysler conceded on the pension issue in 1949, GM was bound to follow. In this way welfare benefits assumed an ever larger part in the negotiations of the 1950s. To some degree, collective bargaining made employers progressive despite themselves, General Motors included.

Welfarism was double-edged, however, capable of fighting unionism as well as buying it off. When General Electric soured on the unions in the postwar period, its industrial-relations director Lemuel Boulware conceived a powerful counterattack, composed partly of a propaganda campaign aimed at winning over employees and communities, and partly of a single-offer bargaining posture designed to show that benefits derived from the company, not the union. Boulwarism, as it came to be known, gave General Electric the upper hand, and it became a model for like-minded companies during the 1950s and after.[19] Alternatively, hostility to unionism might be expressed at the other extreme. This was true, for example, of International Harvester, which suffered from stormy labor relations all through the 1950s. Among other things, Harvester withdrew union-security rights after the war, and in 1953 it stood apart among major UAW employers in rejecting Reuther's living-document theory and refusing to renegotiate its agreement.[20]

The exercise of managerial rights likewise varied widely from the GM norm. In its extensive inquiry into "The Causes of Industrial Peace," the National Planning Association stressed the advantages of flexibility and cooperation. Thus in the case of the glass manufacturer Libbey-Owens-Ford:

> In the contract, management has the *right* to set a new bonus rate . . . yet in practice it gets the union to agree to a rate before it is put into effect. There is no question about management's right to schedule operations, introduce new machinery, and speed up processes, but the union is invariably consulted in advance. . . . In short, the company policy is to implement managerial decisions by making them acceptable to employees.

In a later study of eighteen companies highly regarded for their labor relations, the NPA found a common pattern of joint effort.

> Company executives . . . appeared to look upon the union as means of implementing a large range of managerial functions. For this reason they were not so apprehensive of union interference with the exercise of managerial functions. At the same time the union was actually extending its control of the jobs of its members by assuming some responsibility along with management for exercising these functions. The result was a remarkable degree of compatibility of interests.

This was a strategy for carrying out managerial authority, not for undermining it, the National Planning Association stressed. Industrial-relations experts might argue over whether cooperative practice produced better results than the "arms-length" policy of General Motors. They did not dispute the need for labor to concede management's responsibility "for the conduct of the business." In every NPA case study, the company "wanted freedom to exercise managerial functions and sought, in nearly every instance, some recognition by the union of managerial prerogatives."[21]

Amidst the complexity of the industrial-relations scene, the main thrust could be discerned. A GM executive put it with blunt candor years later: "Give the union the money, the least possible, but give them what it takes. But don't let them take the business away from us."[22] This proved to be an irresistible formula.

In the heady postwar days, collective bargaining had seemed endowed with endless possibilities for redistributing power and authority in American industry. Nothing could have been more mistaken. Of all the circumstances contributing to management's ultimate success, the essential one was that the struggle took place within a bargaining context. It instantly foreclosed any prospects for a comprehensive change of the order of the industrial-council plan. Only the war emergency had prompted the CIO to advance this ambitious scheme, and Philip Murray's lingering hopes for it doubtless accounted in part for his reluctance to see the lifting of the no-strike pledge and economic controls after the war. With the restoration of free collective bargaining, the industrial-council idea was quietly shelved. Reuther then turned to the wage-price demand in part because it seemed a maximum alternative for major reform through collective bargaining. How the General Motors strike was waged tells a great deal about the constraints inherent in the bargaining process.

To begin with, Reuther chose only General Motors as his target, notwithstanding the industry-wide significance of his wage-price demand and the industry-wide scope of all his wartime proposals. During the strike, GM negotiators constantly questioned Reuther's sincerity, charging him on the one hand with dramatizing the issue to advance his own ambitions, and on the other urging him to "get down to the type of job you are supposed to be doing as a trade-union leader, and talk about the money you would like to have for your people."[23] Despite the lip service given to Reuther's economic-stabilization objectives, no one followed his lead—not the UAW departments bargaining with Ford and Chrysler, not the United Electrical Workers (CIO) in its separate agreement with GM, not any other CIO union or national leader. In the end, they all chose to take the money and let the prices go. And so, for that matter, did Reuther after that one great effort. The 1945 program remained on the UAW agenda for many years; it never again became an item of serious negotiation.

Of the lessons to be drawn from this event, the first was the subordination of other purposes to power calculations: simply, more economic pressure would bear on GM if it alone were struck. Second, collective bargaining was a form of labor activity deeply enmeshed in internal union politics. In a variety of ways that did not always meet the eye, events were shaped by factional interest and rivalry entirely independent of what was involved in the strike. For both Reuther and his detractors, the battle with GM was inseparable from the political contest for control of the UAW; if the strike did not freeze automobile prices, it did vault Reuther into the union presidency in 1946. Of most significance, finally, was the bargaining itself. Given that the protagonists were well matched, then everything turned on relative priorities. Protection of its pricing power was indubitably of topmost value to General Motors. Was the intrusion on that prerogative of equal importance to the UAW? If not, then the union was bound to trade prices off for what it wanted more. It was the company's strategy to make the union face up to that choice.

In 1950 the Studebaker Corporation identified an overmanning problem at its South Bend plant. To accomplish a reduction through attrition, the company needed greater flexibility in adjusting rates and making assignments. The obstacle was a group-incentive system. The Studebaker negotiators put the demand for its abolition to the union in this way: "We can't tie up here to a five-year wage agreement [the industry pattern] unless we open the door to getting out some of the excess manpower in this plant."[24] Studebaker's proposition on this commonplace matter did not differ in its essence from the way GM treated Reuther's historic demand for a voice in price determination. In actual practice, of course, a multitude of issues normally had to be balanced out, not a single pair, and other impinging forces made collective bargaining an endlessly complex process—so much so, indeed, as to generate a rich literature by game theorists and social scientists. But the heart of collective bargaining was simple enough to grasp: it was Studebaker's offer to trade an onerous incentive plan against a benefit it believed the union wanted more. Multiply that offer, expand it to include endless combinations and permutations, and one has the bargaining nexus within which organized labor would assert its claims on American industry.

A confident union official had assured Professor Bakke that collective bargaining would cut progressively into management prerogatives because "it's our job to get a voice in whatever affects the men or builds the strength of the union."[25] Only one condition might have validated this easy expectation: that the unions place as high a value on control issues as did management. Here, too, the GM strike revealed the future. As in postwar Detroit, money ordinarily took precedence over industrial democracy.

Consider the union history at General Electric and Westinghouse. Especially among the craft workers, the vanguard of the organizing drives, money itself was not a major issue during the 1930s. The electrical workers were mainly concerned then with job security, speed-up, work rules, and, of course, union recognition. By the mid-1940s, as the voice of the production workers increased, priorities shifted markedly. The demand for shorter hours died out with the Great Depression. Overtime rates the electrical workers now favored for the premium income, not for the inhibiting effect on the long day. When the workday issue revived in later years, significantly, it took the form of involuntary overtime; workers wanted the choice between more free time and more money. When cutbacks threatened in 1945 and 1948, they resisted work-sharing, insisting instead on lay-offs on a strict seniority basis. Most significant was their reversal on incentive pay, which they had earlier assailed as the cause of speed-up, unemployment, and the loss of workers' autonomy. The postwar enthusiasm for incentives derived partly from effective union policing of abuses, even more from the high rates and loose work standards that had crept in during the war. Traditional labor notions about the immorality of incentive pay simply faded away. Finally, there was the overwhelming prominence now given to pay demands. The purpose of the union, proclaimed James Matles at the UE convention in 1944, was to "bring home the gravy to your people." By the mid-1940s, noted the leading student of the subject, "wage increases had become the chief goal of the union movement in the electrical industry."[26]

So they did everywhere in this period. Most potent of the contributing forces was the basic shift from an economy of chronic depression to one of inflation after 1940. Despite the wage freeze, industrial workers kept ahead of rising prices during the war, mainly by dint of long hours. With reconversion, overtime ended and real income plummeted. A price surge of 22.5 per cent following the repeal of federal controls in mid-1946 swallowed up the first postwar wage increases, and prompted a second round in 1947. The very notion of "rounds" of negotiation, regular events in this period, sometimes even in mid-contract as a result of the introduction of reopener clauses, emphasized the monetary purposes of collective bargaining. So did the proliferation of fringe payments. The U.S. Steel contract of 1948, for example, included an incremental increase of one-half cent for each of the thirty-two job classifications; premium pay of four cents an hour for the afternoon shift, six cents for the night shift; time-and-a-half after five consecutive days of work and on holidays; and a guarantee of four hours pay on reporting to work. With the outbreak of the Korean War in June 1950, the upward march of prices resumed (living costs rose 14 per cent in two years) and revived the inflationary pressures on collective bargaining.

At this point, however, the yield began to rise. From 1945 to 1949, industrial earnings barely kept even with higher prices. Thereafter, real income grew steadily. Gross weekly income for production workers in manufacturing went from $54.92 in 1949 to $71.81 (in 1947–49 dollars) in 1959. Despite steeper deductions for social security and income tax, the industrial worker with three dependents had nearly 18 per cent more spendable real income in 1959 than ten years earlier. He gained leisure time as well. In 1946, contracts began to include paid holidays; paid vacations increased from a single week, typical before the war, to as much as four weeks for long-term workers by 1960. The 1950s became the decade of the "affluent" worker—evident in the move to the suburbs (for half of all workers by 1966, three-fourths of those under 40), in rising home ownership, in cars and other consumer durables, and, as infallible as signs of rising expectations, in the high incidence of installment buying and a doubling in the number of working wives between 1945 and 1960. For the industrial worker of this era, the union contract was becoming the passport to a better life. "The labor movement," said Walter Reuther, ". . . is developing a whole new middle class."[27]

Collective bargaining was meanwhile taking on another function. Provisions for security, other than what the worker was able to make on his own, had derived mainly from company welfare programs and, beginning in 1935, from the Social Security Act. The benefit funds of trade unions, important in the pioneering days, had grown outmoded even before the 1930s. Only in rare instances, mainly in the garment trades, had unions tried to incorporate welfare provisions into contracts with employers.

During the 1940s, a major move began in this direction, first among the industrial unions, but soon throughout the labor movement. As with so much else, the initial stimulus came from the war: tax breaks made welfare costs to the employer very low; they offered another way of eluding the wage freeze; and the War Labor Board favored the inclusion of welfare benefits within the contractual labor-management relationship. When John L. Lewis in 1946 extracted from the coal industry a welfare and retirement fund to be financed from a tonnage royalty, he laid down a challenge to the entire labor movement. In the postwar years, moreover, the NLRB consistently broadened the obligatory scope of bargaining to cover welfare issues. More fundamental was the persisting political conservatism of postwar America. No national health plan was in the offing, old-age benefits under the Social Security Act remained frozen at 1935 levels until 1950 (and clearly would never provide for a comfortable retirement), and unemployment benefits varied from state to state and nowhere provided adequate protection. With the welfare state beyond reach—a decisive difference from the experience of European labor—collective bargaining took up the burden.

First incorporated into agreements during the war, health and insurance benefits spread rapidly thereafter without much controversy. Pensions were a different matter, especially on the question of employee contributions. It took a lull in the battle for higher wages during the 1949 recession, a major court decision (*Inland Steel* [1949]), a favorable report by a presidential fact-finding body in steel, and several big strikes, to achieve a general pattern in the basic industries in 1949–50: a pension of $100 a month (social security payments included) at age 65 on a noncontributory basis. Coverage then spread to small-scale industry by the imaginative use of multiemployer plans under joint union-management trusteeships. By the late 1950s, over half of all unionized employees were protected by pension plans, probably three-quarters by health and welfare coverage.

The push for security became self-sustaining, constantly improving the existing benefits, periodically striking out in new directions.[28] In 1955, the UAW scored a major break-through toward its goal of a guaranteed annual wage. Ford agreed to set up a fund (five cents an employee-hour up to a maximum of $400 per worker) from which a supplementary unemployment benefit (SUB) would be paid to guarantee laid-off employees a total, including other income, of 65 per cent of straight-time after-tax pay for twenty-six weeks. Ford's

example was followed by other auto makers, by the steel and
can industries, and by others. Within two years, the total
number of workers covered by some form of income security
reached two million. As Philip Murray had predicted ten
years earlier, the unions chose to "participate actively in the
formulation of plans for security which have become, and will
as time goes on, be increasingly a matter of major concern to
all those who work."[29]

Yet by so doing, they subverted a claim to participation on
matters of management. When it took up the problem of
unstable employment in the auto industry, the UAW had two
choices: either to deal with the causes, or to protect its members from the consequences. By choosing the latter, the UAW
actually conceded away its interest in the former. The union
said as much when its 1953 convention declared that the
"primary goal of a guaranteed annual wage should be to
stimulate management to provide steady full-time employment, week by week, the year round."[30] For its part, the Ford
Motor Company specifically conditioned its acceptance of the
SUB plan on being granted greater flexibility in the operation
of the enterprise. But nothing was conditional on the performance of the company: it had, in effect, paid the union off
by accepting the cost of SUB. And for other forms of income
security, no bones were made that the protection afforded
workers was the price for management's freedom to do what
it wanted to do. This was true, for example, of the landmark
Pacific Longshore agreement (1959) opening the way for the
new container-loading technology, of the experimental Armour agreement (1959) providing for the retraining of
workers displaced by plant closings, and, in general, of the
proliferating severance-pay agreements. Contemplating this
preference "for *income* security rather than *employment* security," Sumner Slichter correctly spoke of "a basic conservatism in the American labor movement." The unions had
thereby "avoid[ed] the necessity of bargaining over such essential management decisions as production schedules, capi-

tal improvement plans, and plant location [and left] management . . . its freedom to make these decisions."[31]

If organized labor readily bargained away some claims, others it defended more tenaciously. The intensity of its interest, in fact, corresponded roughly to the distance from the shop floor. The more remote from the immediate circle of workers' experience, the easier for management to keep an issue from the bargaining table. By the same token, over shop issues the assertion of managerial rights always faced tough sledding. And if this involved taking back earlier contractual concessions or changing established practice, resistance could be very tough, even immovable. Such was the case at Studebaker, whose management admitted in 1962 that, after a decade of trying, its contract remained "a matter of amazement. . . . in the industry and the envy of other unions." Despite its competitive weakness, Studebaker could gain no relief from "the most liberal working practices" in the auto industry.[32] Even so strong a firm as General Electric largely failed to rid itself of a costly piece-rate system, a primary cause of its poisoned union relations and active plant relocation policy during the 1950s. Work standards figured in other important disputes during the decade, including a violent strike at Westinghouse in 1955–56 over time studies of direct day work (that is, hourly-paid production workers) and a 134–day strike at the Pittsburgh Plate Glass Company in 1958.[33] Altogether, roughly one out of four strikes between 1947 and 1960 occurred over job security, work load, and shop conditions.

In 1959, U.S. Steel placed shop issues at the center of its bargaining program. Among eight demands made on the United Steelworkers, the key one involved the local work-practices provision (Section 2-B) in the contracts of the Steel Corporation and a number of other major producers. Section 2-B asserted two principles: that workers had rights in existing working conditions outside the terms of the basic contract, but that management could change those conditions when the "basis" for them was "changed or eliminated." Since its inception in 1947, Section 2-B had been interpreted by umpires along lines evidently unanticipated by management. A series of decisions broadened the definition of the protected local conditions, while linking the management right to make unilateral changes to the introduction of new equipment or production changes. A company could not, for example, cut crew size because of incentives that increased productivity. This particular problem was exacerbated, especially at U.S. Steel, by the withdrawal of the union from an understanding that, as with the wage-rate structure, it would participate in a joint job evaluation/incentive program. The new leadership at U.S. Steel, determined to correct earlier mistakes and emboldened by inflationary pressures and a sympathetic White House, took an approach to the 1959 negotiations contrasting sharply with the conciliatory philosophy of the retired Ben Fairless. Roger Blough and R. Conrad Cooper demanded an end to contract language that had "frozen inefficiency and waste into the operation."

In his autobiography ten years later, former union president David J. McDonald was still puzzling over the industry's strategy. If it was intent on doing so, management had ways of reducing crew size, especially during the rehiring period after layoffs. Outside investigators tended to agree with McDonald. Section 2-B did put a brake on efficiency, but mainly because of its discouraging effect on supervisors. "Inefficiencies which cannot be eliminated under the contract within a reasonable amount of time by an alert management are rare."[34] Having chosen to make an open fight instead, the industry took so stiff a line as to give the union very little leeway for bargaining out a solution. The industry did back away from an initial demand for a freeze on wages and fringes, but insisted that it would bargain on money issues only *after* the union conceded it the freedom "to make operating improvements in the interests of greater efficiency and economy." On the work-rule issue, steel negotiators were unyielding, rejecting, for example, a union proposal for making "reasonableness" rather than past practice the basis for Section 2-B. The industry took an eight-month strike, and, on the central issue, lost.

Of all subjects of negotiation, shop-floor matters were the least tractable within the formal framework of collective bargaining. United States Steel did, in fact, learn this lesson. Relying on the Human Relations Committee set up as part of the 1959 settlement, its management increasingly dealt with productivity issues through "objective problem solving" in an ongoing joint effort with the union. To a large degree, the industry ultimately accomplished by the cooperative route— of which the United Steelworkers had been a leading advocate ever since the 1930s—what it had failed to win by force in 1959. The industrial-relations scholar Jack Stieber applied the lesson to work-rule disputes in manufacturing generally. It was within the means of strong, well-financed management to eliminate "restrictive practices," either by means of technological change or by "buy[ing] them out." "The worst approach is to try to force their elimination because they are 'bad,' 'wrong,' and an infringement of 'management rights.'"[35]

There was a final point to make. By pushing for drastic work-rule changes, the steel industry inevitably brought on the strike. Before the announcement of the industry demands on June 10, 1959, McDonald remembered, the members had been "generally fat and comfortable"; thereafter, they were "fighting mad."[36] McDonald, no enthusiast of industrial war, probably could have held back the steelworkers only at his own peril. Beyond anything else, shop-floor issues were the stuff of rank-and-file militancy. The entire thrust of the union-management relationship aimed at containing that activity. For his part, the prudent manager was ordinarily prepared to concede a good deal, preferably in the form of money and fringe benefits, but, if need be, in some accommodation on shop-floor rights, for the sake of that larger stability. For a brief time, the steel industry acted in a contrary way, which doubtless accounted most of all for David J. McDonald's puzzlement.

World War II had offered an infallible test of ungovernable shop-floor militancy: government denial of maintenance-of-membership privileges to unions with bad records of wildcats and slowdowns. Among the recipients of this recognition was the steel local at the Chicago plant of the Inland Steel Container Company. A new trouble-shooting manager found the supervisory staff demoralized, incapable of maintaining direction over operations, and, in the words of a subsequent investigator, "constantly being pushed around by the union." Aggressive efforts to restore managerial control provoked fierce resistance. When the order came down that henceforth all grievances had to be in writing, paper flooded the system, weekly third-step meetings went on far into the night (with union stewards on time-and-a-half), and endless complaints harassed foremen on the production line. A well-coordinated slowdown followed. The idea was to produce just enough to make the standard rate and forego bonus work, thereby falling far short of production goals but not so short as to precipitate a plant shut-down. Threatened by disciplinary action for loafing, the workers shifted from slowdowns to breakdowns.

> It was a simple matter for an experienced worker to persuade a machine to break down [undetected]. . . . Even if it was only a question of picking a nut up off the floor and screwing it back on the machine, no one would do it. . . . They wouldn't let the foreman do it either because he wasn't supposed to do any work on the line. If the foreman didn't happen to be in the department when the line went down, no one bothered to notify him. The workers just sat down and waited.

A maintenance man would take twenty minutes to show up. He would need help—another twenty minutes. And so on.

After many months of this warfare, an explosion finally came in September 1945 over the company's refusal to pay premium rates for setting up and closing down the line outside the regular eight-hour schedule. For the better part of the next year, the Inland container plant was down on strike.[37]

To a greater or lesser degree, this battle was fought out in industrial plants across the country. As in the Inland plant, the employer counteroffensive everywhere began with the willingness (in the common parlance) "to take a strike." In 1944, as the demand for war production eased, a wave of disciplinary stoppages swept the mass-production industries: in rubber, 18.5 per cent of the workers were out at some time during the year; in steel, 20.3 per cent; in auto, an astonishing 50.5 per cent. According to General Motors, "necessary disciplinary action" caused over half the strikes and almost 83 per cent of all man-hours lost in work stoppages at its plants in 1944.[38]

In the postwar years, great store was placed on a firm, well-defined policy against wildcat strikes, such as Inland Steel adopted in 1952: no discussions on any issue while a wildcat was in progress; definite punishment on a progressive scale; training for supervisory personnel to enable them to maintain the blast furnaces in the event of a sudden stoppage.[39] Beyond firmness—the heart of any labor-relations program, Professor Slichter always insisted—a variety of managerial approaches evolved for maintaining rank-and-file discipline. Once the Taft-Hartley Act (1947) denied foremen collective-bargaining rights, widespread activity began to upgrade first-line supervisors and to integrate them more effectively into the management structure. A renewed interest in methods of labor administration and personnel practices, including a considerable "human-relations" vogue during the 1950s, recalled the era of welfare capitalism. To some degree, technological progress itself served as a disciplining agent, for example, by the persistent efforts in auto plants to incorporate within the assembly line work earlier done on an individual or team basis.[40] But managers did not see shop-floor discipline as their job alone; they expected the help of the unions.

On this point, industry found a ready ally in the labor movement. Contractual responsibility went to the heart of the purposes that American unionism had set for itself. From the outset, even during the turbulent sit-down era, the CIO had officially espoused the sanctity of the contract. The implementation of that principle, of course, was very much subject to collective bargaining. Listen, for example, to the international representative negotiating for the militant local at Inland Container in 1947:

> We are making an agreement here . . . we are going to live up to. . . . The local union has been charged with this responsibility and the officers of the local union have assumed their responsibility and in their last meeting the officers of the local union were virtually taking the hides off some of the people. They are assuming the position of supporting management. . . . We have many situations . . . on wildcats and what have you that happened and as we grow older we can exercise more control than we have exercised in the past. . . . We hope to indicate to management that we are sincere and that we are going to assume our responsibility.
>
> We can see the justification of management being somewhat skeptical, but if we are going to live in the past, then certainly, we are not going to get along too well.[41]

Uttered at a crucial juncture in the negotiations, this statement was intended just in the way it sounded, namely, to extract the key concession needed to wrap up the agreement.

In the immediate postwar period, industry generally demanded "company security" clauses against job actions that violated the agreement. This was management's stated price for the union-security provision in the contract. By making them liable for contract violations, Taft-Hartley further raised the stakes for the unions. They commonly responded by seeking contract clauses absolving them from liability, conceding in exchange tougher company-security provisions that stiffened penalties for individual violators and union procedures for maintaining local discipline.[42] In the case of the highly centralized Steelworkers Union, the international insisted on being the sole signatory to contracts, and a 1948 amendment to its constitution specifically denied the power to any individual or unit to take any action breeching a contract. On imposing a trusteeship over a California local that had engaged in wildcat strikes, the international openly defended its action in court on the grounds that "the duty to maintain its contract with Kaiser Steel Company was paramount to the right of the Local to elect and maintain its own officers . . . [and] must necessarily give way to the rights of the International to maintain and hold inviolate the contract."[43]

The contractual logic itself actually evolved into a pervasive method for containing shop-floor activism. Consider, for example, the issue of relief time at Ford. The 1946 master contract merely indicated that this would receive "due consideration" in setting the speed of the line. Ample scope remained for the will of the assembly-line workers to make itself felt by contesting the specific orders of foremen, by demanding more relief time in hot weather or when job speeds crept up, even by arranging their breaks among themselves. As a result of a major dispute in 1949, the company agreed to employ one relief man for every nineteen production workers. Then relief time was fixed at twenty-four minutes per eight-hour day. The 1961 contract contained further specifics, such as no scheduling of relief periods during the first hour of work and the first hour after lunch (except in emergencies), but, of greater significance, now implementation became subject to local agreement, thereby permitting specification of relief practices to the conditions of the individual plant.[44] Each step expanded the *rights* of Ford workers for relief time, but correspondingly narrowed their *freedom* to work the issue out by their own efforts on the shop floor.

The common tendency everywhere was toward an ever greater expansion of the contractual net, from the great body of umpire rulings compiled in the 517-page *Steelworkers*

Handbook on Arbitration Decisions (1960) to the innumerable specifics incorporated into the local agreements that increasingly supplemented the master contracts in multiplant firms.[45] Contractual rules could never totally penetrate the core of informal shop-floor activity—doubling up by assembly-line workers to get more free time, for example, or banking of extra finished work by machine operators to keep within an informal output limit—any more than could the most vigilant plant management. But the contractual net did progressively narrow the scope of such activity, and, what was no less important, increasingly designate it as extralegal in character. At the point that workers began to accept the underlying premise—if it was not in the contract, it was not a right—half the battle was over.

It only remained to persuade workers that disputes arising under the contract were properly settled by adjudication rather than by job actions. In the postwar years, the grievance procedures of the early contracts developed into elaborate arrangements defining with great precision the number of steps, the authorized personnel, the time limits, the exact prodedures. At each step the decision rested in the hands of management. But if arbitration capped the entire process, the industrial rule of law could be said to have been completed. For then the employer had consented to the submission of his disputed action to the binding judgment of an umpire. The significance of this step elevated arbitration into an index—like the union shop—of the legitimacy of the union relationship. Thus a hostile firm such as International Harvester was notably slow to agree to arbitration, hinged it about with restrictions, and demonstrably resented it for years (as evidenced by the frequent dismissal of umpires).[46] For other firms, by the same token, arbitration lost its symbolic significance along with the acceptance of trade unionism. Employed by the War Labor Board to assure war production, grievance arbitration grew from a rarity in the 1930s to a commonplace in the 1950s, when it appeared in well over 90 per cent of all union contracts.

Precisely because of the limitation on decision-making, however, managers were cruelly torn over arbitration as a practical matter. Manufacturing firms commonly insisted on reserving key decisions, mainly on work standards, and spreading from there, depending on the specific industrial circumstances, to making job assignments, promoting on the basis of merit, setting rates on new work, and so on. These matters were not beyond the grievance procedure. The normal rule applied: the supervisor initiated, the worker grieved. On these reserved matters, however, the final word remained with management. But arbitration had this peculiar property: it stood in a very exact relationship to the right to strike. Ordinarily, the no-strike clause extended only as far as did the scope of arbitration. The Westinghouse and General Electric contracts drew the connection case by case: either party could request arbitration at the end of the grievance process; if neither did, the union could strike over the disputed issue. The steel industry, which gave broad scope to the umpire, likewise had an unreserved no-strike clause.

At some point, every employer had to balance the degree of his own freedom against the freedom left to the other side. In May 1949, sixty thousand Ford workers walked out of the Rouge and Lincoln-Detroit plants over the speed-up of the assembly line, not an arbitrable subject under the contract. To get the men back, the company did submit the disputed issue to arbitration. The settlement included also a series of specific protections against increased work loads (such as were caused by shortages of manpower, the mix of cars on the assembly line, and so on), and a special grievance procedure for non-arbitrable disputes that culminated in a high-level conference.[47] If the principle was preserved, Ford had actually gone far in practice toward conceding its unilateral control over work standards for the sake of labor peace.

Itself only one among innumerable variants, Ford's decision brings neatly into focus the essential nature of the union-management bargain: namely, that every contractual restraint on the workers was also a diminution of managerial discretion—in effect, the reducing of rank-and-file pressures on management authority at the price of the progressive slicing off of pieces of that authority into the terms of a contract. And what of the issues that remained reserved from arbitration? The corresponding right to strike under the contract fell subject to close regulation: first, exhaustion of the grievance procedure; second, due written notice to the employer; finally, proper authorization from the union. The workers' right to strike, insofar as it was formally conceded, was itself placed within the tight confines of rule and procedure. By so agreeing, companies and unions revealed what was, at rock bottom, the common intent of their encompassing contractual relationship—the containment of spontaneous and independent shop-floor activity.

The word *containment* bears emphasis. Given the advanced state of the bargaining system, remarked the industrial-relations expert James W. Kuhn in 1961, "one might think that the wildcat strike, for instance, should disappear from all American industries." But no, the wildcat had not disappeared. The steel industry, according to trade-association records, experienced 788 unauthorized stoppages* costing 729,200 tons of production during 1956–58. Although it maintained no figures on wildcats, the U.S. Bureau of Labor Statistics did keep separate records on short strikes and on strikes occurring during a contract (but without identifying those that were contract violations). Both sets of data suggest a substantial, if moderating, incidence of wildcat strikes during the 1950s. In 1961, one third of all strikes took place while a contract was in effect. Numerous investigations during the decade indicate persistent shop-floor activity covering the full range of pressure tactics from work stoppages to endemic harassment of foremen. And so Professor Kuhn asked himself: "Why, after twenty years of experience with the best grievance procedures which able men could devise, do American workers regularly engage in grievance tactics which are disruptive to production and disruptive of harmonious shop relations?"[48]

Wherever they came into regular contact on the job, wherever they recognized a common identity, factory workers formed bonds, legislated group work standards, and, as best they could, enforced these informal rules on fellow workers and on supervisors. Work-group activity was an expression of the irrepressible social organization of the shop floor. The informal work group long antedated the coming of the unions.[49] It was the activating unit for the rank-and-file militancy of the sitdown era and the war years. And it by no means withered under the influence of the postwar labor-management settlement. The contract gave work groups, whatever their own tactics, a measure of protection from arbitrary reprisal by the employer. And they now had, in the person of the shop steward, a designated leader with formal standing in the factory and with political reasons for supporting their activities. The root sources of the work group, however, went back as always to the technology of the given plant and, to some degree, to the ethno-cultural composition of the workers.

In the rubber industry, tire builders, pitmen and other key groups felt a keen sense of job identity and group pride; day-to-day fluctuations in production conditions (humidity, state of the rubber, etc.) made for constant disputes over rates and work standards; and trouble at any point quickly disrupted the entire tire-making process. "Tire builders are a breed apart," said a local officer. "The pitmen are just as independent, they're famous for their walkouts too. There's been a long history in tire-building and in the pits of the men running the department to suit themselves; they take action on their own."[50] Akron experienced in an extreme form what was a commonplace of American shop-floor life. Wherever group cohesion was high and the capacity to exert pressure strong, there informal work groups remained a potent factor in industrial operations.

They thereby constituted an inherent challenge to the workplace rule of law. They held the means of bypassing the grievance system entirely or, alternatively, of pressuring management to make a favorable finding. The formal proceedings, as Kuhn brilliantly showed through the close analysis of a single grievance case, might actually serve to mask the real event, in which the outcome not only turned on informal bargaining but also dealt with issues not mentioned in the stated grievance.[51] At its best, work-group pressure was particularly effective at disengaging the front-line supervisor from the management structure and extracting from him concessions not countenanced by or known to plant executives. This was what James Kuhn called "fractional bargaining." This was the way by which shop groups commonly sought to shape their working conditions in defiance of the formal adjudicating structure achieved through collective bargaining.

It was, however, an unequal struggle. The force of legitimacy lay on the side of the workplace rule of law. In England, where union contracts did not penetrate down to the factory floor, the shop stewards carved out a bargaining realm quite independent of the union structure.[52] In America, fractional bargaining could not evolve into a comparable shop-bargaining system. The workplace rule of law effectively forestalled the institutionalization of shop-group activity. The denial of legitimacy, moreover, ate at the vitals of the shop-floor impulse. American workers might engage in pressure tactics, but, as Sumner Slichter remarked, they knew they were breaking the rules. It would be hard to imagine a more insidious check on so fundamental a phenomenon as the self-activity of the work group.

Toward the workers, the contract invoked the authority of an industrial rule of law. Between the contracting parties, however, the formal relationship was sustained by a different kind of bargaining. Behind their defined roles as adversaries, as proponents of contending interests, company and union were drawn into unacknowledged collaboration against shop-floor militancy. For the union, hardly less than the company, active work groups posed a troubling challenge. They disrupted the contract. They invaded the union's representative function. And they gave the shop stewards an independent base. While he might exploit rank-and-file militancy on the road to power—as Reuther skillfully did over the no-strike pledge during World War II—ultimately the test of any union leader consisted of his ability at managing the pressure from below. In this endeavor, he needed the help of management. And it, in turn, needed him. What the Libbey-Owens-Ford Company wanted, said a National Planning Association study, was a union willing "to sell the men in the shop on a new bonus rate . . . to say 'no' to men with obviously unjustified grievances. . . . A responsible and good union [is one] able to command the respect of workers and to exert some control over them." Toward that end, remarked the National Planning Association about the firms it studied, management

> was often willing to go more than half-way on some issues. . . .
> Management invariably took into consideration the effects of its
> policy upon the prestige and influence of the incumbent leaders of
> the union. . . . In most cases, the union leaders used their 'will-
> ingness to cooperate' as a very strong bargaining point in making
> demands on management. Both parties tended to defend this sort
> of deal-making as hard-headed and realistic bargaining adapted to
> the environment within which they negotiated.[53]

Such mutuality varied widely, of course, depending as it did on both the industrial-relations philosophy of the employer and the internal politics of the union. But some collaboration was bound to exist, and always with the shared interest in containing the rank and file within the confines of the contract. It was this unsanctified alliance, paradoxically, that underpinned the sanctity of the workplace rule of law.

Nor were its benefits distributed even-handedly within the

plant. If workers disputed a management action, it remained in effect until altered through the grievance procedure. The transgressing worker, on the other hand, was subject to immediate discipline, and was considered guilty until proven innocent. So skewed an arrangement necessarily thrust the initiative on the employer. He was also far better able to exploit a system of rules and procedures. Each accretion to these, each new intricacy, placed a higher premium on the knowledge of the expert and the skills of the lawyer. At the third or fourth step of a grievance, the national union might well meet management on equal terms, but in the daily give-and-take inside the shop the steward and committeeman could not match the professionalism of the industrial-relations man. In a study of Buffalo plants in 1961, George Strauss took note of an increasingly aggressive use of the contract to force concessions from the workers. In a sense, rules and procedures constituted for management the shop-level equivalent of the pressure tactics of the informal work group. Where employers had the upper hand, as they did in the depressed economy of Buffalo, the contract could well be made to "creep" for the company.[54]

These marginal advantages came as a bonus on top of the primary value of the workplace rule of law. In a recent essay, David Lewin reminded employers of the benefits they derived from the orderly resolution of shop-level conflict: first, as compared to the endemic plant strife elsewhere in the industrial world, assurance of continuous production over the life of the contract; second, enforcement of the rules by union officials who, to some degree, thereby acted as the instruments of management; and, finally, the steady flow of data on labor problems from the grievance process that made it, in effect, part of management's information system.[55] The force of Lewin's point, insofar as American industry took it, secured the future of the workplace rule of law. Constructed step by step through collective bargaining, it could be altered, or reversed, only in the same way. Once management assigned a high value to the grievance system, that, like managerial prerogatives earlier, became equally resistant to dilution through the trading processes of collective bargaining. It need hardly be said that the union leadership, through whom local demands had to be filtered, scarcely qualified as fit advocates of contractual changes that would shift authority back toward the shop floor. The collective-bargaining system itself powerfully sustained the workplace rule of law.

Its sturdiest insurance, however, lay within the workers themselves. In the later years of the 1960s, rank-and-file militancy mounted up again. When it began keeping statistics on membership rejections of contracts during these years, the Federal Mediation and Conciliation Service discovered a problem scarcely thought to have existed a decade earlier. In the peak year of 1967, the FMCS reported over a thousand agreements voted down, representing 14.2 per cent of the cases in its annual file.[56] Opposition to established union leadership, likewise hardly known in the 1950s, became commonplace in the 1960s, even in such tightly disciplined unions as the Miners, Steelworkers, and Teamsters. The sources of that dissidence were highly complex and difficult to understand—deriving partly from the protections written into the Landrum-Griffin Act (1959), partly from the social and racial pressures of the Vietnam era, partly from a generational change in the labor force, but certainly also from resentment against oppressive work in American industry. The incidence of strikes occurring with a contract in effect increased from roughly one thousand in 1960 to nearly two in 1969, indicative surely of the mounting importance of shop-floor issues and probably (since the statistics do not distinguish between strikes permitted by and those in violation of the contract) of an increase in the incidence of wildcats.[57] In the auto industry, absenteeism crept up during the 1960s from the norm of 2.5 per cent to 5 per cent, higher around the weekends. At the highly advanced GM assembly plant in Lordstown, Ohio, a three-week strike over speed-up in 1972 became something of a symbol of the revolt against work pressures in the industry.

The impulse behind this upsurge harked back to the shop-floor militancy of the postwar years. "When the men settled things on the floor, it was something they did themselves," remarked a Buffalo union representative in 1961. "They directly participated in determining their working conditions. When things are settled legalistically, through the grievance procedure, it's something foreign. They don't see it."[58] Sense of that remoteness, desire for "settl[ing] things on the floor," ran as an undercurrent through the new wave of rank-and-file militancy. But this discontent seemed incapable of directing itself at the system of plant law that held shop-floor activity in check. It was true that there were protests against grievance procedures, and, as in the case of the miners, demands for an expansion of the right to strike. Not the mechanism itself, however, but only its malfunctioning seemed to be at issue: heavy backlogs of unresolved grievances, evidences of deliberate obstruction by employers, and, to some extent, a sense of disadvantage inherent in highly complex rules and procedures. What was perhaps most telling of the hold of the legalistic system, however, was that, when rank-and-file militants did advocate greater reliance on job action, they should have sought to regain the freedom to strike *in a legal way,* that is, by having the right written into the contract. As for the net of contractual rules specifying the rights of workers, these seemed wholly beyond the scope of rank-and-file attack. The better definition of rules, not their elimination, seemed the only avenue to industrial justice.

The workplace rule of law had deeply implanted itself. It had become part of the environment of the modern factory, and, as such, a permanent brake on the self-activity of American workers.

In his memoir, *The Brothers Reuther* (1976), Victor Reuther wrote feelingly of what collective bargaining had achieved for the auto workers—for themselves, economic equality and decent conditions, for their families, a larger measure of security and dignity. Beyond that, he did not go. Later on, contemplating the inflationary crisis of the 1970s, Victor wondered whether American labor ought not take a page from the European experience, and think "of democratizing the whole process of decision-making at the corporate level, so that the voice of the workers and the voice of the consumers will also be heard in corporate counsels." Precisely these intentions had been Walter Reuther's decades before when he had demanded industrial councils in World War II and when he had confronted General Motors in the reconversion period. So distant had that history become, so unreal the terms of those struggles, that Victor evidently had quite forgotten.[59]

Notes

1. Schlesinger, *Washington Post*, January 1, 1950; J. B. S. Hardman, "The State of the Movement," in J. B. S. Hardman and Maurice F. Neufeld, eds., *The House of Labor* (New York, 1951), p. 53.
2. Ibid., pp. 52–84.
3. Eric Johnston, *America Unlimited* (New York, 1944), p. 176; John M. Clark, *Guideposts in a Time of Change* (New York, 1949), p. 148; Sumner H. Slichter, "Are We Becoming a 'Laboristic' State?" *New York Times Magazine*, May 16, 1948, p. 11.
4. Clark, *Guideposts*, p. 178.
5. Division of Labor Standards, U.S. Department of Labor, *The President's National Labor-Management Conference, November 5–30, 1945*, Bulletin no. 77, 1946, pp. 29, 53–56.
6. William Serrin, *The Company and the Union* (New York, 1973), p. 265; Clayton W. Fountain, *Union Guy* (New York, 1949), p. 172.
7. Clinton S. Golden and Harold J. Ruttenberg, *The Dynamics of Industrial Democracy* (New York, 1942), p. 330.
8. Everett M. Kassalow, "New Patterns of Collective Bargaining," in Richard Lester and Joseph Shister, eds., *Insights into Labor Issues* (New York, 1948), pp. 120–23; E. Wight Bakke, *Mutual Survival* (New York, 1946), p. 42; Sumner H. Slichter, "Profits in a Laboristic Society," *Harvard Business Review* 27 (May 1949): 346.
9. Bakke, *Mutual Survival*, p. 7.
10. Neil W. Chamberlain, *The Union Challenge to Management* (New York, 1948), ch. 4; NAM, "Preserving the Management Functions," reprinted in E. Wight Bakke, ed., *Unions, Management and the Public* (New York, 1960), p. 216; Bakke, *Mutual Survival*, pp. 7, 29.

11. James J. Bambrick and Wade Shurtleff, *Foremanship under Unionism* (Chicago, 1952), pp. 84–85; *Labor-Management Conference,* p. 59; Charles Larrowe, "A Meteor on the Horizon: The Foremen's Association of America," *Labor History* 2 (Fall 1961): 259. The preceding two paragraphs rely substantially on Nelson Lichtenstein, "Wildcats in the UAW: Their Ebb and Flow, 1937–1945" (Paper delivered at the Pacific Coast Branch, American Historical Association, August 1978).

12. Chamberlain, *Union Challenge,* pp. 41, 79, 271.

13. Frederick W. Harbison and Robert Dubin, *Patterns of Union-Management Relations* (Chicago, 1947), p. 57; Chamberlain, *Union Challenge,* pp. 2, 5.

14. Sumner H. Slichter, James J. Healy, and E. Robert Livernash, *The Impact of Collective Bargaining on Management* (Washington, 1960), pp. 666–69, 678–79, 947, 952, 959, 960.

15. Ibid., pp. 11–12.

16. Barton Bernstein, "The GM Strike of 1945–46," *Michigan History* 49 (September 1965): 277; Colston E. Warne, ed., *Labor in Postwar America* (Brooklyn, N.Y., 1949), pp. 409, 412; *Monthly Labor Review* 67 (July 1948): 1–5, and 71 (August 1950): 218–24.

17. Harbison and Dubin, *Patterns,* pp. 45–51; H. W. Anderson, *Today's Job in Labor Relations* (pamphlet: speech delivered before Pacific Northwest Personnel Management Association, November 4, 1949).

18. This idea was first suggested to me by Howell John Harris in his dissertation prospectus, "Getting Everybody Back on the Same Team: An Interpretation of the Industrial Relations Policies of American Business in the 1940s."

19. Herbert Northrup, *Boulwarism* (Ann Arbor, Mich., 1964), *passim.*

20. Robert Ozanne, *A Century of Labor-Management Relations at International Harvester* (Madison, Wis., 1967), pp. 208–13.

21. Frederick H. Harbison and King Carr, *Libbey-Owens-Ford . . . A Case Study,* National Planning Association, Causes of Industrial Peace, Case Studies 2 (Washington, 1948), p. 28; Harbison and John R. Coleman, *Working Harmony in Eighteen Companies: A Case Study,* Ibid., Case Studies 13 (Washington, 1953), p. 42: Clinton S. Golden and Virginia D. Parker, eds., *Causes of Industrial Peace Under Collective Bargaining* (New York, 1955), pp. 35, 40–41.

22. Serrin, *Company and Union,* p. 156.

23. Ibid., p. 161.

24. William M. MacDonald, *Collective Bargaining in the Automobile Industry* (New Haven, 1963), pp. 262–66.

25. Bakke, *Mutual Survival,* p. 61.

26. Ronald Schatz, "American Electrical Workers: Work, Struggles, Aspirations, 1930–1950" (Ph.D. diss., University of Pittsburgh, 1977), p. 216, and ch. 6, *passim.*

27. *Monthly Labor Review* 68 (May 1949): 608, (February 1949): 194–98, 71 (December 1950): 759–61, 83 (December 1960): 1360; Henry Brandon, "A Conversation with Walter Reuther," in Charles M. Rehmus and Doris B. McLaughlin, eds., *Labor and American Politics* (Ann Arbor, Mich., 1967), p. 441.

28. The Bureau of Labor Statistics, for example, reported that for the first six months of 1956, three out of four agreements liberalized one or more of their supplementary benefits. Harold M. Levinson, *Collective Bargaining in the Steel Industry* (Ann Arbor, Mich., 1962), p. 72.

29. Murray (1947), quoted, Abraham Weiss, "Union Welfare Plans," in Hardman and Neufeld, eds., *House of Labor,* pp. 284–85.

30. Quoted, Slichter, Healy and Livernash, *Impact of Collective Bargaining*, p. 458 (my ital.).
31. Ibid., pp. 448, 453.
32. MacDonald, *Collective Bargaining in the Automobile Industry*, p. 284.
33. David Levinson, "The Westinghouse Strike, 1955-56," *Labor Law Journal* 7 (September 1956): 543-51; Schatz, "American Electrical Workers," pp. 156-57.
34. David J. McDonald, *Union Man* (New York, 1969), ch. 20, and pp. 292-93; Garth L. Mangum, "Interaction of Central Administration and Contract Negotiation . . . in Steel," *Labor Law Journal* 12 (September 1961): 846-60.
35. Richard Betheil, "The ENA in Perspective: The Transformation of Collective Bargaining in the Basic Steel Industry," *Review of Radical Political Economics* 10 (Summer 1978): 6-16; Jack Stieber, "Work Rules in Manufacturing," *Proceedings of the Industrial Relations Research Association*, 1961, pp. 401-11.
36. McDonald, *Union Man*, p. 267.
37. William F. Whyte, *Patterns of Industrial Peace* (New York, 1951), pp. 27, 32-51.
38. *Monthly Labor Review* 60 (May 1945): 959, 961; Lichtenstein, "Wildcat Strikes in the UAW," p. 13.
39. Mangum, "Interaction of Central Administration," p. 852.
40. Nelson Lichtenstein, "Auto Worker Militancy and the Structure of Factory Life, 1933-55" (Paper read at the meeting of the Organization of American Historians, April 1979), pp. 18-19.
41. Whyte, *Patterns of Industrial Peace*, pp. 104-105.
42. Warne, ed., *Labor in Postwar America*, pp. 34-35.
43. Lloyd Ulman, *The Government of the Steelworkers Union* (New York, 1962), pp. 52-53.
44. *UAW-Ford Agreement* (1949), pp. 15, 89, and (1961), pp. 21-22.
45. B. J. Widick, *Auto-Work and Its Discontents* (Baltimore, 1976), p. 9.
46. Ozanne, *A Century of Labor-Management Relations*, pp. 208 ff.
47. Bureau of National Affairs, *What's New in Collective Bargaining*, October 28, 1949, pp. 1-2.
48. James W. Kuhn, *Bargaining in Grievance Settlement: The Power of Industrial Work Groups* (New York, 1961), pp. 50-57, and, for a guide to the contemporary scholarship, note 9, p. 193. The BLS began to maintain records on strikes during contract periods only in the 1960s, so Kuhn relied on short-strike statistics for an indication of the fluctuation of wildcat stoppages during the 1950s. Kuhn found "no long-term decline" in these figures and argued that the lower incidence of brief stoppages in the second half of the decade was reflective of the employment cycle. Ibid., pp. 54-55. However, if one follows the series into the 1960s, it becomes clear that the drop in the number of such strikes and strikers during the 1950s represented a longer term decline in the incidence of short strikes. See Jack Stieber, "Grievance Arbitration in the United States," in Royal Commission on Trade Unions and Employers' Associations, *Research Papers 8: Three Studies in Collective Bargaining* (London, 1968), Table I, p. 24. Data on unauthorized stoppages compiled by General Motors, Chrysler, and the major rubber firms likewise indicates a long-term drop during the 1950s. I am indebted to Sean Flaherty and Charles Jesceck for making this data available to me.
49. See, e.g., Stanley B. Mathewson, *Restriction of Output among Unorganized Workers* (New York, 1931).
50. Kuhn, *Bargaining in Grievance Settlement*, pp. 147-66.
51. Ibid., ch. 4.

52. See, e.g., J.F.B. Goodman and T. G. Whittingham, *Shop Stewards in British Industry* (Maidenhead, Berkshire, England, 1969).

53. Harbison and Carr, *Libbey-Owens-Ford,* pp. 28–29; Harbison and Coleman, *Working Harmony in Eighteen Companies,* pp. 38–40.

54. George Strauss, "The Shifting Power Balance in the Plant," *Industrial Relations* 1 (May 1962): 65–96.

55. David Lewin, "The Impact of Unionism on American Business: Evidence for an Assessment," *Columbia Journal of World Business* 13 (Winter 1978): 89–103. It need hardly be pointed out, however, that the workplace rule of law was not the only means of containing shop-floor activity. An employer might attack the problem directly by rearranging work processes, by introducing new technology, and by using a variety of industrial-relations techniques designed to foster good feelings and to thwart the formation of strong work groups. The current resurgence of open-shop sentiment in American industry may well stem partly from a rising confidence in the ability to control workers in a "union-free environment."

56. *Monthly Labor Review* 92 (July 1969): 22.

57. U.S. Bureau of Labor Statistics, *Analysis of Work Stoppages,* Bulletin #1339 [1961],.p. 9, #1687 [1969], p. 17. Company data, referred to in Note 48, also indicate a rise in unauthorized strikes in the late 1960s.

56. *Monthly Labor Review* 92 (July 1969): 22.

57. Ibid., p. 23.

58. Strauss, "The Shifting Power Balance," p. 90.

59. Victor Reuther, *The Brothers Reuther* (Boston, 1976), pp. 304, 320–21. In its negotiation with Chrysler in 1976, the UAW actually demanded two seats on the board of directors. The bid failed, amid widespread expressions of disapproval both from other unions and from industry generally. But three years later, on the verge of bankruptcy, Chrysler offered the union one seat as part of an emergency package of concessions to help the firm through its troubles. *New York Times,* May 13, June 27, November 15, 1976; *Newsweek,* November 5, 1979, p. 82.

6
The Uses of Power II:
Political Action

Political action, like collective bargaining, held out seemingly boundless opportunity for the exertion of labor's power at the close of World War II. It did not appear beyond reason to anticipate a role comparable to that played by the labor movement in British political life. In the end, the American unions settled for a good deal less. As in the industrial sector, they accommodated themselves to a secondary place, functioning to far greater effect than had been permitted the old AFL, but so confined as to foreclose a dominant part in the political system. The comparable outcomes were not accidental. Insofar as it was its own master, insofar as the labor movement had choices to make, the course it took in both political action and collective bargaining derived from a common intellectual heritage deeply rooted in the American trade-union past.

Only the breaks with that past held people's attention at the outset. During the 1940s, labor's public concerns broadened dramatically. What had characterized voluntarism had been not so much the exclusion of politics—an impossibility, Gompers well knew—as an insistence on holding labor's political concerns to those issues immediately relevant to trade unions and their memberships. This explained the heavy trade-union involvement in local political life even at the height of voluntarist sentiment in the AFL. As labor's concerns fell more and more within the orbit of Congress, the AFL stepped up its activity in national politics. From the Bill of Grievances of 1906 to the furious lobbying for the Wagner Act in 1935, there ran a continuing thrust of interest-group politicking that in no wise lessened in intensity after the New Deal. But, starting in the 1930s, the labor movement began to concern itself with a broader range of social issues. "It is a new departure," Philip Murray proclaimed in 1944, "for American labor to lead . . . a national movement devoted to the general welfare just as much as to the particular interests of labor groups."[1]

The sources of this transformation, never wholly articulated, derived partly from the discovery in the Great Depression that labor's well-being could not be insulated from the healthy functioning of the larger society, partly from the strong identification with the New Deal, partly from the infusion of radicals and progressive intellectuals, partly from the very explosion of numbers and resources that obligated organized labor to look beyond its narrow interests. In Detroit during the early 1940s, the UAW championed the cause of blacks on housing and police brutality and forged a durable political alliance with a black community hitherto deeply distrustful of the labor movement. In their account of this, August Meier and Elliott Rudwick offer a provocative compensatory explanation: it was easier to fight for civil rights in public than it was to guarantee black auto workers equal treatment in the plants or even inside the UAW.[2] Clearly, in any case, labor's impulse to adopt the cause of the common man as its own was deeply felt, and not only in the CIO, but, if somewhat more belatedly and moderately, in the AFL as well.

The labor movement attached itself to the welfare-state program enunciated by wartime progressives and fervently articulated by Vice President Henry Wallace. Their agenda took form in President Roosevelt's Economic Bill of Rights (January 1944), which elevated basic security to the status of human rights and expanded the scope of those rights beyond income to include health, education, and housing. Pushing past FDR's generalities, the progressives advocated national planning on the one hand, and, on the other, an economic policy designed to assure full employment. "When the war is over we will have a people anxious to have jobs for all," pronounced the CIO. "What we must not lack is a plan to keep our industries going full blast, and a president and a Congress who will assume the responsibility for all the people's needs."[3]

Larger purposes perforce expanded labor's political activity. It was no longer enough to circulate a list of labor's friends and labor's enemies, and leave it to union people as voters to do their duty. In 1936, Labor's Non-Partisan League—mainly CIO, but with some AFL support—had shown what could be done to raise money and get out the vote for FDR. The LNPL, however, fell victim to internecine warfare, immobilized while John L. Lewis and FDR quarreled, and then carried off by Lewis when he quit the CIO. The disastrous congressional election of 1942—by the estimate of a CIO lobbyist, only a quarter of the new House could be considered friendly—and the passage of the antilabor Smith-Connally War Labor Disputes Act of 1943 over Roosevelt's veto convinced the CIO of the need for a more concerted effort.[4] The Political Action Committee, headed by Sidney Hillman, did yeoman work in the election of 1944. Fourteen regional offices covered the country, an organizational network went down to the precinct level in areas of labor strength, and the field staff of the major industrial unions devoted the better part of their time to political work in the final months of the campaign. Altogether, the PAC and its nonlabor satellite, the National Citizens-PAC, raised nearly $1.4 million. Made a permanent arm of the CIO midway through the campaign, the PAC signified the new importance attached to political involvement by the industrial-union wing of the labor movement. Forced to the same conclusion by the passage of the Taft-Hartley Act in 1947, the AFL set up its own Labor's League for Political Education, and in the 1948 election nearly matched the political expenditure of the CIO.

But what role would organized labor take in American politics? The question did not especially trouble the AFL. To step up the Federation's political activity, said Secretary-Treasurer George Meany, was "by no means a departure from the old political philosophy of the A.F. of L. of 'defeating your enemies and rewarding your friends'. . . . That policy is just as valid today as when it was initiated many years ago by Samuel Gompers." It was true that, of all political approaches, nonpartisanship was most likely to end in inactivity, since it eschewed any formal connection with other political structures and did not necessarily call for a continuing organization (the AFL had never maintained a political department or staff prior to the LLPE). But, with a strong impetus behind it, a nonpartisan stance had much to recommend it, both by fostering progressive candidacies and, no less important, by strengthening labor's bargaining power with the two parties. Moreover, nonpartisanship was deeply rooted in trade-union thinking, and by no means only in the AFL. The desire for an independent identity and the suspicion of entangling ties stirred CIO industrial unionists as well. "Speaking for myself individually," burst out Philip Murray in 1943, "I am not in a state of mind . . . to say to the Democratic Party, to any other party, 'Here we are, meek and humble of spirit, prepared to give our bodies and our souls in a state of abject surrender!'"⁵ In point of fact, the CIO-PAC always formally espoused nonpartisanship, and the underlying sentiment would make itself felt persistently on labor's participation in American public life.

Yet the political environment grew ever more inhospitable to genuine nonpartisanship. The rough equivalence between the two major parties—Gomper's central premise—no longer held true. The labor vote, once substantially shared by the two parties, had shifted heavily into the Democratic column since the Wilsonian years. And so had the labor proclivity of the Democratic party, demonstrably so under Al Smith during the 1920s, and then in a quantum leap under the New Deal. Nonpartisanship had also assumed the modesty of labor's political goals. The AFL's activism did not threaten its older philosophy, George Meany said, because its efforts were prompted not by interest in "running the country but for the purpose of protecting ourselves."[6] As the scope of labor's public concerns expanded, however, so did its incapacity for treating the parties evenhandedly. When the progressive Republican Wayne Morse pleaded for union support for the liberal wings of both parties, Walter Reuther answered "that in that case no party will ever have the clear-cut policy and the leadership to translate and implement policy, *because the power of the party will be diluted on basic questions*."[7]

From the outset, the planners of the CIO-PAC saw its actual mission to be the advancement of the Democratic party. It was idle to "pretend that there is the slightest possibility of our achieving genuine influence in the Republican Party. . . . We recommend that work be carried out largely within the Democratic Party."[8] In practice, in spite of a formally nonpartisan position, this meant that whenever there was a viable Democratic candidate, he could normally count on PAC support, irrespective of the merits of his opponent. It was Democratic partiality that helped explain the defeat of so tried and true a friend as Wisconsin's Senator Robert LaFollete, Jr. in 1946, and that later forced Wayne Morse into the Democratic party. The figure of FDR, the enthusiasm for the New Deal, carried the CIO comparatively easily along this course. But the underlying logic pushed the AFL in the same direction. The Federation had always drawn the line on presidential endorsements, tantamount in its view to party endorsements. In 1952 this symbol of nonpartisanship finally fell: the AFL came out for Adlai Stevenson.

Cutting athwart the *de facto* Democratic connection stood an altogether different brand of labor partisanship. From the start, the rise of the CIO had stirred old dreams of an independent party, building from the militant industrial unions into a broad-based political movement of workers, farmers, and others (such as the groups John L. Lewis addressed in the first half of 1940 when he was actively thinking about a third party—the National Youth Congress, the NAACP, the American Negro Congress, the Townsend Old Age Movement).

World War II revived third-party enthusiasms, partly in reaction to the rightward drift of wartime politics, partly as the political expression of rank-and-file militancy in the industrial unions. In New York, the American Labor party, which had been created in 1936 by the CIO to corral the large socialist vote for FDR, declared its independence of the Democratic party by fielding its own gubernatorial candidate in the 1942 race. In July 1943, the ALP sponsored a trade-union conference that endorsed efforts "to organize labor's forces independently on the political field." In Michigan, where the CIO had come out for an independent third party, Detroit auto unionists the following March formed the Michigan Commonwealth Federation modeled on the Canadian Commonwealth Federation across the border in Ontario. The significance of this insurgency, which spread to several other industrial states and involved important elements of the garment trades, textiles, and the UAW, could be measured by the response of the labor supporters of the Democratic party. In his autobiography, David McDonald actually suggested that the Political Action Committee was started so as to head off third-party activity. If that exaggerates the challenge, certainly the PAC did wholly dissociate itself from labor-party sentiment and, as Philip Murray said, "discourage every move in that direction." A good deal of its energy was expended in stamping out such political insurgency before the 1944 campaign got well underway. FDR's victory, said the CIO afterward, confirmed "the correctness of our decision. . . . We reaffirm that decision and reject any and all proposals for a third party."[9]

When the sociologist E. Wright Mills surveyed labor leaders in 1946, he discovered a telling discrepancy in their thinking about a new labor party. Asked if they would favor such a move within two or three years, 23 per cent of CIO officials and 13 per cent of AFL officials said yes. Ten years hence? The positive responses leaped to 52 per cent for CIO, 23 per cent for AFL. And for CIO national officers—the key group— the shift went from 8 per cent to a remarkable 65 per cent.[10] What this signified was the intractable political dilemma confronting the labor movement. On the one hand, the idea of a labor party evoked much sympathy. Indeed, for all its unrelenting opposition, the PAC came back regularly to the issue. The original planners did not preclude "consideration of the need of a new labor party later on." And, on first announcing the start of the PAC, Sidney Hillman expressed opposition "to the formation of a third party *at this time*." On the other hand, an independent effort seemed sure to cost the labor movement heavily in the short run. Murray put the standard argument before the 1944 election: "A third party would only serve to divide labor and progressive forces, resulting in the election of political enemies."[11]

Might the time ever come when organized labor would pay that price for the sake of laying the basis of a new party? Not, surely, while FDR lived. Not even the wartime advocates of a third party had opposed his re-election for a fourth term; the state parties they wanted to form independent of the Democratic organization would support FDR on a national ticket. His hold remained firm until the end, notwithstanding the absence of any reward for labor's unstinting help in the 1944 election. Not only did Roosevelt make no move to moderate the hated Little Steel wage-freeze formula, but he also came out in January 1945 for a national service law bitterly opposed by labor, and this time without the linkage to a progressive tax program that earlier had offered at least the semblance of equal sacrifice. With the passing in April 1945 of the

"Champion," as the CIO sorrowfully eulogized him, that binding tie to the Democratic party dissolved.

Harry Truman was no Roosevelt. It was true that FDR and his party lieutenants had so skillfully managed the vice-presidential race at the 1944 convention, in part by the manufacture of a false boom for the conservative Senator James F. Byrnes, in part by the clever deployment of the loyal Hillman, as to secure the reluctant assent of the CIO for dumping Vice President Henry Wallace.[12] It was true also that Harry Truman made an earnest effort to take up the mantle of Roosevelt's Economic Bill of Rights. But labor's initial warmth soon cooled. For one thing, Truman's reconversion program proved almost a total loss. With Truman's failure to establish his authority over his congressional party, the conservative coalition re-emerged stronger than ever. One by one, his postwar proposals foundered: tax reform, national unemployment insurance, a higher minimum wage, a genuine full employment bill, effective price control. Truman's legislative ineptness was bad enough, but his heavy-handed reaction to the postwar strike wave bothered unions even more. In December 1945 his proposal for fact-finding boards and cooling-off periods (during which strikes would be illegal) provoked a bitter reaction from Philip Murray, who accused the president of betraying the New Deal. When a nationwide railroad strike broke out in May 1946, Truman called for sweeping powers authorizing the government to seize vital industries, to draft strikers who refused to return to work, and to fine and imprison uncooperative union leaders. Every segment of the labor movement condemned Truman. President A. F. Whitney of the Railway Trainmen characterized his proposal as "of the warp and woof of fascism" and pledged every penny in his union's treasury to defeat Truman in 1948.[13]

If ever labor's normal political calculations seemed inoperable, it was in this turbulent reconversion period. "The time is now ripe for labor to divorce itself from the two old parties and resolve to build the base for an independent, indigenous national party," proclaimed Victor Reuther in December 1945. On September 20, 1946, Truman sacked that New Deal symbol Henry Wallace from the cabinet. The next week, three hundred CIO delegates and assorted allies condemned the administration at a Chicago Conference of Progressives. The upshot was the formation in December 1946 of the Progressive Citizens of America, which specifically warned that "if the Democratic party woos privilege and betrays the people it will die and deserve to die. We cannot therefore rule out the possibility of a new political party."[14]

That threat did materialize. The PCA evolved during 1947 into a third party. With Henry Wallace as its standard-bearer, the Progressive party mounted a challenge comparable in the scope of its effort to the Progressive party of 1924 and the Populist party of the 1890s. But the Wallace movement did not become the vehicle of organized labor. On the contrary, it wedded trade unionism to the two-party system. The injury done in 1947–48 to a new labor politics was devastating and irreparable.

The coming of the Cold War had produced a fundamental realignment of liberal forces in the country. On the one side stood the PCA, which gathered in all those elements that blamed the United States for the breakdown of the Grand Alliance. On the other side, the Americans for Democratic Action carried on the anticommunism that its predecessor, the Union for Democratic Action, had stubbornly sustained against the popular-front tide of the war years. "We reject any association with Communists or sympathizers with communism in the United States," proclaimed the ADA, defining thereby what it conceived to be the fundamental divergence from the PCA.[15] On foreign policy, the ADA moved from considerable ambivalence to outright support for the Truman administration, particularly after the Marshall Plan, with its promise of massive economic aid for shattered Europe, lent a New Deal cast to the strategy of containment. There was little to choose between on domestic reform. Both PCA and ADA proclaimed themselves the inheritors of the New Deal, although campaign exigencies did evoke from the Wallace group a more radical rhetoric. Their positions were, in any case, close enough so as to preclude among ADA adherents any sense of sacrifice of reform principles for the sake of foreign policy and anticommunism. The final distinction between these emergent configurations, crucial to the future of labor politics, touched the question of political alignments: it was the PCA that captured the third-party impulse, and the ADA that firmly identified itself with the fortunes of the Democratic party.

A remarkable redeployment of forces took place on this new political terrain. Among the first labor adherents of the ADA, indeed founding members, were David Dubinsky of the AFL's International Ladies Garment Workers Union, Emil Rieve of the CIO Textile Workers Union, and Walter Reuther. Up to this point, these three had formed the heart of third-party activity within the labor movement.

No less compelling a sign of the unsettling impact of the Cold War was the countermarch of the popular-front elements. During the war, the Roosevelt administration had found no more avid boosters than the Communists, both in the CIO-PAC and in its auxiliary middle-class bodies. To advance the fortunes of the Democratic party, this "left" wing (it was a sign of the confusion of the times that the advocates of independent politics, social reform, and militant trade unionism were dubbed the "right" within the wartime CIO) had not been above supporting Tammany candidates in New York and the corrupt Hague machine in New Jersey. And, by the same token, the popular fronters took a leading part in the PAC campaign against third-party activity in 1943–44, teaming up with Sidney Hillman to capture Dubinsky's American Labor party in New York, pushing the Farmer-Labor party to merge with the Democrats in Minnesota, and, in general, furiously branding as divisive and unpatriotic the least sign of third-party sentiment. This notion, however, appeared in a quite different light with the onset of the Cold War, and with the transformation of President Truman into a warmonger. It was these erstwhile popular fronters who led the way into the Progressive Citizens of America.

As for the main CIO party, answerable to Philip Murray, it initially went along with its wartime allies on the left, more out of animus against Truman's domestic performance than from any disagreement with his foreign policy. The disastrous congressional elections of 1946, which gave the Republicans control of both houses and demonstrated the high political toll for any further association with the left, caused the CIO to beat a hasty retreat. Having thus been burned, Murray's first impulse was to pull back to a safe neutrality applying impartially to both the PCA and the ADA. But as the PCA became a third party with the potential for handing the Republicans victory in 1948, and as the ADA established itself as the voice of the new anticommunist liberal consensus, the force of events pushed Murray into the ADA camp. For the first time, the CIO committed itself to the kind of close, functional relationship with others on which a new labor-liberal politics might have been built. Only this activity was devoted, not to a third party, but to the re-election of Harry Truman.

Inside the CIO, political issues merged with a growing crisis over the Communists. They had figured prominently in the affairs of the CIO from the outset. Philip Murray, like John L. Lewis before him, had accepted the Communists for the potent contribution they were making to the industrial-union movement, careful to control them within the CIO national office (and in his own Steelworkers Union), but leaving them free to make their way in the affiliated unions. At the close of World War II, Communists led 14 of 31 CIO international unions (representing, however, only 15 per cent of the total CIO membership) and shared or contested for power in half the others. At the 1946 convention, the left wing commanded nearly a third of the delegate strength.[16] By then, however, Communism had become an explosive internal issue, setting off bitter factional battles in some unions and, everywhere, dividing the entire movement over Cold War policy and, more ominously, over questions of loyalty and patriotism. A devout Catholic under pressure from the anticommunist Association of Catholic Trade Unionists, Murray himself was demonstrably losing patience. At his instigation, the 1946 convention adopted a resolution condemning "efforts of the Communist Party or other political parties and their adherents to interfere in the affairs of the CIO."[17] A new constitutional amendment prohibited state and city bodies—many of them Communist strong points—from taking positions in conflict with CIO policy or from associating with organizations not recognized by the CIO. The autonomy principle prevented this rule from being applied to the international unions. In any case, however, the Communists were hunkering down: they themselves voted for the resolution denouncing Communist interference in the CIO.

The third-party issue brought the crisis to a head. After the 1946 Republican victories, Congress passed the Taft-Hartley Act, which the labor movement universally condemned at the time as a punitive attack on its basic rights. Truman's veto, notwithstanding that it had been overridden, reminded trade-unionists again of the value of a friend in the White House: Taft-Hartley would have been a good deal harsher but for the need of its proponents for moderate votes in anticipation of Truman's veto. Taft-Hartley brought the labor movement sharply back to earth. If the hated law was to be repealed, the Democrats would have to win in 1948. Taft-Hartley also went a long way toward restoring Truman's credit with labor. For his part, Truman began to rebuild his bridges to the movement, and to reassert his commitment to liberal reform. If the unions would have preferred someone else (at one point, the CIO-PAC wanted to draft General Eisenhower), they settled for Truman. In the end, he had the support of virtually every labor leader save John L. Lewis, even of so bitter a critic as the Trainmen's A. F. Whitney.

At the executive board meeting in January 1948, the CIO threw down the gauntlet to the Communists: a vote of 33 to 13 condemned the Wallace candidacy. By then, however, after many months of indecision, the Communists had committed themselves to the Progressive party. While trade-union Communists had not normally submitted themselves to regular party discipline, still less sympathizers, on this particular issue, invested with the moral weight of war and peace and publicly defined as it was, CIO left wingers had little choice but to take a stand (or, as with Mike Quill of the Transit Workers, defect). In fact, the Wallace campaign received only halfhearted support from the CIO left, in many instances not even the official endorsement of unions led by Communists. This was not enough for the CIO administration. With Truman unexpectedly victorious, and with the internal power balance swinging decisively to the right, the CIO moved against the Communists. The 1948 election had become a test of loyalties. "Are they going to be loyal to the CIO or loyal to the Communist Party?" asked Walter Reuther. To support Wallace meant putting political purposes before concrete trade-union needs. This was the unpardonable violation that led to the expulsion of the Communist-led unions in 1949.

The Communist presence had long inhibited the third-party impulse within the CIO, partly by fragmenting the natural constituency on the left, even more by a basic disregard for the sources of that impulse. But the very events that eliminated the Communists as spoilers also burned out the roots of an independent labor politics. At its convention immediately following the 1948 election, the CIO reaffirmed its "nonpartisan policy" of supporting "the progressive forces in both major parties" and rejecting a third party as divisive of those forces in "the interest of reaction." The only opposition came from the doomed Communists.[18]

Unobserved, meanwhile, the Cold War was drawing the noncommunist unions into a functional relationship with the federal government. The AFL had, in fact, carried on its own

Cold War while Washington had still been celebrating the Grand Alliance. With the fighting still on in Europe, the Federation had been making ready, raising funds and setting up a special staff to aid in the "reestablishment of powerful free and democratic [European] trade unions" that would be resistant to Communist domination.[19] A key man in this AFL effort, amidst its unimpeachable pure-and-simple unionists, was David Dubinsky, leader of the third-party movement in New York, and in some ways the dominant figure in the political insurgency of the war period. (One of his aides, Jay Lovestone, became the chief strategist of the AFL's international program.) The CIO, on the other hand, had willingly joined with the British Trade Union Congress, along with European Communists and Soviet organizations, to establish the World Federation of Trade Unions in 1945. The build-up of international tensions, especially over the Marshall Plan, brought the CIO into increasing conflict with the Communists. By 1948, the CIO was working side by side with the AFL to foster European trade-union participation in economic recovery programs, and the next year the American rivals joined together to help set up the International Confederation of Free Trade Unions in opposition to the Communist-dominated WFTU.

This international involvement did more than color labor's perception of domestic politics. To carry on their work in Europe (and later in the Third World), the American unions needed the resources and cooperation of the government, and it in turn quickly discovered in the unions effective instruments of American foreign policy. An interlocking relationship developed that grew more intimate during the 1950s.[20] Beyond union resolutions of support for cold-war policy, these working ties deeply inhibited any impulse toward independent labor politics.

A durable consensus emerged within the CIO that increasingly encompassed the AFL as well. As the rivals drew closer together in the early 1950s, labor's political future settled on a fixed course. The merger of the AFL and CIO in 1955, and the combining of their political forces in the Committee on Political Education (COPE), marked an irrevocable commitment to the two-party system.

In his more reflective moments, Franklin D. Roosevelt had been known to dwell on an inevitable realignment of the major parties. This expectation exerted a potent reconciling influence on the new generation of labor progressives. "We felt that instead of trying to create a third party—a labor party," Walter Reuther told a British journalist in 1960, ". . . that we ought to bring about a realignment and get the liberal forces in one party and the conservatives in another." Nor was there any doubt, despite the official obeisance to nonpartisanship, who would carry labor's banner. "The Democratic Party adopts a good policy, a good program at every convention—just as advanced as the Labour Party," Reuther continued. "But . . . when the party gets power, because it's 'all things to all men,' it lacks the internal discipline to translate party platform into specific legislation. . . ."[21] Thus from the postwar crisis arose the political purpose of the modern labor movement: to complete the transformation begun by the New Deal and make the Democrats the genuine party of the common man in America.

Formidable resources were brought to that task. Building on the foundations of CIO-PAC and AFL-LLPE, the AFL-CIO's Committee on Political Education operated on a nationwide basis paralleling the country's political structure. In highly unionized areas, it was organized down to the precinct level. COPE was capable of mobilizing large numbers of volunteers for campaign work—191,000 in the week before the election of 1968, for example. In fact, however, a high degree of professionalism characterized its work: full-time directors not only for the states, but also for principal cities and even some congressional districts; a heavy reliance on union staffers and organizers to assume political duties during campaign months; an apparatus always in place and ready to go; and a sophisticated technical capacity (when the NAM once wanted to put out a get-out-the-vote manual, it reprinted COPE's). Beyond its campaign support, the labor movement became the most reliable source of funds for Democratic candidates, providing as much as two-thirds of the money in a heavily unionized state such as Michigan, and roughly 25 per cent nationally. In 1968, unions contributed a record $7.6 million to the Democratic campaign.[22] Congressional efforts to curb this activity caused certain bookkeeping distinctions and forced a greater reliance on fundraising than otherwise might have happened—since union dues could not go directly to candidates—but did not significantly inhibit the role of organized labor, in the words of one political scientist, "as the most important nation-wide electoral organization for the Democratic Party."[23]

The extent to which this contribution translated into party influence varied widely. In Detroit, where the UAW was very strong and the Democratic organization nearly moribund, the CIO-PAC moved in and virtually took over the party in 1948. In Chicago, on the other hand, the powerful Democratic organization operated on traditional machine lines and held the unions to a satellite role. However the balance was struck with the existing party organization, labor devoted its efforts persistently toward remaking the Democratic party along liberal lines.

In his seminal *Labor in American Politics* (1969), J. David Greenstone defined labor as "an organized constituency" of the Democratic party, that is, one that acted not solely as representative of a specific group, but more out of conern for the broader purposes and direction of the party. As the Solid South began to crack after World War II, for example, organized labor consistently encouraged party realignment, teaming up (not always with the approval of its members and local bodies) with civil-rights groups on behalf of liberal Democrats, and even tacitly supporting Republicans in preference to con-

servative Democrats. By 1965, 17 of 106 Southern congress-
men were Republicans, and 24 of the 89 Democrats were
moderately liberal or better (that is, they voted with COPE
half or more of the time). The erosion of the entrenched
Democratic wing, reflective as it was of a social and legal
revolution going on in the modern South, was testimony also
to labor's unremitting role as a liberalizing "constituent" within
the party. Nor was this function expressed only through the
selection of candidates. The unions also tried to activate
potential constituencies by registration drives in ghetto areas
and by fostering minority political leaders and organizations.
Perhaps most fully observed in the UAW-black coalition in
Detroit, such activities took place in urban areas across the
country. "Labor was acting more as the party's electoral arm
than as a separate pressure group," Professor Greenstone
pointed out, for it was helping "aggregate groups that are
much more completely in the *party's* political constituency
rather than in the ranks of union members themselves."[24]

The test of all this party effort, of course, resided in the
programmatic results. Labor's broad welfare-egalitarian goals
were given expression in union resolutions and in testimony
before the platform committees at party conventions. But, as
Reuther had remarked, it was one thing to write a good
platform, quite another to translate it into national policy.
Following the Democratic capture of the White House in
1960, and especially after President Kennedy's assassination
generated a popular mandate for congressional action, labor
came into its own as a legislative force. In a sphere carefully
separated from COPE, the AFL-CIO maintained formidable
lobbying capabilities: a Legislative Department headed by a
highly knowledgeable former congressman, an Industrial
Union Department which, under Walter Reuther, practiced
an aggressive social advocacy; the cooperation of the lobbyists of many affiliated (and sometimes, unaffiliated) international unions; and rich support facilities in research, publicity, and communications.

In two ways, the deployment of these resources went beyond ordinary pressure-group activities. First, the union effort generally occurred within a coalition of forces, with labor doing much of the initiating and organizing, and always shouldering the operational burden. In the successful campaign for Medicare, for example, unions helped build up the grass-roots organizations of the elderly, a labor official ran the umbrella National Council for Senior Citizens, and the crucial technical and financial backing came from the AFL-CIO. Without labor, said Greenstone, "the entire pro-Medicare campaign might never have attained the formidable level [it] reached in the mid–1960s."[25] Equally distinctive was the reliance on labor by the Democratic leadership on Capitol Hill and in the White House. In legislative battles on which party leaders could not exert strong direction, labor stepped in and took over some part of their role. This happened, for example, in the debates over job discrimination and the poll tax in the civil-rights bills of 1964 and 1965, and, to a fuller extent, in defense of the Supreme Court decision on reapportionment of state legislatures from rural-conservative attacks in 1961 and 1964–65.

On the whole, it could be argued, the AFL-CIO proved a better champion of the general welfare than of its own narrow interests. The unions made a mess of their effort to stave off labor-reform demands arising from the revelations of corruption and undemocratic practices in the McClellan hearings of 1957–58. On this kind of challenge, labor fell into disarray, lost its sure legislative touch, and exchanged the tone of high-minded social advocacy for an unyielding, often strident, opposition. The Landrum-Griffin bill that passed the House on August 14, 1959, was "the worst defeat for organized labor on Capitol Hill" since Taft-Hartley twelve years before; and, while the compromise version emerging from conference moderated especially the restraints on labor's economic powers, the union movement ended with regulatory legislation a good deal tougher than might have been the case had it played a wiser hand.[26] With the best of efforts, however, labor's activities as a pressure group differed fundamentally from its functions as social advocate. It was, in fact, the particular attribute of labor's participation in the Democratic party to be at once narrowly interested and broadly concerned. And if a choice had to be made?

In the course of the legislative work resulting in the Civil Rights Act of 1964, sentiment developed for a fair-employment section. To get through, the ban against job discrimination would have to apply to unions as well as employers. AFL-CIO President Meany could well have blocked union inclusion. Instead he supported it, thereby clearing the way for fundamental advance in the economic rights of minorities. Meany's choice did involve an element of ambivalence, since, as he publicly conceded, the AFL-CIO itself lacked the power to stop the discriminatory practices of affiliated unions.

There could, however, be no ambivalence about the hated right-to-work provision (Section 14b) of the Taft-Hartley Act. By 1965, nineteen states had passed laws prohibiting the union shop, and only the most determined efforts had staved off right-to-work laws in many other states. Organized labor desired no other objective so warmly as the elimination of Section 14b. In the wake of Lyndon Johnson's landslide victory of 1964, and with Johnson's pledge of support for repeal, the AFL-CIO launched a maximum lobbying effort in the eighty-ninth Congress. Twice a choice had to be made. The first was over President Johnson's request for a delay on 14b until after consideration of his Great Society program, thus increasing the vulnerability of right-to-work repeal to a Senate filibuster. The second was during the battle over reapportionment. Senator Everett Dirksen had authored a constitutional amendment diluting the Supreme Court decision. He was also slated to lead the filibuster against the repeal of 14b. The AFL-CIO could have bartered with Dirksen. On both occasions, organized labor put the larger interest before its own, and eventually lost right-to-work repeal to Dirksen's filibuster.[27]

The trade unions had forged a big place for themselves in American political life. They constituted, remarked the British political scientist Vivian Vale in 1971, "by far the largest and most stable body supporting liberal causes in the United States today."[28] Professor Greenstone characterized their role within the Democratic party as "a partial equivalence to the Social Democratic [formerly socialist] party-trade union alliance in much of Western Europe." That is, by pitching its political efforts to the broader party constituency rather than primarily to the narrow concerns of its own members, the labor movement was itself acting in an "aggregating" way "often thought to be a distinguishing attribute of major political parties in two-party systems." Greenstone, indeed, speculated in 1969 that American labor was on the verge of creating a new form of class politics, one pitting consumers, with labor as the core, against producers.[29]

In light of future events, it might have been more pertinent to ask: why did the labor movement so limit its role? For, if it was something more than an interest group, organized labor was something less than the controlling force within the Democratic party. And it was less by conscious and deliberate choice.

"The essential problem for the labor movement is to learn to work with a party without trying to capture it," Walter Reuther had said. In the same breath in which he identified the Democrats as America's liberal party, he specifically opposed "the labor movement trying to capture the Democratic Party."[30] Well, why not? Why should a union movement representing so enormous a bloc of voters and committed so genuinely to a broad program of political action not seek to "capture" the party of its choice?

Organized labor had paused even before the first step in

that direction. In the political crisis of 1947–48, the CIO had formally entered the ADA, taking seats on the governing board and contributing to its finances. Those official ties were broken after Truman's victory and never restored.[31] If organized labor did not relish an official place in the ADA, still less did it in the Democratic party. The representation that the TUC claimed in the British Labor Party, for example, was not desired by the AFL-CIO. Labor leaders were active in party affairs; upwards of three hundred might serve as delegates to the Democratic conventions. But they came as party people elected by the same processes as any other delegates, not as representatives sent by the labor movement. The fact was that the labor movement, for all its importance to the Democratic party, had no wish to share in matters of governance, either within the party or in its responsibilities in office (excepting perhaps over the Department of Labor, toward which the AFL-CIO asserted some proprietary claim).

This self-denial was grounded on quite basic historic assumptions. Organized labor still retained that progressive suspicion of party politics which, for better or worse, had shaped the American political reform tradition. As David Dubinsky once put it: "Labor must be in social politics, not in party politics."[32] This distancing from party rule, in point of fact, had much to recommend it in practice. By asserting its primary concern for issues, labor could engage in a highly productive division of duties with responsible Democratic leaders. Free of the constraints they faced in accommodating the party's right wing, at key moments union people acted in their stead to carry the progressive legislation of the eighty-ninth Congress. Labor's independence was not merely tactical, however. The suspicion of party went to more fundamental concerns that kept alive the formal adherence to nonpartisanship.

At its merger convention, the AFL-CIO "reaffirm[ed] labor's traditional policy of avoiding entangling alliances . . . and of supporting worthy candidates regardless of . . . party affiliation. . . . We seek neither to capture any organization *nor will we submit our identity to any group in any manner.*"³³ If nonpartisanship as Gompers had conceived it had long since gone, the underlying reasoning remained very much alive. The AFL-CIO, strong as it was, still felt Gompers's anxiety for asserting labor's separateness and independence. This in turn rested on labor's conception of how it was regarded by the larger American society, the final determinant of labor's maximum place in American politics.

"I think that at the point the labor movement captures the Democratic Party," Walter Reuther declared flatly, "you then destroy the broad base that is essential to translate sound policy into governmental action." The UAW itself acted on this premise. While the Michigan Democratic party was virtually taken over by the unions, the face it presented to the public was not unlike that of Democratic parties in other northern industrial states. And when the UAW did put forward labor candidates—in the Detroit mayoral races of 1943 and 1945, for example—they did badly. It all came down to the question of social class, Reuther told his English interviewer. The most the labor movement could aspire to in American politics was "to learn to work with a party without trying to capture it."³⁴

This was of a piece with labor's confined role in the industrial sector. No one, of course, would want to equate the modern UAW-GM contract with any union agreement of the pre-New Deal era, or the role of the AFL-CIO inside the Democratic party in 1968 with anything dreamt of by Samuel Gompers. It is the underlying perspective that carried on, the assumption that labor's place was inherently limited, that its sphere was necessarily circumscribed in the nation's industrial and political life. And, if one listened closely, Gompers's words could be heard echoing long decades after his death. "Our goals as trade unionists are modest," said George Meany the year of the merger, "for we do not seek to recast American society . . . we seek a rising standard of living." And in

1966: "The one word that best describes [the] day-to-day operation of the labor movement program is 'practical'. . . . We avoid preconceived notions, and we do not try to fit our program into some theoretical, all-embracing structure."[35] If the Walter Reuthers voiced a headier social rhetoric, if they grew restless under the burden of Meany's philosophy, in practice they adhered to the same trade-union precepts confining the power of the labor movement.

After World War II, organized labor had marked out for itself a political role that, in a fundamental sense, conformed to its historic notion of limits in American life. Midway through the 1960s, the wisdom of that choice could scarcely have seemed in doubt: it had made labor a force in the Democratic party and had yielded great advances in social policy under Kennedy and Johnson.

Just at that time, as it happened, I had begun to study the labor history of the New Deal era. I was especially struck by the general pessimism toward the labor movement at the start of the 1930s. Even the most knowledgeable of observers, I discovered, had written off the trade unions just as they were about to enter a period of dramatic revival. In a lecture at Johns Hopkins in early 1966, I proposed that this miscalculation really was suggestive of something basic about the labor movement. Having made a modest assessment of its place in the larger society, American trade unionism relied on its institutional resilience, its capacity for growth under favorable circumstances, for survival in adversity (if necessary, as in the 1920s, by a ruthless policy of retrenchment). The labor movement was thus, by definition, a responsive, not a shaping, force—"essentially a passive agent in relation to its surrounding environment." Back in the dark days of 1932, no one could have predicted its imminent upsurge because "the trigger was not in the labor movement, but in the larger environment."[36] That conclusion told me enough in 1966 to know that labor's current politics was predicated on the existence of a particular political environment. What I could not know was the extent to which that environment was about to change.

Vietnam shattered the cold-war consensus among American liberals. By 1968, there had been wholesale defections from President Johnson's prosecution of the war in Southeast Asia, and, thereafter, a broadening repudiation of the entire containment strategy that had endured for twenty years. Long after its middle-class allies had reversed course, the AFL-CIO supported the Vietnam war, after the Tet offensive of January 1968, even after the disastrous invasion of Cambodia in May 1970. Impelled by an abiding anticommunism, the AFL-CIO adhered to its cold-war stance in the face of the move toward detente with the Soviet Union in the early 1970s. Hardly less divisive were the host of cultural and generational issues that ranged union people against the liberal impulses of the Vietnam era. They were, on the whole, repelled by the assault on traditional values and institutions inspired by the antiwar and student movements. In an age enamored with environmental issues and increasingly suspicious of government, finally, not even welfare-state reforms any longer provided a firm bond between labor and other liberals. A touchstone to these changes could be found in the discussion draft of the New Democratic Coalition when it decided not to support Hubert Humphrey in the 1968 presidential campaign: organized labor, Humphrey's strongest backer, was written off as a satisfied and conservative force and the "present liberalism of the Democratic Party [as] stale and irrelevant." This animus the AFL-CIO heartily reciprocated. As the balance tipped decisively after the 1968 election, George Meany spoke scornfully of "the extremists . . . these so-called liberals or new lefts, or whatever you want to call them, [who] have taken over the Democratic Party." So appalled was the AFL-CIO by the nomination of George McGovern in 1972 that, in a historic reversal of policy, labor withheld its endorsement and sat out the election. The new liberals, warned an AFL-CIO spokesman afterward, "want to take over the Democratic party, even if it means throwing out the labor movement."[37]

The divisiveness of the Vietnam era undermined an essential premise of modern labor politics: namely, the existence of a core of issues that could rally a broad range of liberal agreement. A second premise, in some ways more fundamental to its aggregating role, was the ability of the labor movement to identify its political purposes with the general interest. In the years since the Great Society, organized labor has been pressed inexorably into the mold of an interest group.

Such, for example, has been the undoubted result of the inflationary spiral that began during the Vietnam War. It might have been otherwise under the stringent, comprehensive economic controls favored by the AFL-CIO (a political consideration that might well have recommended this policy to labor), but not under the program sprung on the nation by the Nixon administration in August 1971. Symptomatically, labor's loudest complaint was on the narrowest ground: the ninety-day wage freeze constituted an abrogation of union contracts scheduled to go into effect during that period. On the broader front, the laxness toward prices as compared to wages, the failure to include profits and dividends under the economic controls, cast organized labor in the role of the defender of the narrow interests of its own constituency. Nor has it been possible to escape this part, either in Washington or at the bargaining table, since the abandonment of the Nixon controls in 1974. If anything, the substitution of voluntary wage and price guidelines has served only to compound the dilemma of unions who, in order to do the best they can for their members, must stand in public defiance of pious pleas for restraint from the White House. A telling article appeared in the liberal *New Republic* in early 1979 caustically entitled "The New Feudalism." Its argument was that inflation had created an economic jungle which consumed the weak and fattened the organized and well-connected. Among the best-protected the *New Republic* ranked the trade unions.

It offered these facts in evidence: in the ten years since 1967, while living costs had more than doubled and the real income of many Americans had fallen, real average hourly earnings had advanced 33 per cent in steel, 23 per cent in auto.[38] In these corrosive times, the labor movement found increasing difficulty putting itself forward as the advocate of the public interest.

Nor was inflation alone in undermining labor's aggregating political role. A hallmark of its postwar liberalism had been its stand on trade policy. During the 1960s, foreign competition started to eat away at American markets, in 1971 capturing 70 per cent of radios and television sets, 35 per cent of apparel, nearly 20 per cent of steel, 15 per cent of automobiles. Estimating a loss of 900,000 jobs since 1966, the AFL-CIO in 1971 began to espouse the cause of protectionism.[39] Anxiety over jobs, in fact, ranged organized labor against a host of new liberal causes: federal funding for a supersonic transport, the building of nuclear-energy plants, pollution-control standards for industry, development versus the protection of the natural environment. It was not that individual unions had not always battled for laws advancing their narrow interests. What was new was the shift of the balance away from general-interest politics. To the extent that this was a response to economic forces, the political balance might swing again with an easing of inflationary pressures and a tightening of the job market, or possibly even through a re-evaluation of labor's interests in the new economy that was emerging in the 1970s. But in one respect a permanent change had occurred affecting labor's capacity to act as an aggregating force in American liberal politics.

The 1960s saw a remarkable trade-union penetration of the rapidly growing public sector. The extent of organization among public employees, not one in ten at the start of the decade, leaped to better than one in two by 1972. The giants of the labor movement now included the American Federation of Teachers, the American Federation of Government Employees, and the American Federation of State, County and Municipal Workers. No less significant was the transformation of such professional bodies as the National Education Association, the American Nurses Association, and the Assembly of Governmental Employees (a confederation of state associations) into collective-bargaining agencies, although not yet formally part of the labor movement. Of all the professional bodies, the NEA made the fullest transition to trade unionism, authorizing 122 strikes during the 1972–73 school year and acting in practice not a whit less militant than the rival AFT. Whatever else this phenomenon might mean for the future of American trade unionism, politically the immediate effect was to reinforce the perception of organized labor as a special-interest group. For the collective bargaining of public-employee unionism took place squarely in the public arena. In the era of ample public funding and rapid governmental expansion, the implications did not clearly emerge. But the tax revolt which hit with a vengeance during the later 1970s drove home the fact that, for public-employee unionism, political action was before anything else the way to increase the paycheck.

The force of these changes in turn attacked yet a third premise underlying labor's aggregating political role: the ability of the movement to speak with a common voice on basic public issues. United on foreign policy ever since the suppression of the Communist wing at the onset of the Cold War, organized labor split over Vietnam. When the ADA turned against the Johnson administration in March 1968, a number of leading labor members withdrew in protest, but nine, including Walter Reuther, favored its endorsement of Eugene McCarthy. Antiwar sentiment, although always in the minority, grew bolder as the Southeast Asian struggle went on and evolved into a dissident group broadly critical of the public stance of the AFL-CIO. The UAW disaffiliated in 1968, charging the Federation with blind adherence to cold-war politics and with "failing in the broad social responsibilities it has to the total community of America."[40] The UAW, even after the death of Reuther in an airplane crash in 1970, served as the rallying point for unions discontented with the intransigent leadership of George Meany. And this dis-affection propagated a political independence among the unions unknown in earlier years. The Federation's declaration of neutrality did not prevent considerable labor support from going to McGovern, even among central labor bodies con-stitutionally subject to official policy. When the Federation took a hands-off stance toward the Democratic caucuses and primaries four years later, nine dissident unions, six of them affiliates, coordinated their political activities through the Labor Clearinghouse Coalition entirely independent of the AFL-CIO.

The tensions of the Vietnam era had meanwhile reached down into the union rank-and-file. Capitalizing on the anxie-ties of white workers over the civil-rights revolution and the middle-class assault on traditional values, Alabama's George Wallace made heavy inroads in a number of northern in-dustrial states during the 1968 campaign. Only a massive union countereffort kept in check the labor vote for Wallace (who, despite his skill at exploiting working-class frustrations, was highly vulnerable to charges of reactionary social and labor policies in his own state). Even so, the episode left lingering doubts about the capacity of the union leadership to speak for its own members. The question resurfaced in later years especially over the costs of public-employee unionism. "The public workers have an extremely difficult problem," conceded a UAW leader. "A trade unionist will fight like hell to help raise wages at Ford—even though that may raise car prices—but he won't vote to increase property taxes to raise teacher salaries."[41] The strains on the solidarity between pri-vate and public workers could only grow worse in the tax-revolt atmosphere that produced the California referendum on Proposition 13 in June 1978. That vote to slash property taxes afforded, indeed, a classic instance in which the labor movement achieved a paper unity, only to be undercut by massive defections among the rank-and-file.

Labor's political disarray was, however, only partly caused by the changing nature of the issues. Within the political institutions, fundamental changes were also at work. The party structure itself was undergoing progressive deterioration in these years. Without some institutional weakening, as J. David Greenstone has noted, the unions could not have carved out their place within the Democratic party in the first place. But once inside, the interests of the labor movement lay in institutional stability. By the early 1970s, the Democratic party was no longer capable of meeting labor's expectations for a predictable return on its efforts as a partisan force.

In the wake of the turbulent Chicago convention of 1968, the Democratic party inaugurated sweeping internal reforms to "open up" participation in its national conventions: prohibiting the unit rule in the selection of state delegates; requiring that all delegates from nonprimary states be chosen by some kind of election; and directing state parties to take "affirmative steps" to assure representation of minorities, women, and young people "in reasonable relationship to their presence in the population of the State." Recognizing the likely impact, the AFL-CIO stood in unavailing opposition to the reform movement inside the Democratic party. By 1972, too, the proliferating state primaries were selecting a majority of the delegates to the national convention. Beyond these changes in formal procedures were the equally important advances in the techniques of campaign organization and media manipulation. With a personal organization staffed by professionals, highly skilled at packaging him for television, and capable of independent fund-raising (augmented by federal funding for presidential candidates), an outsider could capture a nomination and run successfully for office with little regard for the preferences of the established party leadership and with little support among the party cadre. From the mid–1960s onward, nearly every major state saw the emergence of such candidates, and so did the nation in the mid-1970s. This new breed, almost by definition hostile or indifferent to responsible party politics, by the same token hardly was attuned to treat the labor movement on the terms that it received from the party organization.

The political ferment accompanying these party changes at first obscured their full meaning. The dissident unions sympathetic to the McGovern wing believed that, by aligning themselves with progressive candidates and by seeking to penetrate the delegate selection process, they could become a part of the new political mainstream.[42] Given the alienation it felt, the AFL–CIO itself had little stomach for the new politics. Having dismissed the Democrats in 1970 as no longer "the so-called liberal party that it was a few years ago," George Meany kept his organization on the political sidelines while the new elements were in the ascendency.

Following McGovern's disastrous campaign in 1972, the balance swung back within the Democratic party. With its planks on national health insurance, tax reform, full employment, and labor-law reform, the 1976 platform highly pleased organized labor. Jimmy Carter's selection of Walter Mondale (a product of the Minnesota Farmer-Labor party and protegé of Hubert Humphrey) as his running mate seemed to seal the bargain. Both COPE and its counterparts among the independents mounted a major effort in the 1976 campaign. With Carter in the White House and the Congress heavily Democratic, an AFL-CIO writer remarked two years later, labor had expected to "see a resurgence of the kind of liberal legislation that marked the Kennedy-Johnson years." What the adjourning ninety-fifth Congress left behind, however, was "not a monument to forward-looking social legislation[,] but a tombstone," the demise of nearly the whole of an ambitious program.[43]

This bleak outcome offered compelling testimony to the transformation of the party system over the past decade. Products of the new personal politics, the Democrats elected to

Congress in 1974 and 1976 felt little obligation to submit themselves either to the leadership or the platform of the party. "The sense of party loyalty just isn't there," remarked chief AFL-CIO lobbyist A. J. Biemiller. "They lack any political philosophy or ideology," added Douglas Fraser of the UAW. "The only commitment is to get reelected. The Democratic Party is in disarray."[44] Nor was the party cause much helped by the man in the White House, for Jimmy Carter was himself an unseasoned outsider who had capitalized on the new politics to gain the Democratic nomination. Once in office, he lacked both the skills and means to provide the kind of party leadership that had characterized previous Democratic presidencies. Without strong roots in the party, moreover, his commitment to the party platform was only superficial, and readily abandoned under the pressures of the inflationary spiral and the energy crisis.

Organized labor learned a hard lesson from the ninety-fifth Congress: the breakdown of party politics meant that a partisan effort no longer translated into the kind of ongoing, predictable influence the unions had exerted within the Democratic party for the twenty years after World War II.

Structural change could not, however, by itself account for the record of failure on Capitol Hill in 1977–78. If labor could not count on the Democrats, it could still compete for their votes. And if it lost in that competition, this told of the rising potency of labor's opponents. The ninety-fifth Congress carried this final, ominous meaning for the labor movement. It could no longer assume the balance of political forces that had been one expression of the labor-management settlement of the postwar era.

No more telling battle took place in the ninety-fifth Congress than over the reform of the National Labor Relations Act. Over the years, this cornerstone law had lost much of its original force as a guarantee of the rights of workers to organize and engage in collective bargaining, partly as a result of

Taft-Hartley amendments, partly by the process of reinterpretation by the NLRB and the courts, but mainly through the unremitting efforts of an army of resourceful lawyers and consultants chipping away at the law. It was widely held that any determined employer who was prepared to spend the money could frustrate the intent of the law.

The legal history of J. P. Stevens and Co. served as a grim object lesson. The second largest textile manufacturer in the country had been fending off organizing efforts since 1963. J. P. Stevens fired the leaders of that first drive, then resorted to delaying tactics that stretched the resulting unfair-labor practice cases over five years. Finally ordered to reinstate the discharged workers with full back pay and seniority, J. P. Stevens doubtless felt it had got its money's worth: its tactics had long since sapped the union's strength. When the United Textile Workers did manage to win elections at the Roanoke Rapids, North Carolina, plants in 1974, the company could not be drawn into negotiations that would lead to a contract. This was another standard strategy: long delay was likely to deprive any union of its majority standing, either by discouraging enough workers, or, if the union chose to strike, by enabling the company to bring in nonunion replacements.[45] After sixteen years, J. P. Stevens deservedly stood as a testament to the erosion of the Wagner Act.[46]

The proposed changes would have speeded up unfair-labor practice cases and representation elections; increased penalties for violations of the law, including compensation in refusal-to-bargain cases and the withholding of federal contracts to "willful" violators; and, to counter the captive-audience advantage of employers, given organizers equal opportunity to address employees in representation campaigns. In labor's view, these were entirely conservative reforms designed to assure rights already granted to workers by the law. "Labor law reform would not have organized a single worker or put unions at any kind of new advantage," contended the AFL-CIO. The dean of the Michigan Law

School thought the bill created "the smallest possible target by concentrating on the problems of delay and the most urgently needed remedies . . . rather than on substantive regulation that would shift the balance of collective bargaining power as between unions and organized employers."[47] Yet labor-law reform set off a furious legislative battle.

Not in many years had American business formed so united a front. Virtually the entire spectrum came together on this issue, from the National Right To Work Committee to the corporate liberals on the prestigious Labor-Management Group. That struggle, along with the fight against the common situs picketing bill for the building trades, commented one lobbyist for the U.S. Chamber of Commerce, generated "one hell of a coordinated effort by the business community." The campaign was marked by the recent operational advances in direct-mail techniques for money-raising and focusing grass-roots pressure and by a surge of political activism among businessmen as evidenced in the proliferating political action committees in corporations and trade associations. Most notable was the untrammeled animus with which the antireform campaign was waged. The tactics struck Douglas Fraser "as the most vicious, unfair attack upon the labor movement in more than 30 years." In that battle could be seen the formidable dimensions of the new bloc—"a heavily-financed, well orchestrated coalition between big business and right-wing extremists," George Meany called it—that confronted and bested labor in the ninety-fifth Congress.[48]

The meaning of this assault on labor reform went beyond the political arena. The open shop was once again on the march—evident in such new groups as the NAM's Committee for a Union-Free Environment, in the booming business of labor-management consultant firms, and in the resistance organizers regularly encountered in new plants even of unionized firms. No less a company than General Motors was trying to fend off the UAW at plants it was opening in the South. The giant corporation, protested the union president, "has received responsibility, productivity and cooperation from the UAW and its members. In return, GM has given us a Southern strategy designed to set up a non-union network that threatens the hard-fought gains won by the UAW. We have given stability and been rewarded with hostility." With his eye on European industrial relations, the labor economist Everett M. Kassalow saw "almost a bizarre quality" in GM's stand. "The resistance of U.S. employers to unionizing efforts simply has no serious industry counterpart in Western Europe today," Professor Kassalow remarked. The irreducible fact was, said *Business Week,* that "American business has by and large never really accepted unionism."[49]

The incentive to act on that rooted animus stemmed partly from the inflationary, slow-growing economy, partly from the more effective means at hand. During the 1970s, management became increasingly wily and sophisticated: surveys of employee attitudes, training and promotion programs, even "conflict resolution systems" modeled on union grievance procedures. Generally careful to match union rates and conditions, open-shop firms took the stance of the enlightened employer who, in the words of one consultant, wants "to remain union-free because he prefers to deal with you directly in our concern for your welfare."[50] Under the smiling veneer, however, the hard fist still lurked. In 1977, the NLRB received 42,802 complaints charging discrimination against union workers, six times the number in the mid–1950s. There was also the problem of the "runaway shop." Migration of industry continued unabated to the inhospitable Sunbelt, where, despite the best efforts of the unions, organization stood at half the level of the rest of the country at the end of the 1970s. The rate of union success in representation elections was in steady decline: from a high of 80 per cent in 1946, to 60.7 per cent in 1967, to a low of 47 per cent in 1977. Beyond the employer-made difficulties, impersonal forces were eroding the economic base of American trade unionism: foreign competition consuming union jobs; computer technology decimating even so anchored an organization as the International Typographical Union; steady expansion of white-collar work in manufacturing; and the long-term shrinkage of the economic sector represented by industry, mining, construction, and transportation (from half of nonagricultural employment in 1950 to barely a third in 1980). Surveying the scene in 1978, the veteran labor reporter A. H. Raskin was struck by "a sense of insecurity that is growing rapidly in the upper echelons of labor."[51]

On July 19, 1978, shortly after the labor-reform bill fell victim to a Senate filibuster, Douglas Fraser did the unthinkable: he resigned, in a blaze of publicity, from the Labor-Management Group. Even on this high-level body advisory to the president, the veritable embodiment of corporate liberalism, business leaders had "broken and discarded the fragile, unwritten compact previously existing during a past period of growth and progress." They had, charged the UAW president, joined the unconscionable attack on labor-law reform, become uncompromising in their opposition to social legislation, and, in the case of General Motors, tried to undermine his own union through a "Southern strategy." In all these ways, they were violating the "unwritten compact" that had prevailed for the thirty years past. American industry, concluded Fraser, had "chosen to wage a one-sided class war," to court "confrontation, rather than cooperation." Fraser could no longer stay on the Labor-Management Group "seeking unity with leaders of American industry, while they try to destroy us and ruin the lives of the people I represent."[52]

With that gesture, Fraser signaled the onset of a political crisis for the labor movement. On the economic side, it was an open question as to how far the postwar labor-management settlement had broken down. The AFL-CIO leadership, as surprised as anyone by Fraser's resignation, agreed with the specifics of his indictment, but doubted the need for so sweeping a conclusion. When the time came to bargain, Meany dryly remarked, employers would still sit down to negotiate agreements.[53] Within a few weeks, in fact, the UAW was happy to announce that GM had repeated its assurances (having previously so pledged during the 1976 negotiations) that it would not resist the union in the South and, on a particular sore point, that it would not try to screen out UAW members in hiring for new plants. The company had doubtless concluded that the open-shop benefits in the South did not outweigh the trouble threatening at its union facilities. On the whole, where the bargaining system was well rooted, the stabilizing benefits to the employer—or the costs of attempt at dislodgement—counterbalanced the lure of the open shop, notwithstanding its ominous appeal throughout American industry. [54] For his part, Fraser approached the 1979 round of auto negotiations very much with the air of business-as-usual.

It was the political system that immediately registered the destabilization of the postwar labor-management settlement. How serious this seemed could be gauged by the alternative Fraser posed to labor's partnership with corporate business. Its "one-sided class war" was being waged "against working people, the unemployed, the poor, the minorities, the very young and the very old, and even many in the middle-class of our society." Fraser would rather sit with the victims of social injustice "than with those whose religion is the status quo, whose goal is profit and whose hearts are cold. We in the UAW intend to reforge the links with those who believe in struggle." Within this rhetorical flourish was a hard truth: if business brushed aside the political restraint prescribed by the labor-management settlement, and if the trade unions lost the postwar dynamism that had first brought about the accommodation, then the political initiative could not be regained within the confines of that settlement. Hence Fraser's impulse to break out, to chart a new political course based on a broad coalition of the progressive forces in the country. The exploratory conference called by Fraser on October 17, 1978, was remarkable for the spectrum of groups that it brought together. These included not only representatives of thirty activist unions (both AFL-CIO affiliates and independents) but also of seventy-one other organizations ranging from the NAACP, the National Farmers Union, and the National Women's Political Caucus, to many single-issue groups (environmentalists, tax reformers, consumer advocates), to the ADA and other progressive elements within the Democratic party. At a second meeting on January 15, 1979, this "coalition of coalitions" formally constituted itself as the Progressive Alliance.[55]

For the present, this activity seemed significant mainly as a measure of labor's deep political distress. Initially, at any rate, the Progressive Alliance looked like a paper organization, without real capacity either for generating grass-roots support or for undertaking political work. For the future, however, there were certain signs of promise. Organized labor had given evidence of a reviving ability to rally a broad liberal coalition, encompassing a vastly different mix of concerns than in the days of the Great Society (this applied also to some degree to the AFL-CIO establishment, notwithstanding that it held aloof from the Progressive Alliance). A second hopeful sign was labor's capacity, crucial to its role as the builder of a new progressive coalition, for incorporating within the movement elements of the groups with which it sought alliance.

In the recent past, American trade unionism had demonstrated its continuing utility as a mode of action for the powerless and exploited. In the nation's hospitals, in agriculture, in food processing, in the service trades, in Southern textile and garment factories, low-wage workers organized in growing numbers during the 1960s and after. Mainly women, Spanish-speaking, or black, the working poor helped to replenish labor's stock of social idealism that had been depleted by the successes of collective bargaining. It was this felt need, indeed, that largely prompted the flow of aid from other trade unions to the California grape-harvest hands, to black hospital workers in Charleston, South Carolina, and to the Chicano garment makers of the Farrah Manufacturing Co. in Texas. The resulting unions upheld within the labor movement the spirit of struggle that Fraser espoused in his attack on the Labor-Management Group.[56]

If they could not pretend to so inspiring a role, white-collar workers held still greater potential for the labor movement. By 1980 they were more numerous in the labor force than all other workers combined (service, agricultural, production). The extent of organization among American white-collar workers in 1977—one in eight—was barely half that of the next lowest among white-collar workers of the leading Western industrial nations.[57] Yet this in fact represented substantial progress for the American labor movement, primarily as a result of the recent union surge in the public sector. At the end of the 1970s, fully a fourth of all American workers covered by collective bargaining, well over five million, were in white-collar jobs. Relatively few, however, came from the private sector. These salaried workers, highly resistant in the past, constituted a future challenge of the first magnitude to American trade unionism, and not only because of the numbers involved. Organized labor had shaped itself on a narrow conception of its class appeal in American society. A continuing influx of white-collar workers might well alter its deep-rooted sense of limits and revive lines of thought closed off since the days of Samuel Gompers. As it was, the white-collar presence was already sufficient for building linkages between the labor movement and middle-class reform in contemporary America. Union advances among both low-wage and white-collar workers lent some substance to Douglas Fraser's talk of "making new alliances[,] forming new coalitions to help our nation find its way."

In the meantime, however, there was the immediate political crisis to be faced. What had so magnified the conservative thrust in the ninety-fifth Congress had been the concurrent deterioration of the party order. Quite simply, weak loyalty and discipline had enabled the potent right-wing lobby to pull away enough Democratic votes to kill labor's program. (It would have taken two more ayes to end the Senate filibuster on the labor-reform bill; among the Democrats voting against cloture had been three elected with strong labor support.)[58] As Cesar Chavez put it: "You elect Democrats, and they end up voting Republican."[59] On quitting the Labor-Management Group, indeed, Fraser had reserved his bitterest words for the party politics that engendered in citizens, especially the poor and the minorities, "the sense of helplessness and inability to affect the system in any way. The Republican Party remains controlled by and the Democratic Party heavily influenced by business interests. The reality is that both are weak and ineffective as parties, with no visible, clear-cut ideological differences between them, because of business domination."

Where did this leave the labor movement? In their distress, the unions reverted back to the old terms of political debate, and, with that, to the old dilemmas. Fraser's denunciation of both major parties added fuel to the mounting talk about a labor party. The old objections still applied, however, and Fraser himself pronounced a third party "not a good idea at the present time."[60] Never abandoned in principle by the AFL-CIO, nor wholly in practice either, nonpartisanship also took on fresh appeal. Even so progressive a union leader as Jerry Wurf of the State, County and Municipal Workers, while urging other Democrats to challenge President Carter for the nomination, was not above suggesting that he could go with the Republicans if they produced a better presidential candidate in 1980.[61] For nonpartisanship, however, as with a labor party, past objections prevailed. The Republicans fielded all too few acceptable candidates. And, by cutting the unions off from party affairs, nonpartisanship ran counter to the abiding hope for restructured parties that would offer voters a real ideological choice. So, for practical purposes, labor remained stuck with the Democrats. One widely shared impulse was to try to improve the existing partisan approach: monitor voting records more closely; discriminate more carefully in granting support; and, above all, raise the rewards (contributions, volunteers, logistical support) granted to good candidates and withheld from bad ones. But, especially on the left, thoughts turned also to party reform. In September 1978, the UAW's *Solidarity* carried a bell-weather article on Canadian politics and the labor-farmer New Democratic Party: the point was that, under the parliamentary system, the NDP did enforce discipline—on pain of expulsion—in pursuit of the platform on which it had run. Had this principle applied to the Democratic party, the ninety-fifth Congress would have been a triumph for labor, not a disaster. The Progressive Alliance, after wide-ranging discussion, set as a goal "political parties that are accountable, issue-oriented, and disciplined to abide by their platform commitments."[62] What remained to be seen was how the Democratic party might be so transformed in a system lacking a parliamentary framework and engendering powerful currents for what Fraser called the "politics of personality."

It is, by way of conclusion, perhaps sufficient to observe in these anxious efforts the distance from the time twenty years before when Walter Reuther, predecessor to Douglas Fraser, had spoken so confidently of the labor movement fulfilling its political destiny within a Democratic party that served as the American equivalent of a European social-democratic party.

Back in 1948, Sumner Slichter had asked: "Are we becoming a 'laboristic' state?" In our own time—in 1980—it takes an act of historical imagination to retrieve the sense of awe at labor's power and vitality that lay behind Professor Slichter's question. Today, union membership stands at over twenty million. But this represents fewer than one in four in the nonfarm labor force, compared to one in three after World War II. And while for the next thirty years the labor movement grew steadily, if not at the pace of the total labor force, since the mid-1970s it has begun to suffer an absolute decline in numbers. "A widespread erosion is under way in union membership and power," warns the journalist A. H. Raskin. Far from serving as the cutting edge of social change, moreover, trade unionism appears today to be a largely spent force in the national life. "The American labor movement is having less and less impact on society," says Jerry Wurf. The future is never foreclosed. But it is hard to envisage the day near at hand when people will again say, as Sumner Slichter did in 1948, that the union movement has placed the country "on the threshold of major changes in its economic and political institutions."[63]

Notes

1. Joseph Gaer, *The First Round* (New York, 1944), p. 68.
2. August Meier and Elliott Rudwick, *Black Detroit and the Rise of the UAW* (New York, 1979), ch. 4.
3. Gaer, *First Round,* p. 92.
4. Nelson Lichtenstein, "Industrial Unionism Under the No-Strike Pledge" (Ph.D. diss., University of California, Berkeley, 1974), p. 526.
5. Philip Taft, *Organized Labor in American History* (New York, 1964), p. 614; Lichtenstein, "Industrial Unionism," pp. 548-49.
6. Taft, *Organized Labor,* p. 614.
7. Henry Brandon, "Conversation with Reuther," in Charles M. Rehmus and Doris B. McLaughlin, eds., *Labor and American Politics* (Ann Arbor, Mich., 1967), p. 441 (my ital.).
8. James C. Foster, *The Union Politic: The CIO Political Action Committee* (Columbia, Mo., 1975), pp. 9, 197.
9. Lichtenstein, "Industrial Unionism," pp. 23, 534, 544; David J. McDonald, *Union Man* (New York, 1969) p. 169; Gaer, *First Round,* p. 61; Taft, *Organized Labor,* p. 611.
10. C. Wright Mills, *The New Men of Power* (New York, 1948), pp. 211-12.
11. Foster, *Union Politic,* p. 9; Lichtenstein, "Industrial Unionism," p. 546; Gaer, *First Round,* p. 61 (my ital.).
12. Norman Markowitz, *The Rise and Fall of the People's Century* (New York, 1973), ch. 3.
13. Mary H. Hinchey, "The Frustration of the New Deal Revival," (Ph.D. diss., University of Missouri, 1965), pp. 188-89; Arthur F. McClure, *The Truman Administration and the Problems of Postwar Labor* (Rutherford, N.J., 1969), pp. 82-83; Joel Seidman, *American Labor From Defense to Reconversion* (Chicago, 1953), pp. 150-57.
14. Irving Howe and B. J. Widick, *Walter Reuther and the UAW* (New York, 1949), p. 275; Markowitz, *The People's Century,* pp. 155 ff. 221; Foster, *Union Politic,* p. 65.
15. Markowitz, *The People's Century,* p. 223.
16. Max Kampelman, *The Communist Party vs. the CIO* (New York, 1957), pp. 45-46, 58.

17. Bert Cochran, *Labor and Communism* (Princeton, 1977), p. 267.
18. Ibid., pp. 304, 305, 306, 308–309.
19. Philip Taft, *Defending Freedom* (Los Angeles, 1973), pp. 68–69.
20. See, for example, Roy Godson, *American Labor and European Politics* (New York, 1976), pp. 182–84 and Appendix C; Joseph Goulden, *Meany* (New York, 1972), p. 377 ff.
21. Brandon, "A Conversation with Reuther," p. 443.
22. Fay Calkins, *The CIO and the Democratic Party* (Chicago, 1952), p. 131; Harry M. Scoble, "The Magnitude and Method of Labor's Involvement in Politics," in Rehmus and McLaughlin, *Labor and American Politics,* pp. 364–65.
23. J. David Greenstone, *Labor in American Politics* (New York, 1969), p. 69–70.
24. Ibid., pp. 261, 325–30, 352.
25. Ibid., p. 338.
26. Sar A. Levitan, "Union Lobbyists' Contribution to Tough Labor Legislation," in Rehmus and McLaughlin, *Labor and American Politics,* p. 250; Alan K. McAdams, *Power and Politics in Labor Legislation* (New York, 1964), pp. 265–66.
27. Greenstone, *Labor in American Politics,* pp. 332–33, 342, 350–51. For Meany's pungent response to Dirksen's suggestion, see Goulden, *Meany,* p. 348.
28. Vivian Vale, *Labour in American Politics* (London, 1971), p. 160.
29. Greenstone, *Labor in American Politics,* pp. 361–62, chap. 11.
30. Brandon, "Conversation with Reuther," p. 443.
31. Foster, *Union Politic,* pp. 90–91, 133–35.
32. Mills, *New Men of Power,* p. 163.
33. Harry W. Laidler, "Labor's Role in American Politics," *Current History* 36 (June 1959): 325 (my ital.).
34. Brandon, "Conversation with Reuther," pp. 440–41, 443.
35. Goulden, *Meany,* pp. 465–66.
36. David Brody, "The Expansion of the American Labor Movement: Institutional Sources of Stimulus and Restraint," in Stephen E. Ambrose, ed., *Institutions in Modern America* (Baltimore, 1967), pp. 11–36.
37. Herbert S. Parmet, *The Democrats: The Years After FDR* (New York, 1975), pp. 290–91, 301; Goulden, *Meany,* p. 415.
38. Eliot Marshall, "The New Feudalism," *The New Republic,* January 20, 1979, pp. 13–16.
39. *Fortune* 87 (March 1973): 94–95.
40. Parmet, *Democrats,* p. 252; Goulden, *Meany,* p. 388.
41. *Business Week,* July 21, 1975, p. 56.
42. See, for example, "Six Million Workers Minus George Meany," *The New Republic,* January 3, 1976, pp. 6–8.
43. *AFL-CIO News,* October 28, 1978, p. 5.
44. *American Federationist* 86 (January 1979): 15; *Solidarity,* November 1–15, 1978, p. 5.
45. See, for example, *U.S. News and World Report,* January 10, 1977, pp. 73–74; U.S., Congress, House, Committee on Labor and Education, *Hearings on the Labor Reform Act of 1977,* 95th Congress, 1st sess., 1977, I, pp. 631–33.
46. In February 1978, an appeals court order took effect against J. P. Stevens, containing broad cease-and-desist provisions, strong directives for remedial measures, and an unprecedentedly heavy schedule of fines for failure to comply. *Monthly Labor Review* 101 (April 1978): 51.
47. *AFL-CIO News,* October 28, 1978, p. 5; Theodore J. St. Antoine, "Proposed Labor Reform," *Proceedings of the Industrial Relations Research Association,*

1977, p. 165. For a full range of views, see *Hearings on the Labor Reform Act, passim.*

48. *Solidarity,* July 1978, p. 3; *AFL-CIO News,* October 21, 1978, p. 4.

49. *Solidarity,* July 1978, pp. 3-4; Everett M. Kassalow, "How Some European Nations Avoided U.S. Levels of Industrial Conflict," *Monthly Labor Review* 101 (April 1978): 97; *Business Week,* December 4, 1978, p. 56.

50. *Newsweek,* April 22, 1974, p. 95. After shrugging them off for many years, the AFL-CIO in 1979 officially acknowledged the threat being posed by labor-management consultants. *San Francisco Chronicle,* February 24, 1979. See also, Charles McDonald and Dick Wilson, "Peddling the 'Union Free' Guarantee," *American Federationist* 86 (April 1979): 12-19.

51. A. H. Raskin, "The Big Squeeze on Labor Unions," *Atlantic* 242 (October 1978): 43.

52. *Solidarity,* July 1978, pp. 3-4. The press release and complete letter are reprinted in *Radical History Review,* no. 18 (Fall 1978): 117-22. For editorial comment, see *New York Times,* July 30, 1978.

53. *AFL-CIO News,* August 12, 1978, p. 3.

54. The statistics do not suggest a significant deterioration of union strength in organized areas. The number of workers reverting to nonunion status as a result of decertification elections in 1977 was 21,600. While this was four times greater than in 1967, it amounted to only .2 per cent of the union labor force. See *Business Week,* December 4, 1978, p. 56. Among production workers in manufacturing, the percentage organized varied as follows between 1956 and 1976: 1956, 65.9%; 1958, 69.7%; 1960, 68.3%; 1962, 64.5%; 1964, 65.3%; 1966, 61.3%; 1968, 63.5%; 1970, 65.4%; 1972, 63.9%; 1974, 62.6%; 1976, 62.1% (Source: Myron Roomkin and Hervey A. Juris, "Unions in the Traditional Sectors," *Proceedings of the Industrial Relations Research Association,* 1976, Table 1, p. 213).

55. *Solidarity,* October 15-30, 1978, pp. 3-6, and February 1979, pp. 10-11.

56. Laurie D. Cummings, "The Employed Poor," *Monthly Labor Review* 88 (July 1965): 828-35; Jack Barbash, "The Emergence of Low-Wage Unionism," *Monthly Labor Review* 97 (April 1974): 51-52. The best account of the rise of the United Farm Workers is Dick Meister and Anne Loftis, *A Long Time Coming* (New York, 1977). On the hospital workers, see A. H. Raskin, "A Union with 'Soul'," *New York Times Magazine,* March 22, 1970, p. 24 ff.

57. Everett M. Kassalow, "White-Collar Unions and the Work Humanization Movement," *Monthly Labor Review* 100 (May 1977): 10-11.

58. *AFL-CIO News,* October 28, 1978, p. 4.

59. *Solidarity,* October 15-30, 1978, p. 3.

60. Ibid., p. 3.

61. *San Francisco Chronicle,* July 13, 1979.

62. *Solidarity,* February 1979, p. 11.

63. Sumner H. Slichter, "Are We Becoming a 'Laboristic' State?" *New York Times Magazine,* May 16, 1948, p. 11; Raskin, "Big Squeeze on Labor Unions," p. 43; Wurf quoted, *Business Week,* December 4, 1978, p. 55.

7
A Movement in Crisis

The first edition of this book appeared in 1980. It now turns out, some thirteen years later, that the ominous events described in the concluding pages of that first edition [pp. 229–239 of the present edition] marked the onset of a new stage in the history of the American labor movement. The absolute loss of membership that set in during the mid-1970s was not stemmed. On the contrary, in the course of the 1980s, trade unions suffered a further net loss of over 3 million members. At a time when the labor force was rapidly growing—21 million new jobs were created during the decade—these losses translated into a stunning shrinkage in the scope of union representation in the country. In the private sector, only 12 per cent of the labor force remained organized in 1990 (compared to 20 per cent in 1980). But for its hold on the public sector, which is over a third unionized, the labor movement would be down perilously close to pre-New Deal levels.

Since the mid-1970s, transforming changes have everywhere swept across the economic landscape. Beginning in the Carter administration, a policy of deregulation set in motion competitive forces that undercut long-standing collective-bargaining relationships in the airlines, trucking, and telephone communications. In manufacturing, the problem was foreign competition. For some American industries, the recession of 1982–83 was a crushing event. Not even the most

Revised and reprinted, with permission, from *Dissent* (Winter 1992): 32–41.

robust of union responses could stem the loss of jobs. Under Lynn Williams, for example, the Steelworkers Union literally broke the mold of conventional collective bargaining and, at a time of fearful industry losses and cutbacks, managed to preserve its contracts with the basic producers.[1] But between 1983 and 1988, 166,000 production jobs were lost; over the longer term since 1975, union membership declined by half. The United Auto Workers were just as hard hit. Nothing the domestic automakers did seemed to make much of a dent against Japanese competition, which was closing on a third of the American market by the early 1990s. Even the mightiest of them all—General Motors—was reeling from huge losses; in December 1991 it announced a sweeping new round of plant shutdowns and layoffs.

Coal mining, on the other hand, was a strictly domestic industry that, after half a century of decline, underwent a substantial revival beginning in the 1960s. What undermined the union was not increased competition, but on the contrary, a restructuring process that eliminated the cutthroat market conditions against which John L. Lewis had devised his particularly potent form of industry-wide bargaining. The Mine Workers, losing ground for several decades, saw over half their remaining members depart during the 1980s: scarcely 15 per cent of the mine labor force remained organized at the end of the decade. The building trades, another historic bastion of union strength, were overtaken not so much by structural change as by a rapidly expanding nonunion sector that ruthlessly underbid high-wage union labor.

However complex and varied in its particularities, the downward pathway of American unions has been remarkably consistent: in the private sector, collective-bargaining systems are everywhere under siege, and anti-unionism is resurgent. The labor-management settlement of the postwar era has, for practical purposes, been nullified.

The labor movement is the victim, manifestly, of powerful economic forces mostly beyond its capacity to control. But market competition and structural change do not automatically translate into trade-union decline. What is happening in the United States is after all part of a global phenomenon, affecting, if not necessarily to the same degree or in precisely the same ways, the labor markets of all the advanced industrial economies. In the view of some political economists,[2] a new stage of late capitalism has set in worldwide, displacing the regulated national economies with a global economic order characterized by capital mobility and competitive labor markets.

No other labor movement, however, has been so hard hit by these global developments. Of fifteen industrialized countries, only in three others did the percentage of organized workers actually fall between 1970 and 1985/86, and nowhere with anything like the magnitude of the American decline. In 1970, the United States was at the bottom end of the scale, but it shared the 30 to 39 per cent decile with six other countries. At 17 per cent in 1985/86, it stood in a class by itself, eleven points behind the next most laggard movement.[3] If we measure union strength by collective-bargaining coverage, the disparity is even greater than these numbers would suggest. In Germany, for example, roughly 45 per cent of workers belonged to unions in the mid-1980s, but union agreements covered 90 per cent; for Britain, the respective figures were 45 to 50 per cent and 75 per cent. In the United States, on the other hand, contract coverage extends only a few percentage points beyond the proportion of workers belonging to unions.[4] So, as compared to other countries, the decline of union densities translates much more completely into an actual reduction in the scope of representation. The American economy really is becoming distinguished in the industrial world as a "union-free environment."

The following discussion seeks to take a reading on the painfully reduced circumstances of the labor movement today and, in particular, to place its current distress in some kind of historical and comparative perspective.

We can perhaps best get at the predicament of the American movement by comparing it to what happened to trade unionism in English-speaking Canada in these years. No two movements could have been more alike in institutional make-up and historical experience. The early and persisting tendency of Canadian local unions to affiliate with the emerging national trade unions south of the border—not the contrary impulses of Canadian nationalism—was the determining fact in the evolution of Canadian unionism. The decisive moment came in 1902, when the Trades and Labour Congress (the Canadian counterpart to the American Federation of Labor) expelled the Knights of Labor bodies and adopted the AFL principle of opposition to dual unionism, thereby granting the Canadian branches of the U.S. internationals (so designated precisely because they included Canadian locals) a virtual monopoly over trade-union representation in the TLC. It became, in effect, the Canadian wing of the American movement. And thereafter, with certain deviations,[5] the two movements came close to having a unitary institutional history, with the Canadians generally marching a half step to the rear. There was the same split over industrial unionism in the 1930s, a Canadian version of the Wagner Act in 1944, anticommunist purges in 1949–50, and in the wake of AFL-CIO reunification in 1955, the Canadian Labour Congress the next year. At that time, 70 per cent of all organized workers in Canada belonged to AFL-CIO unions. The 1950s marked the apex of the historic tendency toward an integrated North American labor movement.

That tendency no longer governs. From the 1960s onward, the Canadian unions entered a period of sustained growth, more than doubling their membership in twenty years and, by the early 1980s, boasting a unionized sector approaching 40 per cent—this in stark contrast to the devastating spiral down below 20 per cent in the United States. The historic linkages between the two movements are disintegrating. Increasingly, the Canadian branches have been inclined to go their own way, either by asserting more autonomy, or as the Canadian Auto Workers did in 1984, by declaring their independence. A dwindling share of the Canadian movement—35 per cent or less by the late 1980s—retains ties to the AFL-CIO, and the sense that the Canadian movement has a separate destiny is palpable. The Canadian Auto Workers split off from the UAW citing the responsibility they had "to play a lead role" in fulfilling "a Canadian labour movement programme."[6]

How are we to account for this remarkable divergence of institutional fortunes? For auto, an economic explanation might suffice. The Canadian industry boomed after the 1982 recession. With output and employment on the rise—the Canadian share of North American production expanded by 25 per cent during the decade—Canadian auto workers were spared the plant closings and draconian cost-cutting demands confronting their U.S. brothers and sisters. The vaunted Canadian militancy against concessions was well grounded in a markedly more favorable bargaining environment. But for Canada as a whole that was decidedly not the case. Since 1973, manufacturing productivity increased even more slowly than in the United States, the unemployment rate ran almost consistently higher during the 1980s, and as in the United States, the downward pressure on wages has been (in the words of the Canadian scholar Daniel Drache) "far-reaching and broad-based."[7] It cannot be said that economic environment for collective bargaining is more favorable in Canada than in the United States.

What has become more favorable is, in the broadest sense, political. In the United States, the legal framework for collective bargaining has deeply eroded since the glory days of the Wagner Act, so that employers today feel free to thwart the unionization of their employees and, perhaps even more important in the current economic climate, to break out of established contractual relations—hence the urgency with which the AFL-CIO is lobbying for legislation prohibiting the permanent replacement of strikers.

In Canada, on the other hand, the collective bargaining process is closely regulated by conciliation requirements, strike votes, and prohibitions against stoppages during the life of contracts (with mandatory arbitration of grievances required). In flush times, these state restraints might seem burdensome (in practice, of course, they become incorporated into the bargaining strategy of the parties), but under adverse conditions, they preserve the collective-bargaining process itself. The rights of workers to organize and bargain collectively are much more effectively protected under Canadian law, in particular, because of swift certification procedures and the mandatory signing of first agreements. And in a variety of ways—in the agency-shop requirements in the major provinces (as compared to the right-to-work laws in many states), for example, and in limitations on the freedom of employers to move from unionized sites—Canadian law signals the legitimacy of collective bargaining. This is reflected in the bargaining rights granted public employees, who are organized at twice the U.S. rate and are identified with the militant wing of the Canadian movement. Corporate employers—even those with nasty records south of the border—do not sing the praises of a union-free environment in Canada, and of course, there is no Canadian counterpart to the emblematic action by the Reagan administration breaking the strike of federal air controllers in 1981. There has emerged what the Canadian scholar Christopher Huxley and his associates have called a distinctively Canadian "labor regime."

By way of explanation, the sociologist Seymour Lipset and others point to collectivist values inhering in the Canadian political culture that accord legitimacy to the labor movement and shelter it from the market-driven anti-unionism rampant in the United States. There is much to be said for this as a basic explanation, of course. But the fact is that, while Canadian statist tendencies go far back (for example, to

MacKenzie King's Industrial Disputes Investigative Act of 1907), the legal and political climate was no more favorable to trade unionism, nor the unionized sector larger, in Canada than in the United States up to quite recent times. The catalytic element sparking Canada's modern labor regime is to be found in the country's changing party system, and in a new path taken by Canadian labor. In the 1960s, a political divergence occurred no less remarkable than the divergence of institutional fortunes of the two movements.

The AFL-CIO remained steadfastly nonpartisan, although, as compared to the old AFL, with far more potent force and in firm alliance to the Democratic party. In Canada, on the other hand, the two-party system itself came under attack, initially by the Cooperative Commonwealth Federation in the western provinces, and then more decisively after the New Democratic party was launched in 1961. Canadian labor threw off the nonpartisanship fostered by the AFL-CIO linkage and entered into an increasingly robust social-democratic third-party politics. As the NDP made headway—its progress capped by the capture of Ontario in the 1990 elections—Canadian unionism not only gained political muscle, but increasingly became a progressive force in the nation's political life. It assumed the mantle of what the Canadian scholar Pradeep Kumar calls "social unionism."[8] In the meanwhile, the AFL-CIO fell on hard political times, becoming more marginal to electoral politics after the collapse of the Johnson administration in 1968, and reduced increasingly to fighting for its own sectional interests rather than for the larger social-justice objectives that since the New Deal had animated labor's legislative agenda. In the 1980s the political standing of the AFL-CIO went into a tailspin, driven down on the one side by the hostility of the Reagan administration and on the other by the growing disarray and impotence of the Democratic party. This is "the most striking difference," remark Huxley and his associates—"the increasing importance of more adversarial and political unionism in Canada, marked above all by the interdependence and mutual aid between key unions and the New Democratic Party, and analogous developments in Quebec. . . ."[9]

Are we to conclude that U.S. labor took a historic misstep and should have followed the Canadian example? By no means. The more apt historical question runs the other way: why was Canadian labor so long in finding the empowering political role it currently enjoys? The comparative history in which I have indulged of course does pose an inescapable question on the American side: What was there about the nation's politics that denied such an empowering role to U.S. labor? But, inviting as that question is, it is not one that can be pursued in this essay.[10] If we can agree that, at least after the triumph of the New Deal, the fundamental conditions of American politics did preclude the Canadian option, that will suffice for my purposes. For what I want to argue is that American labor's recent decline should not be seen as a contingent event, one that, with better leaders or bolder policies, might have turned out differently, but rather that, given the changes in the U.S. economy, its decline was historically determined. In short: no other labor movement—not even one otherwise so alike in its institutional characteristics—stands so exposed to the forces of its economic environment.[11]

The Canadian comparison suggests the insulating powers of a more favoring political culture. But it does not explain how, in the absence of such a culture, the American movement made headway in the past. So, in thinking about prospects for its future recovery, we have to turn to the best historical instance we have of how trade unionism has triumphed in the American environment—the 1930s.

In 1929, organized labor was an arrested movement. In the areas of its historical strength—construction, mining, and transportation—it represented in the range of 25 to 30 per cent of eligible workers. The modern movement represents roughly the same proportion of workers in the sectors of its historical strength (that is, as of 1950). At both moments, the crisis confronting the labor movement came not primarily from these mature sectors, which even totally organized could by themselves not have sustained a robust national movement, but from the dynamic new sectors of economic growth seemingly beyond the reach of trade unionism. In 1929, of course, the dynamic core was the technologically advanced mass-production industries. Today it is the white-collar sector, which has two kinds of workers. One is the semiskilled—store clerks, bank tellers, data processers, clerical workers—whose routinized work is increasingly subject to automation. Increasing more rapidly are the employees that Charles Heckscher designates as "semiprofessional," including middle managers, engineers, nurses, teachers, computer programmers, technicians, accountants, sales representatives and the like. While manufacturing employment has slipped below 20 per cent, white-collar workers constitute well over half the labor force today, and the semiprofessionals among them fully a third of the labor force.[12] The surge of white-collar employment, in turn, reflects the transformation of the American economy from producer of goods to producer of services and information.

It would be hard to say whether the changing complexion of the modern movement, which is already over half white-collar, gives it any relative advantage over the 1929 movement, where the craft/industrial mix had shifted much less—only a quarter of the organized came from the manufacturing sector in 1929—but also where class barriers did not stand so formidably between the unorganized and trade unionism as they do today. No one would argue, however, that the obstacles facing organized labor seemed any less daunting in 1929 than they do in 1993.

There are, too, quite striking parallels in how the labor movement responded to adversity. In politics, for example, there were comparably desperate initiatives: the abortive entry into the Democratic party nominating process in 1984 has a counterpart in the farmer-labor insurgency within the party primaries that petered out in LaFollette's Progressive ticket of 1924. And there was an eerily familiar retreat in the 1920s from adversarial unionism, evident not only in the sharp decline in strike activity, but more significantly in the AFL's conversion to co-operative labor-management relations that bears a striking similarity to the anxious receptivity of today's trade unions toward a more flexible and mutualistic system of labor relations. The Baltimore and Ohio Railroad had very much the same cachet for the 1920s that GM's NUMMI plant has today.

The breakthrough of the 1930s, of course, came from an entirely different direction. With the onset of the Great Depression, the balance of forces in the United States shifted dramatically. The elemental events were, first, the rise of the New Deal, and, second, the rebellion of the industrial workers. And from these events there issued the particular conditions making possible the unionization of the mass-production sector. First, the state began to protect the rights of workers to organize and engage in collective bargaining, initially under Section 7a of the National Industrial Recovery Act (1933) and then decisively with the passage of the Wagner Act (1935). Employers were deprived of the enormous power advantage they had long enjoyed in the struggle over collective bargaining.

At the same time, the New Deal moved to mitigate the market pressures that had driven employer anti-unionism. Section 7a was part of the industrial recovery legislation that, through codes of fair competition, enabled industries to cartelize their depression-ridden markets. The exchange was entirely deliberate—representational rights for workers as a price for market controls for industry. This key linkage survived the early demise of the National Industrial Recovery Act. The Wagner Act contained an explicit economic rationale: collective bargaining would give rise to the mass purchasing power necessary for sustained economic growth.

This, in turn, prefigured the Keynesian economic policy that became the government's way of underwriting the New Deal collective bargaining system. With macroeconomic policy (as specified by the Employment Act of 1946) responsible for long-term demand and price competition firmly controlled by the restored oligipolistic structures or, as in the transport and communications sectors, by direct state regulation, the market-driven basis for American anti-unionism had seemingly run its course after World War II.

Much the same could be said for the labor-process sources of anti-unionism. The struggle over job control touched off by Taylorism had passed by the 1930s. In the mass-production sector, what remained at issue was no longer whether managers had the authority, but only how they exercised it. There were, moreover, compelling reasons, almost systemic in nature, for the formalization of work rules. Where tasks were subdivided and precisely defined, for example, job classification necessarily followed and from that came the principle of pay equity. Time-and-motion study meant objective—that is, testable—standards for the pace of work. Internal labor markets implied uniform rules governing layoff, recall, and even promotion. Corporate commitment to this formalized system was imperfect, however, and broke down entirely in the early years of the Great Depression.

Rank-and-file fury over job insecurity and intolerable speed-up forced management's hand during the NRA period. Between 1933 and 1936—*before* collective bargaining began —all the elements of the modern workplace regime were more or less in place: specified, uniform rights for workers (beginning with seniority and pay equity); a formal procedure for adjudicating grievances arising from those rights; and a structure of shop-floor representation to implement the grievance procedure. Corporate employers would have much preferred to operate this regime under nonunion conditions. Indeed, it had taken shape in the course of their efforts to implant the employee-representation plans (that is, company unions) that employers hoped would satisfy the requirements of New Deal labor policy. But when that strategy failed, they were prepared to have the workplace regime incorporated into contractual relations with independent unions under the terms of the Wagner Act.

Thus there emerged the key elements—the legal framework, the market regulation, an agreed-upon workplace regime—buttressing the modern collective-bargaining system. It is, of course, the breakdown of these sustaining elements that accounts for labor's recent decline, and, by the same token, something like them in new forms will have to take shape to bring into being the next expansionist period.

But what does the history I have described say about the labor movement as the agent of its own revival? It was a bystander in the cataclysmic economic collapse that set things in motion, and a very minor player in the emergence of the New Deal and upsurge of rank-and-file militancy. Nor was it ever in a position to make or break the key developments in law, economic policy, or workplace relations on which labor's future depended. The AFL never had the power to shape the environment within which it operated. But what it did have was an acute and true sense of what, as a job-conscious labor movement, it wanted from that environment. That may sound like an odd claim, given the notorious failure of the AFL to surmount the jurisdictional impasse over industrial unionism that split the movement in 1935. But, at a more fundamental level, the labor movement—both the AFL and CIO wings—was unerring and, at the critical junctures, astonishingly successful in advancing its trade-union interests.

This is best observed in the battle over New Deal collective bargaining policy. What was at issue, once Section 7a was adopted, was really a competition between rival conceptions of labor organization. Corporate employers argued that labor's rights could be fulfilled through employee representation plans, that is, by a system of works councils. In resisting that claim, the AFL faced a hard, uphill struggle. For one thing, corporate industry seized the initiative, put the ERPs into place unilaterally in 1933, and thereafter largely defined the terms of the debate. The AFL never had the power during the NRA period to impose collective bargaining on unwilling employers. Nor was much help forthcoming from the New Deal. The ERP scheme, as it evolved from its transparently cynical beginnings, became attractive to many in the administration, including Roosevelt himself, as an alternative to collective bargaining.

What the AFL had on its side, in the long, dispiriting battle over Section 7a, was an absolutely clear and unwavering conception of what it wanted: a system of state regulation that conformed to its conception of collective bargaining through trade-union representation. And in the Wagner Act, against all odds, the labor movement prevailed. Everything in the law's provisions was keyed to promoting collective bargaining: majority rule in the selection of bargaining agents; exclusive representation by the certified bargaining agents; the obligation of good-faith bargaining imposed on employers; labor's right to strike specifically guaranteed. Yet, despite its far reach, the law was specifically circumscribed, setting collective bargaining in motion, but leaving the process itself within the realm of contractual freedom. A voluntaristic labor movement would not have had it otherwise. Never mind that in later years a darker side to the law would be revealed, and the wisdom of departing from Gompers's anti-statist principles called into question. At the time, the Wagner Act represented a remarkable triumph for American trade unionism.

The rise of industrial unionism enables us to identify the enduring historical determinants of the fate of organized labor in the American environment. The essential developments at the time in politics, market structure, and workplace relations have to be taken as autonomous events. Yes, the labor movement played a role; it joined the New Deal, advocated market regulation, participated in the workplace struggles of 1933–36; in any proper history, all this would have to be fully explicated.[13] But these transforming events were not of labor's making. Nor can we expect that they will be when—if—another historic moment like the 1930s arrives. What we can hope is that the labor movement will know how to seize that moment, and that depends, as it did in the 1930s, on a sure sense of its job-conscious character.

Back in the darkest days of the 1982 recession, the business analyst Peter Drucker wrote a column for the *Wall Street Journal* (September 22, 1982) entitled, "Are Unions Becoming Irrelevant?" There was something very particular—and prescient—about how Drucker put that question. It suggested some fundamental disjuncture: the industrial order had gone off in one direction, the labor movement in another, and in so doing, was in danger of becoming "irrelevant." Drucker's question has had a remarkable resonance: it defines the dominant strain of current thinking about the problems of American labor. And, from that perspective, there seems to have developed a broad consensus about the locus of that fatal disjuncture. It is at the workplace.

In a highly influential recent analysis, the industrial relations scholars Thomas Kochan, Harry Katz, and Robert McKersie write:

> . . . Over the course of the past half century union and nonunion systems traded positions as the innovative force in industrial relations. . . . An alternative human resources management system . . . gradually overtook collective bargaining and emerged as the pacesetter by emphasizing high employee involvement and commitment and flexibility in the utilization of individual employees.[14]

Involvement, commitment, flexibility—these are the watchwords of the new industrial relations, and they are required, the labor relations expert Ben Fischer tells us, "by very new forces in the patterns of ownership, management and market

behavior, along with radical new technology. . . . The type of
work being performed by workers is changing. The manner in
which performance is sought contrasts drastically with yesterday's strategies."[15] The conclusion drawn by a distinguished
panel of business and labor leaders for the Economic Policy
Council is that

> . . . a "them and us" system of workplace relations [is] simply
> inadequate in today's social and economic environment. Finding
> the common interests of employees and employers, of unions and
> managers, and developing a process for overcoming the division
> between workers and managers, is the critical challenge that labor
> and capital must address in the decade ahead.[16]

The foregoing quotations, which could be replicated many
times over, fairly convey a broad consensus of what might be
called "progressive" thinking (including inside the labor movement) about the obsolescence of the contractual system of
workplace relations that took shape under industrial unionism.

The attack on that system has powerful programmatic
implications. The way Peter Drucker initially defined the
question—are unions becoming irrelevant?—embodied the
most important part of the answer: namely, it identified
the unions as the problem. And if the gap between institution
and environment were wide enough, then it would follow—as
indeed Drucker says—that "the labor union will have to
transform itself drastically." And those who have focused on
the workplace (as Drucker himself did not) draw the same
conclusion. To adapt to the new industrial relations, says Ben
Fischer, "will dictate a redefinition of what is a union." So
labor's crisis has brought the movement to a juncture where
this question is seriously contemplated: should institutional
change be undertaken of the scope needed to promote a shift
from adversarial to cooperative workplace relations?

Let us assume, for the sake of argument, that the mass-
production regime to which that adversarial system was responsive is in fact coming to an end. Why should we believe

that the succeeding regime will not in its turn set in motion a process that, like the one we have just surveyed, will end with a new adversarial system, a postmodern version, so to speak, of what Sumner Slichter half a century ago called industrial jurisprudence?[17] The answer, at its most basic, would have to be that past experience no longer applies. Indeed, that is precisely what Ben Fischer does say about "the new face of much of industrial relations": it "is not a replay of history."

If that is true, then of course not much can be learned from labor's past. But we need to specify quite precisely the historical discontinuity that must transpire: namely, that the new industrial relations not give rise to a crisis over industrial justice.

Proponents do indeed make that assumption. New modes of flexible production and knowledge-based operation, they argue, require an abandonment of the Taylorist reliance on hierarchical control and a rationalized division of labor. The emerging post-Taylorist system of industrial relations is characterized by what Charles Heckscher calls "managerialism," whose aim it is "that *every* employee be a manager, involved in decisions and contributing intelligently to the goals of the corporation." To achieve these results, corporations have enlisted a sophisticated human resources science that Kochan, Katz, and McKersie assure us has mastered the mysteries of employee motivation. Under its guidance, a wide range of programs have taken shape—all-salaried compensation, profit sharing, work sharing, flexible work schedules, payment for knowledge, autonomous work teams, ingenious systems of communication, and grievance handling. "At its best," concludes Heckscher, "the managerialist order offers genuine improvements in the situation of employees as well as in the effectiveness of the organization."[18]

If the managerialist order at its "best" becomes the norm, what are the prospects for the labor movement? The critical question is really not how successful the existing unions can be at transforming their relations with organized employers.

Without penetrating the new dynamic sectors, as it did in mass production fifty years ago, the labor movement can look forward only to stagnation and decline. In these sectors, no amount of union enthusiasm for cooperative relations and employee involvement is likely to persuade employers that collective bargaining is preferable to a union-free environment. And if Heckscher's managerialist order lives up to its promise, what incentive would their employees have for joining a union?[19]

But there are contrary facts to consider. "Nonunion firms are subject to the same market and technological pressures as are union firms," concede Kochan, Katz, and McKersie. And, writing in the mid-1980s, they already could see that many of the nonunion growth firms of the 1960s and 1970s "are now facing the challenge of adapting their human resource management practices to maturing, more price-competitive markets." Under economic pressure, strategies that "valued low turnover and high commitment" might give way to "strategies that depend on low labor costs." What had seemed unassailable on its own terms—"the innovative force in industrial relations"—turns out to be hostage to the marketplace after all.

And which were the vulnerable firms? In the mid-1980s, Kochan, Katz, and McKersie thought only smaller and mid-sized companies, especially those "most highly exposed to market pressures." Surely not the great exemplars of innovative human resource management like IBM. Indeed, IBM served as Kochan, Katz, and McKersie's model instance of corporate responsibility: in the hard times of the early 1980s, it was "achieving substantial manpower shifts without breaching its historic commitment to employment continuity."[20] Half a dozen years later, no one could speak with such confidence of IBM's intentions. At the end of 1991, performing poorly in a depressed computer market, the giant firm announced a sweeping corporate decentralization intended to gain for it the benefits of more robust competition: its major units would henceforth operate autonomously and be judged by their market performance and profitability. IBM had already undertaken a massive cost-cutting program that had eliminated 65,000 jobs between 1986 and 1991; another 20,000 was planned for 1992. Thus far, the cuts had been achieved through attrition, voluntary buy-outs, and early retirements. But, with IBM stock prices at a nine-year low, the company chairman told Wall Street analysts in December 1991 that he no longer ruled out layoffs.[21]

Other embattled members of the nonunion pantheon had long since given up the pretence of a no-layoff policy. Across the white-collar service sector, major employers hitherto sheltered from hard times—Citicorp in banking, Aetna in insurance, Sears in retailing, Xerox in information processing, and TRW, Inc., widely hailed as a model practitioner of the new industrial relations—were among the leading job-cutters in the stagnant economy of the early 1990s. The structural problems that had afflicted manufacturing in the 1980s seemed now to be overtaking the service sector, which suffered from bloated payrolls, from lagging productivity gains (a mere .7 per cent annually), and for many firms, from heavy debts burdens incurred by the leveraged buyouts of the expansionary 1980s. Where earlier one white-collar job had been lost for every four blue-collar jobs, in the early 1990s the gap was down to one for every two. White-collar unemployment stood at 4.2 per cent in October 1991, and by all accounts, desk jobs had become a prime target of corporate cost-cutting programs.[22]

Suddenly, instead of celebrations of the new industrial relations, there are lamentations over the corrosive effects of job insecurity on employee motivation. ". . . It's very costly in terms of morale and trust that is lost," warns the human resources vice-president of the Intel Corporation. And, predictably, there is much talk about the need—to quote a bellwether commentary in the business section of *New York Times*—for "Restoring Loyalty to the Workplace."[23]

Dissatisfaction among white-collar employees, however, seems to have been on the rise long before the current wave of layoffs. Consider what the Opinion Research Corporation found in surveys among managers at about 200 companies over a thirty-year period from the 1950s to the early 1980s: those who rated their companies favorably in terms of fair application of policies and rules dropped from almost 80 per cent to less than 40 per cent, those who felt secure in their jobs declined from nearly 100 per cent to 65 per cent, those who thought their company was a better place to work than when they had started stood at a little higher than 25 per cent. Among clerical workers, ORC figures indicated an approval rating of company fairness down from 70 per cent in the 1950s to 20 per cent in 1979. The sharpest break occurred around 1975, just at the onset of intensifying market pressures on the American economy generally.[24] But it is not only the long-term erosion of the privileged status of white-collar employees that accounts for these rising levels of dissatisfaction. At least equally important is the other side of the equation: the sense of entitlement that employees today feel over their job rights.

Until quite recently, there was no such thing in law as "job rights." The basic common-law principle was "employment at will"—save for binding contracts to the contrary, employers enjoyed an unlimited prerogative to discipline and discharge workers for any or indeed for no reason. The Wagner Act had established the one major exception: employees could not be fired or punished for engaging in union activities. Then came Title VII of the Civil Rights Act of 1964, which prohibited job discrimination because of race, color, religion, national origin, or sex. Antidiscrimination protections expanded in later years to cover age, physical disability, and, in a variety of state laws, sexual orientation, political affiliation, marital status, and pregnancy. The right not to be discriminated against has in fact achieved an ironic universality as a result of the intensifying assault on affirmative action: "reverse discrimination," validated by conservative court decisions and by the new Civil Rights Act of 1991, stirs the rights consciousness of even the most unreconstructed of WASP males. A second form of job entitlement derives from the surge of regulatory laws covering occupational safety and health, pollution control, and other business activities. These laws specifically protect whistle-blowing employees from punishment by employers.

Finally, the "at will" doctrine has come under siege at a more fundamental level. Since the mid-1970s, a number of state courts have begun to assert in their decisions the principle of "wrongful discharge," limiting the rights of employers where there is evidence of an "implied contract"—in which employees have been given reason to believe that they would not be discharged arbitrarily or without cause—or where dismissal is deemed to be inconsistent with "public policy," variably defined by the courts to include not only statutory expressions of public policy but extending more broadly to basic rights as freedom of conscience and personal privacy and freedom from sexual harassment.

The cumulative effect of these remarkable legal developments, writes Charles Heckscher, "has been to greatly weaken the fabric of the legal veil of managerial prerogative," and, correlatively, to strengthen the expectations of employees to be treated fairly. Heckscher, indeed, sees signs of an emergent movement among white-collar employees, still inchoate and divided among many interest groups, but acting "on a single premise: that corporations, while they may have property rights, have no right to abuse their employees."[25]

"This is quite different from the premise that fueled industrial unionism," Heckscher adds. His error here is fundamental, masking as it does a vital continuity between past and present. Recall the moment at which industrial unionism crystallized during the 1930s. There had been a prior period of struggle driven, as now, by a deepening sense of industrial injustice among factory workers. That its roots may have been somewhat different from those animating the incipient movement that Heckscher describes seems to me not especially germaine, so long as we are not prepared to say that injustice is less potent a conception for industrial workers than for semiprofessional white-collar employees and less potent if it arises from the factory regime than from a sense of legal entitlement (although, with the adoption of Section 7a, there developed in the minds of industrial workers as well a strong sense of legal entitlement). During the battles over employee representation of the NRA period, the terms of a just workplace system took shape and gained the broad assent of all parties (including, in large measure, management). Empowered by the Wagner Act, the industrial unions then seized that system, gave it contractual form, and in short, made themselves the institutional embodiment of the job interests of the mass-production workers.

In this achievement resides the essential historical continuity on which I am insisting: that what made trade unionism compelling to American workers in the past—and is likely to do so in the future—was its job-conscious capacity to link itself to their aspirations for industrial justice. The labor movement cannot itself define those aspirations, nor very much influence the processes that give rise to them. This was true for the industrial workers of the 1930s and true likewise of the incipient movement for employee rights to which Heckscher calls our attention. Should that movement reach crisis proportions, however, the stage would be set, so to speak, for the next CIO.[26]

American industrial relations has arrived at an odd juncture. How can we be moving at once toward a cooperative labor-management system and also toward a deepening crisis over employee rights? The explanation would seem to be that basic structural forces are in contradiction: postindustrial technology demands involvement and commitment from employees, but the competitive market and corporate restructuring now deny to all but the most sheltered firms the means for assuring the job security and predictable treatment on which employee commitment depends. How that contradiction is resolved remains to be seen, but on its resolution probably rides the future of the American labor movement. Insofar as the outcome favors managerialism, to that extent labor's prospects are surely foreclosed. It was because the contrary happened in the 1930s—because welfare capitalism failed under the stress of the Great Depression—that the occasion was provided for the rise of the industrial unions.

Embattled as it is, the labor movement hears on all sides today calls for an end to "adversarialism." Insofar as this means responsiveness to the logic of a post-Taylorist system of production, the advise is sound and altogether consistent with historical experience. It bears repeating that, after all, the "adversarial" work-rules system now so roundly condemned was adopted not in opposition to, but directly in conformity with the logic of the mass-production regime. But retreating from "them and us" as a basic orientation is a different matter. The labor movement will not prevail by trying to persuade nonunion employers.[27] It is their employees that have to be persuaded, and if and when that time comes, what will persuade them will be the only kind of appeal that has worked with American workers since the days of Samuel Gompers: namely, the identification of the union with their demand for industrial justice. The source of that appeal is the abiding job-consciousness of American trade unionism. In this sense, labor's past is deeply and irrevocably implicated in whatever future it has.

Notes

1. For a vivid and detailed account, see John P. Hoerr, *And the Wolf Finally Came: The Decline of the American Steel Industry* (Pittsburgh, 1988).
2. This view is advanced, for example, by the Régulation school of French political

economy. The key postwar development, according to the Régulationists, was collective bargaining, which became a wage-setting mechanism for the entire society. Wages became linked to productivity growth, not the labor market. A kind of regulated capitalism resulted, characterized by sustained economic growth, social stability, and Keynesian state administration of markets. The system made for relatively prosperous working classes without altering fundamental economic relations. Daniel Drache and Meric S. Gertler, eds., *The New Era of Global Competition* (Montreal, 1991), pp. xiii–xv, and ch. 1.

3. Only France, not included in the survey, was almost as thinly organized, but not because of any sudden drop-off: the French movement has hovered in the 20 per cent range since 1960. For the survey data, see Richard Freeman, Appendix 1, in Wei-Chiao Huang, ed., *Organized Labor at the Crossroads* (Kalamazoo, Mich., 1989).

4. Gary N. Chaison and Joseph B. Rose, "The Macrodeterminants of Union Growth and Decline," in George Strauss et al., eds., *The State of the Unions* (Madison, Wisc., 1991), pp. 11–12.

5. Probably most significant, in retrospect, was the One Big Union that sprang up after World War I in the western provinces. Unlike the IWW, the OBU was not a dual-union movement, but rather was rooted in the mainstream trade-union structure. After its early collapse, the OBU left a tradition of radicalism and political activism in the western Canadian branches that fostered third-party politics in the western provinces from the early 1930s onward.

6. Quoted in Christopher Huxley, David Kettler, and James Struthers, "Is Canada's Experience 'Especially Instructive'?" in Seymour M. Lipset, ed., *Unions in Transition: Entering the Second Century* (San Francisco, 1986), p. 114.

7. "The Systematic Search for Flexibility: National Competitiveness and New Work Relations," in Drache and Gertler, *The New Era of Global Competition*, p. 251.

8. Pradeep Kumar, "Organized Labour in Canada and the United States: Similarities and Differences," in John A. Wiles, *Labour Relations in Canada* (Scarborough, Ont., 1989), p. 25.

9. Huxley et al. in Lipset, *Unions in Transitions*, p. 131.

10. Readers who are curious about my own views on the history of American labor politics are invited to see my essay in Jack Greene, ed., *The Encyclopedia of American Political History* (New York, 1983).

11. How the Canadian movement will fare under the Free Trade Agreement of 1989, or should the free-market enthusiasms of the Mulrooney government persist, is of course an open question. For a full-scale recent assessment see Drache and Gertler, *The New Era of Global Competition*, especially the essays in Part 4.

12. Charles H. Heckscher, *The New Unionism: Employee Involvement in the Modern Corporation* (New York, 1988), pp. 67–70 and note 41 (chap. 4).

13. From Steven Fraser's splendid new biography *Labor Will Rule: Sidney Hillman and the Rise of American Labor* (New York, 1991), for example, we can appreciate more fully the presence of at least one progressive labor leader among the proto-Keynesian shapers of New Deal policy.

14. *The Transformation of American Industrial Relations* (New York, 1986), pp. 226–27.

15. Ben Fischer, speech, August 14, 1989, reprinted in *Daily Labor Report* (September 19, 1989).

16. "The Common Interests of Employees and Employers in the 1990s," *Report of the Economic Policy Council Panel of the United Nations Association* (New York, 1990) [introductory pamphlet].

17. Slichter meant by the phrase "a method of introducing civil rights into industry, that is, of requiring that management be conducted by rule rather than by arbitrary decision." He assumed industrial jurisprudence would apply to the mass production industries just in the process of being organized at the time he was conducting his research, but his book mostly described union practices in the traditionally organized fields, and his view was that industrial jurisprudence, although widely varying in its specifics, was a general characteristic of American trade-union practice. Sumner Slichter, *Union Policies and Industrial Management* (Washington, D.C., 1941), pp. 1–3, and *passim*.

18. Heckscher, *The New Unionism*, p. 85.

19. The AFL-CIO hopes to answer that question, in the immediate term, by offering associate memberships to individuals and, through its Union Privilege program, providing them with credit cards, group insurance, mail-order pharmaceuticals, and other useful services. Some observers see in this the beginnings of a transformation of organized labor from an economic to a human services movement. What the associate-member program surely does reveal is the uphill struggle the unions know they face in the organizing field. For a survey of union programs, see Arthur B. Shostak, *Robust Unionism: Innovation in the Labor Movement* (Ithaca, N.Y., 1991), which is truly an exercise in the power of positive thinking.

20. Kochan et al., *The Transformation of American Industrial Relations*, pp. 246–47.

21. *New York Times*, December 10, 1991. For bitter statements attacking IBM's personnel evaluation policy, which requires giving failing grades to 10 per cent of its employees, see *New York Times*, February 16 and March 22, 1992. Wrote one former employee: IBM "has turned from a challenging and caring employer to one ruled by fear and intimidation."

22. *New York Times*, December 16, 1991. On the lagging fortunes of the service sector, see *New York Times*, September 24, 1991; January 2, 1992.

23. *New York Times*, December 15, 16, 1991.

24. The survey data in this paragraph are taken from Heckscher, *The New Unionism*, ch. 12; and Kochan et al., *The Transformation of American Industrial Relations*, pp. 214–15.

25. Heckscher, *The New Unionism*, pp. 238, 242. Much of Heckscher's analysis, it should be noted, is taken up with new forms of unionism—what he calls "associational unionism"—that he thinks are more likely to be effective under current conditions.

26. In this discussion I am focusing on what Dorothy Sue Cobble has recently characterized as "worksite unionism," in which job rights are defined in relationship to a particular site and employer. But, as she rightly notes, an increasing portion of the service sector is made up of workers ranging from highly skilled contract computer programmers to part-time, mostly female clericals who lack that relationship. For relatively mobile workers such as these, industrial justice would have a quite different content, arising in varying degrees from their concerns with occupational identity, control over the labor supply, portable rights and benefits, and peer determination of performance standards and workplace discipline. For such workers, the challenge to the labor movement is to come forth with a new institutional form that Cobble calls "occupational unionism." But its roots are, as she argues, already well established in the history of craft unionism and, indeed, Cobble's insights derive from her historical study of organized waitresses. Dorothy Sue Cobble, "Organizing the Postindustrial Workforce: Lessons from the History of Waitress Unionism," *Industrial and*

Labor Relations Review 44 (April 1991): 419–36. Both Cobble and Heckscher offer imaginative prescriptions for the labor law and institutional changes needed before the white-collar private sector can be organized. Whether the existing unions are incapable of transformation, as Heckscher is inclined to believe (p. 237), seems to me something of an open question: after all, old-line AFL unions like the Teamsters, Machinists, and Meat Cutters proved extraordinarily resilient once challenged by the CIO, and current unions are much more flexible jurisdictionally than those of the 1930s. But it does not actually matter very much whether established unions do it, or whether new institutions emerge, or as happened in the public sector, professional associations evolve into unions, so long as the end result is trade unionist in function.

27. For most employers, anti-unionism is an entirely rational choice. On the one hand: collective bargaining cuts profits. Recent studies show that union employers earn significantly less on capital investment—19 per cent less, for example, among 902 firms surveyed during the 1970s—than comparable nonunion firms. Richard B. Freeman and James L. Medoff, *What Do Unions Do?* (New York, 1984), p. 183 [table 12-1], and for a full treatment of the union impact on wages, productivity, and profits, chaps. 3, 11, 12. This holds cross-nationally as well: the economic costs of collective bargaining to employers are substantially higher in the United States than in other advanced industrial countries. David G. Blanchflower and Richard B. Freeman, "Unionism in the United States and Other Advanced OECD Countries," *Industrial Relations* 31 (Winter 1992): 80–94. On the other hand: American employers are eager for—and capitalize on—the freedom of the action that comes from not having to deal with unions. On the matter of distributing the burdens of market fluctuations, for example, a recent statistical analysis reveals that for every dollar of company earnings lost because of output decline in the United States, the income of workers falls by 48 cents and profits by 52 cents. In no other advanced industrial economy surveyed by an NBER study was so heavy a burden shifted to workers, and in Japan virtually 100 per cent of the costs of output decline were borne by stockholders. Frank R. Lichtenberg, "In a Downturn, Cut Profits Before Jobs," *New York Times*, February 16, 1992. If one sought to explain the "exceptionalism" revealed in the comparative decline of American unionism with which this essay opened, he or she could do worse than by starting with these kinds of economic numbers.